Advance Praise for Anne Speckhard & **Fetal Abduction**

Fetal Abduction is a unique study exploring a horrific new crime, a perpetrator with multiple personalities, and the inside story of the trial of Annette Morales Rodriguez. Through the twists and turns of this story the reader comes to understand the motives of a woman abused as a child - her mind split in two, and how a normal desire turned into an obsession that ended in murder. Anne Speckhard is able to poignantly humanize Morales Rodriguez and also sheds light on the failings of the U.S. criminal justice system.

—Dr. Richard G. Zevitz – Marquette University

FETAL ABDUCTION

THE TRUE STORY OF MULTIPLE PERSONALITIES AND MURDER

ANNE SPECHARD, PH.D.

First published 2012
by Advances Press
McLean, VA

Book Design by Nikki Hensley (www.hensleygraphics.com)
Editing by Jayne Pillemer
Cover Design by Jessica Speckhard (www.speckhardsavc.com)

Every effort has been made to contact and acknowledge copyright own-
ers, but the author and publishers would be pleased to have any errors or
omissions brought to their attention so that corrections may be published
at a later printing.

Library of Congress Control Number: 2012922031

ISBN 978-1-935866-56-5 – Fetal Abduction: A True Story of Multiple Personalities and Murder - Hardcover
ISBN 978-1-935866-57-2 – Fetal Abduction: A True Story of Multiple Personalities and Murder - E Pub
ISBN 978-1-935866-58-9 – Fetal Abduction: A True Story of Multiple Personalities and Murder - Paperback

DEDICATION

To all the children – boys and girls – who *now* as we read these words suffer under the cruel hands of sexual assault, incest and rape. May they be delivered into kinder, loving circumstances and find their paths to freedom and health. May they never visit upon others the cruelties they endured.

TABLE OF CONTENTS

PREFACE

There are so many sick stories in our day. As I worked on this one I found myself fascinated with it and despite it being a story of blood and gore, I knew I needed to tell it. But why fill the pages of a yet another book with yet one more story of sickness, cruelty and evil when there are already so many such stories?

Perhaps because it begins with a child. We were all children once, born innocent into this world—our genes programmed in expectation of loving arms, smiling eyes, kindhearted nurture. Our brains were pre-wired for relationship, for love, joy and laughter.

But some children are born into tears. And they grow up to cause more tears. Annette Morales Rodriguez is one of those stories. Her mind was fractured by the betrayal of those entrusted to care for and nurture her. And when she became first a mother herself, trying to protect and nurture her own children, she encountered even more betrayal: the attempted sexual assault of her daughter, the removal of her children from her care and mind-breakingly, learning when she thought she was pregnant that a doctor had years ago tied her tubes and rendered her sterile without her understanding the gravity of this decision.

But a mother's heart was not the only heart Annette Morales Rodriguez possessed. Unremitting years of childhood sexual abuse had created another self: a hater and a taker who could plot the death of another mother and take her baby from her by holding her down and literally cutting it from her womb.

Why? This book is an attempt to answer that question. It is the story as I found it when I served briefly as an expert witness in her case. In that capacity I was tasked with trying to understand the psychological reasons for her crime and if she understood right from wrong at the time she perpetrated it. Like her fragmented mind,

the shards of her broken life that I was able to discover and piece together certainly do not contain the whole of her story.

I met Annette for two full days in the Spring of 2012 in the Milwaukee County Jail and there as I interviewed her about her life, I witnessed her alternating between her two very distinct personalities: Annette, a quiet, fearful woman who sounded like she was also a loving mother, and Lara, a cold hearted psychopath whose only interest was to ensure Annette's well-being as she understood it and to protect her by holding all the pain, evil, and assaults she had endured earlier in her life inside her portion of the mind.

* * *

Most of us understand posttraumatic and dissociative amnesia when it comes to war traumas and sudden accidents or disaster—but amnesia for an entire portion of one's life? Ongoing amnesias every time a part of the persona emerges that takes executive control of the mind and body? Multiple personalities? These things are very difficult to fathom and hard to believe.

But I can assure they do occur. I have personally encountered in my clinical practice eleven cases of Dissociative Identity Disorder in which fully-formed personalities were evident with amnesias between them. I also found many other patients who did not at the beginning of therapy have full or, in some cases, any conscious recall of deeply traumatic events that had occurred in their childhood or adult lives. And I know that these things did occur as some were verified by emergency room and medical visits or by the testimony of relatives who witnessed events my patients had somehow managed to sequester and lock away in parts of their minds for many years. I learned in my years of providing psychotherapy and healing many wounded persons that the mind is capable of hiding all types of horrors if doing so serves some useful purpose. Usually dissociating from a traumatic memory allows us to continue to find some respite, grow and hopefully escape beyond the horrors.

Dissociative Identity Disorder, a diagnosis found in the American Psychiatric Association's Diagnostic and Statistical Manual of Mental Disorders (DSM-IV-TR, 2000) is the diagnosis I gave to Annette Morales Rodrigues after meeting with and observing her for two full days.

> The criteria for DSM IV TR 300.14 Dissociative Identity Disorder include the following:[1]
>
> A. The presence of two or more distinct identities or personality states (each with its own relatively enduring pattern of perceiving, relating to, and thinking about the environment and self).
>
> B. At least two of these identities or personality states recurringly take control of the person's behavior.
>
> C. Inability to recall important personal information that is too extensive to be explained by ordinary forgetfulness.
>
> D. The disturbance is not due to the direct physiological effects of a substance (e.g., blackouts or chaotic behavior during alcohol intoxication) or a general medical condition (e.g., complex partial seizures).

Dissociative Identity Disorder (DID) (also known prior to 1994 as Multiple Personality Disorder-MPD) occurs in early childhood in response to severe childhood trauma—usually repeated, life threatening and emotionally terrifying physical, sexual, and/or emotional abuse that has occurred during a sensitive period of development (usually pre-puberty). Posttraumatic Stress Disorder (PTSD), often co-morbid with Dissociative Identity Disorder, is present in approximately eight percent of the population whereas DID is thought to appear in one percent of the population.[2] DID is also thought to be

more prevalent in women, and girls have been found in research to be more dissociative in response to trauma whereas boys more often develop conduct disorders.[3] The severe dissociation witnessed in DID usually develops in direct relationship to the inability of the child to escape from ongoing traumatization and to deal with what is occurring—often on a daily basis.

Dissociation, which occurs in both posttraumatic stress disorder, and much more pervasively in dissociative identity disorder, is a disconnection between a person's thoughts, memories, feelings, actions, or sense of who he or she is. In healthy functioning people, normal dissociation occurs along a spectrum and may include experiences such as daydreaming and losing awareness of time while driving (as in "highway hypnosis"), getting lost in work or heavily absorbed in a book or movie, all of which involve losing touch with awareness of one's immediate surroundings for a short period of time.

Peri-traumatic dissociation is also a normal phenomenon occurring in healthy people during or surrounding the time period of a traumatic event. In these cases, during and shortly after the trauma, one may become disconnected from one's emotions, thoughts or other cognitive functions. This is quite common in response to traumatic exposure and is resolved for most people over a short period of time. For example during a car accident, a personal assault or a natural disaster, many people may report a sense of time slowing down and then re-experience a series of flashbacks of what occurred until they can piece together the fragmented pieces of memory into a narrative recall of what actually occurred under terrifying circumstances. The occurrence of peri-traumatic dissociation may be a predictor of the onset of PTSD.

Persons who experience repeated terror states long after a traumatic episode may not have been able to fully integrate their terrifying experience into consciousness and the memories remain dissociated from continuous normal conscious awareness—except when

they are triggered by reminders of it. For example, a rape survivor who cannot integrate her horrific experience into normal consciousness may continue well beyond the traumatic episode to undergo a cycle of flashbacks, avoidance and hyper-arousal, or panicked bodily responses to triggers and reminders of the original trauma. He or she may then become caught up in a dysfunctional cycle in which they avoid traumatic triggers and flashbacks along with highly aroused mind/body states so much so that normal functioning becomes impaired. This is the essence of PTSD.

Dissociative identity disorder is a far more severe disorder than PTSD. In children who develop DID in response to childhood sexual abuse, the terror of being assaulted repeatedly at a tender age leads to dissociation that is so severe and uncontrollable that near to complete amnesias exist for the actual assaults and "alter" personalities emerge to deal with the trauma and continue to exist for the purpose of sequestering the terror of the repetitive episodes or assaults from the "host" personality. At the onset of the dissociative identity disorder, the child typically dissociates the memory of the event, the circumstances surrounding it, and the horror, terror and other overwhelming negative feelings about the event to mentally escape from the fear, pain, and horror and may be unable to later recall the details of the experience. This process, when repeated over time during sensitive periods in a child's development, gives birth to an "alter" personality (or series of them) which holds the overwhelming pain, emotional numbness, terror, shame and horror of having been a recurring victim of childhood sexual abuse (or other overwhelming repetitive traumas). The "alter" personalities often remain separated in the mind and may even take on lives of their own continuing to emerge into adulthood when experiences occur that trigger reminders of the traumatic episodes.

Dissociation to this extreme in children arises as an automatic (i.e. unconscious) defense and functions as a means of tolerating an experience that is terrifying, repetitive and inescapable. DID typically arises when the child is too terrified to tell anyone about the abuse,

finds no way to stop it and cannot cope with the terror and pain. Dissociation to this severe and ongoing degree allows the child to function while enduring inescapable traumatic and recurring abuse. During abuse, the "alter's" ability to take executive control of the mind/body and dissociate thoughts, feelings, memories and perceptions of the trauma allows the terror, inescapability and horror of the abuse to be separated in the mind. The child or "host" personality "goes away"—or drops out of consciousness—while the "alter" personality emerges to endure and record memories of the abuse.

Severe dissociation of this nature is a very effective coping mechanism. However, the same mechanism that protects a child from the painful awareness of the shame, terror and emotionally overwhelming events in childhood, may create a debilitating disorder in which the "alter" personality persists into adulthood having developed an internal (and perhaps even external) life of it's own, emerging automatically in response to post-traumatic triggers and acting outside of the "host" personalities conscious control with full ability to take over executive function of the mind and body.

In adult cases of DID, "alter" personalities often continue to exist and appear unbidden to overtake the "host" personality whenever emotionally challenging, painful and overwhelming events occur, including memories that trigger the original traumas. Often the current situation is not as threatening as the past, but the threat is misperceived, and as with PTSD, is misinterpreted, causing an automatic response of "switching" to the alter personality.

In dissociative identity disorder, alters are often fully aware, while the "host" personality by contrast typically suffers severe and total amnesias for when the dissociative "alter" takes control of the mind and body – usually in response to any circumstance of perceived threat – especially those that match or are reminders of the original threat in childhood. As the alter takes control there is a consequent dropping out of cognitive functions, emotional responses, decision-making, moral awareness etc. that has become deeply entrained in

childhood during the abuse and continues throughout adulthood—or until their DID is discovered and treated.

For the "host" personality, the alters emergence at any sign of threat and taking over executive control of the mind/body results in a discontinuous sense of self, confusion, and shame over being unable to explain "blank" spaces in memory, behaviors that are inexplicable and often out of normal character, relationships that the individual doesn't even know she has, and other events carried out by the deeply emotionally pained alter(s) that carries all the memories and emotional pain of the childhood abuse.

Likewise, it must be understood that despite being referred to and experienced as different personalities, the alters are not fully formed personalities by any means. Have "split" off of the main host personality, they are fragments of personality that exist only to handle anger, terror, shame or other painful emotions and terrifying experiences. They emerged in childhood as a means of surviving childhood traumas and typically do not mature with the host personality into complete selves. This is because they are separate fragments of the mind that emerge for limited functions, and have the specific purpose of coping with and sequestering overwhelming and terrifying memories of childhood abuse. Thus, they typically lack fully-developed adult cognitive functions, decision-making skills and moral development. They may literally think like a child and are therefore unable to deal with the situation at hand.

MRI studies of persons with DID and PTSD (to a lesser extent) demonstrate that in an traumatically aroused state, many of the normally active neural connections in the brain "drop out" as entire parts of the brain cease communicating in a unified and normal fashion. This means that normal impulse control, decision-making, the ability to feel emotions, narrative memory or even the ability to speak can drop out of conscious availability to the person while in an altered state of consciousness, i.e. an alter personality or a traumatic memory and state of hyperarousal.

Anne Speckhard

Often alter personalities come out to handle sexual encounters—even consensual and loving ones, as these can be traumatic reminders of previous sexual abuse. Alters that hold the painful memories of childhood traumas may also come "out" to seek out licit or illicit substances to numb difficult emotions that remain painfully present in the alter. However their protective attempts to shield the host personality from reminders of previous sexual abuse and their behaviors to numb emotional pain often cause new problems. Alcoholism or drug abuse is often co-morbid with a DID diagnosis as substances are often used to self medicate and dull the emotional pain in the alter personality from memories of the abuse. Other co-morbid diagnosis may include depression, posttraumatic stress disorder, panic attacks, obsessive-compulsive symptoms, phobias, and self-harming behavior such as cutting, eating disorders, and high-risk sexual behaviors. These are, however, all secondary diagnoses to the primary dissociative disorder. If the primary problem is not well addressed by working through the dissociated memories of abuse and integrating the personality fragments, recovery is generally short-lived.

A person with DID is often completely unaware of her extreme dissociative tendencies and typically has amnesias and perplexing evidence of strange behaviors that are attributed to her for which she has no memory. These behaviors only come to her conscious awareness as she learns about them from others, finds clues left over from "blank spots" in consciousness, or partial memories "bleed" into consciousness through flashbacks and confused "memories" of what the alter endured or did when it was "out". The host usually cannot control the alter personality's decisions and behaviors and often finds evidence of unhealthy sexual decisions and substance abuse. Often they cause her deep shame, more emotional pain and a sense of discontinuity and consternation. Habitual and severe defensive dissociation often leads to serious dysfunction in school, work, social, and daily activities.

As persons with DID suffer from frequent blanks in their consciousness, they may also find that they have skills in one personality that they lack in another and that others report to them behaviors, abilities, even relationships that they have no knowledge about. Likewise the host personality may suffer from extreme confusion, depression and mood swings (from extreme sadness and other painful emotions from the abuse seeping into consciousness), suicidal thoughts or attempts, sleep disorders (insomnia, night terrors, and sleep walking), panic attacks and phobias (flashbacks, reactions to reminders of the trauma) as the traumatic memories break through into the host personality's consciousness. The host personality may also experience headaches, amnesias, time loss, trances, "out-of-body experiences" and psychotic-like symptoms due to the confusion of the alter personalities taking over executive function of the mind and body.

DID patients may be misdiagnosed as psychotic or with schizophrenia due to voices and visual hallucinations they experience when an alter personality's memories or thoughts "bleed" into consciousness in what seems to be an auditory or visual or other perceptual hallucination. Bipolar disorder may also be misdiagnosed due to the rapid cycling between alter personalities.

DID persons often experience headaches when memories of the abuse or threat is perceived and if the threat or memory becomes too strong, they may "switch" to an alter personality. These "switches" are often accompanied by a trance-like state, eyes rolling back into the head, rapid eye blinking and then sudden movement into an alter personality. Family members, friends, coworkers, neighbors, and others with whom a DID patient interacts on a daily basis may be aware of the eyes rolling up and rapid eye blinking that accompanies the sudden shift in personality but not realize what they are witnessing. They often attribute the amnesic blanks and personality changes in their loved one to "spaciness" and moodiness while not realizing the person they are dealing with is highly and chronically dissociative. The host personality often has clues that her psycho-

logical life is not normal and may even hear voices or have hallu-
cinatory flashbacks of things experienced in the alter personalities,
but since these are confusing and she typically suffers amnesia for
when the alter personality takes executive function, she may feel
very fearful of and also have a very difficult time articulating and
understanding the mental illness from which she suffers.

With good intensive psychotherapy over years (cognitive behavioral therapy usually being the treatment of choice with the possible
adjuncts of group, art, or hypnotherapy), DID patients can have a
good prognosis. Treatment for DID should be expected to be long-
term, intensive, and involves remembering and working through
the dissociated traumatic experiences. Under treatment, the goal of
therapy is for the alters to ultimately merge into a single, continuous
whole personality, with the host personality reclaiming the awareness, identity, and history previously held by the individual parts.
Individuals with DID have been successfully treated to carry on
normal lives post treatment. However, many also drop out of treatment and have difficult lives in which violence, substance abuse and
chaos reigns.[4]

* * *

At the time of Annette Morales Rodriguez's arrest, her case was
the fourteenth such occurrence of fetal abduction in the U.S. since
1987. I was unaware that such events ever occurred, and I found it
horrific and inexplicable why a woman would opt to cut a fetal child
from another woman's body—thereby committing murder—when
kidnapping an infant seemed so much simpler. It seemed to me that
there must be some internal justification for taking a child out of another woman's womb—that perhaps having lost a fetal child herself,
a woman might opt to carry out such a violent assault. There had to
be a reason for resorting to this bizarre option.

In conducting my evaluation of Annette Morales Rodriguez, I
was to learn why she committed her crime. Of course I was limited
in my perspective, but I was also as thorough in conducting her eval-

uation as time, funds and logistics allowed me to be. I took a much longer time—two full days—than most experts do questioning her, trying to get to the bottom of things. I requested all her medical, police, and court related records and pored over those I was provided. I also attempted to interview Ramón[5], her live in boyfriend at the time as well as her best friend and older children, and her still-living family members (i.e. siblings, father, husband, etc.). Some records were not forthcoming and interviewing in her larger family and community circle also did not come to pass due to logistics. Thus I did not find out the whole story behind her children being alone in the house when the assault of her oldest child occurred and Child Protective Services took Annette's children from her. I also did not find the truth behind Annette's oldest daughter's statement to the police after her crime that Annette and Ramón fought all the time – probably referring to when Annette was in her Lara personality and drinking, but I never did learn more about that. Nor was I able to corroborate Annette's stories of childhood abuse—although witnessing her dissociative switches between personalities convinced me that something serious must have indeed happened to her in childhood to cause that. I also did not learn how or why her sister died. But I did learn a lot and what I learned is shared here in an attempt to explain how and why childhood victims of chronic, inescapable and horrific sexual crimes can grow into having true multiple personalities, as well as how they may also transition from victim to perpetrator.

When one is examining another person's life and trying to get to the truth, it is always a crude approximation, an interpretation of what records and stories are available to evaluate. In writing this account I base it on what I believe to be her true story, based on her account and those of the police, their description of interviews with her friends and family members, hospital records and reports from her health care providers. I use her own words for the most part, or a paraphrase of them to recreate conversations for life events she described to me. I tried to stay as true as I could to what she told me. At times she relayed what had been said to her, but I admit that this

account is only a version of the truth, not the entirety, not a perfect picture of who she was and all the suffering that she both endured and later caused.

Most of the names in this book are the actual names of those involved but some I have changed in order to protect their identities and in those cases it is always noted in the text. In the case of Annette's most recent boyfriend, I had to recreate him and attribute words and thoughts from Annette's limited descriptions, and I didn't feel it was fair to use his real name, so it is changed here. I also, out of respect for her death and the grief of her family, changed the victim's name in this account to Eva Alvarez Mendoza (changed even in news quotes, etc.) although her true name is easily discoverable. Others who still bear their actual names are represented as they appear in official records, their own reports, by the reports of others, etc., but of course they are still only limited versions of their totality and I hope I have been as fair as I can in recreating them and the statements they were said by others to have made.

* * *

As I was writing this book a friend of mine whose daughter is studying psychology told me a story of a patient in the hospital where she is doing her internship in London. This young man had brutally killed his parents and his sibling after enduring years of abuse at their hands. He is now locked in a psychiatric facility where the psychologist who was trying to help him became his next victim. Plotting ahead of time, he arranged to have a container of bleach ready that upon meeting her, he then poured into her eyes while he held her down, blinding her forever.

"Why?" my friend asked me, "would a man who was an abuse victim himself ever grow up to become a perpetrator? Why aren't those who are abused themselves the most gentle and the most understanding of how harmful violent acts can be?"

This is a thorny question indeed. That children learn, in one part of the mind, at least that the overpowering abuser holds all the pow-

er whereas the victim is powerless and feels only pain leaves them with the bitter choice of identifying with power versus pain. For many identifying with the powerful abuser is far more acceptable than identifying oneself as the victim being raped, burned, assault, and identifying with the powerful aggressor can keep the pain of victimhood at bay—separating it from consciousness. Then when flashbacks of trauma occur, this same identification reoccurs in a DID patient in an alter personality, causing the victims themselves to move into the role of abuser in order to keep the pain away. This is the theory many psychologists would use to explain the passing down of sexual assault and coldhearted violence from one victim to another.

However, understanding how a victim becomes a perpetrator does not stop it from happening. Perhaps much more important is to bring into our consciousness the shocking reality and to acknowledge just how many children are sexual assaulted each and every day. Most people know many victims of molestation, sexual assault, and rape. But do these victims feel free to share their pain? Do they know where to go for help? Or do they struggle alone – still tied up by the threats of their abusers –fearful, shamed and in the constant hell of frequent flashbacks and intrusive and confusing mind/body states and then perhaps in one of these fugue states commit atrocities on others.

I heard an expert once claim that most of our prisons are filled with adults who were these children. It may be true. And as long as we continue to turn our heads and refuse to acknowledge the depth and breadth of the problem—how common sexual assault and child-hood abuse is—and as long as we allow rapists, child molesters and sexual assaulters to go unhindered, they will continue to ruin the lives of thousands more.

This is one story being brought to light. I pray it may help many others to be saved from such a fate.

Annette Morales Rodriguez committed murder. She killed a nearly born child as well. And she was severely mentally ill. In her trial, I was shocked to watch as her lawyers allowed her to plead not guilty without invoking the insanity defense! In our court system, we do not try persons who are incompetent to stand trial by virtue of a mental defect or disease, nor do we typically find guilty those who were so mentally ill that they were unaware of the moral gravity of their actions. Surely as one reads the story of Annette Morales Rodriguez they will see that this woman needs to be in a locked psychiatric ward, not a prison!

* * *

As I write this account, I realize that one day Eva Alvarez Mendoza's children and husband may read it. I did not focus on their pain, horror or trauma in this book, but I certainly acknowledge it. I pray comfort for them in their horrific loss and hope perhaps understanding how truly sick and dehumanized the perpetrator of this crime was can offer them some freedom from its horror. Nothing will ever replace their beloved mother and wife. And perhaps they wish for Annette to be punished more. I can assure, that from what I saw of her in jail, she lived in a daily hell.

Annette's children and Ramón may also read this book. Rest assured, dear children, such sickness and evil does not pass generationally by genes. Our genes are made for love and health, and they instinctively seek nurture and peace. Annette's pain was passed to her behaviorally from the hands of an abuser into her heart and mind, fractured as it became. I pray healing for her and freedom for the pain of her children over having such a mother. May she one day return from prison healed, her mind knit into a cohesive whole, her cold-hearted perpetrator self left long behind and may she find a way to make whatever amends are possible for what she has done.

May all children grow up in safety with love surrounding them. May none of us turn our backs upon those children who sadly and horrifically need us now to intervene, to call for help, to reach out

and love them back into the human family. Those are my prayers as I write this book. May all our prayers be answered now.

PROLOGUE:

ABUELA'S FUNERAL

Until the age of sixteen, Annette Morales Rodriguez has no idea of her dissociative identity disorder. Most persons with this condition don't understand. That's the whole point of a split mind—to hide life's horrors from conscious awareness.

Annette first learns of her multiple personalities in the tiny village of Arresto at Abuela's funeral.[6] It is amidst their shared grief for Abuela's passing, the only mother they'd had since Mama ran off to New York city when Annette was twelve-years-old, that "Lara" broke through.

Mama is home from New York for the funeral. But it isn't the first time she's returned to Puerto Rico. The first was for Annette's Quinceañera—her fifteenth birthday, the biggest day in a young girl's life, the day she passes from being a girl to becoming a woman. And that celebration was ruined with Mama's sudden return.

"Baby, it's so good to hear you!" Mama's voice, unchanged over the years had rung through the line. Anger, no rage, was all Annette felt. *Who did she think she was, calling now, right before her birthday, after so many years of silence?*

"How's life in New York with your *new boyfriend?*" Annette wanted to shout into the phone. "How does a mother *abandon her three daughters? How does it feel to forget your own children?*" She wanted all the pain in her voice would rip through the phone lines and fill Mama's ears so that she would know the years of built up tears, hurt and sorrow that all three of her daughters had been feeling for years now. But instead, her voice just went dead and she

1

didn't express any of it—no pain, no hurt, no "happy to hear from you!" either. Just silence.

"Annette, honey, I'm home, here at Tia Lisa's. I'm here to help with your party! We're going to make you a big celebration!" Mama had said.

No, there will be no party! Not now, not with you back! Annette answered in the cold silence of her mind. *Nothing to celebrate.* And as Annette's heart went cold and hard, her numb hand put the receiver back down on the phone, cutting the line.

Why did she have to call? Annette fumed. *Does she think she can just walk back into my life and take over again? That I even want to see her?*

Of course Mama called again. But Annette just left the phone ringing and ringing. No answer—just like Mama had left her little girls years ago waiting and hoping for an answer, for some explanation of how a mother can just walk out on her family! *Let her wait and hope now. Let her suffer!* Annette seethed as she walked away, picked up Papa's clothes and took them to put into the washer. Soon her sisters would be coming for dinner and there was a lot more work to be done. *Damn her for calling anyway! She's got no rights here anymore!*

Mama's arriving just in time for Annette's Quinceañera was arriving three years too late as far as Annette was concerned. Maria and Linda accepted Mama back without questions, just let her slip right back into their lives as easily as she had slipped out. Mama with her matching crocodile shoes and handbags and fancy dresses. Mama with her New York life.

Annette refused to see her, didn't go to Aunt's house when Mama was in town and refused to have her Quinceañera party. But today they will see each other at Abuela's funeral.

Abuela is my real mother! Annette thinks to herself now as she reaches for her black dress and veil. *Abuela raised me, not her!* Tears course down Annette's cheeks as she puts her sleek black

dress over her head. Wiping away her tears she smiles grimly into the mirror as she pins on the old-fashioned lace mantilla, the one that Abuela gave her when she turned fifteen and *didn't* have a party. It's long, black and hangs loosely on both sides of her dark, long wavy hair, framing her face in black lace - just like the ones Abuela always wore to Catholic mass long after Vatican II decided they were no longer necessary. *There,* Annette thinks to herself as she adjusts it. *Abuela would like this!*

Before leaving the house Annette walks outside to the bushes and snaps off three branches of pink flowers. Carrying them back into the house she places them on the shelf underneath the feet of the porcelain Virgin Mary. *Take her to heaven si Dios quiere [God willing]!* Annette prays as she bends to kiss the cold ceramic feet of the Virgin. *Cold, like Abuela lying in her coffin,* Annette thinks as she walks silently to the car to join Papa and her two sisters to the wake.

Standing now in front of the coffin Annette suddenly feels weak, her legs buckling. Annette swoons and falls to the floor almost hitting her head as Papa reaches out to break her crash. Coming to, Annette is confused.

Where am I? She thinks looking around her. *Why is everyone in black?*

It's Abuela. She's dead! A voice answers in her head. *We have no one to watch over us now! And that bitch of our mother is here pretending to cry. Look at her with her matching heels and crocodile bag! She's such a bitch!*

Who are you? Annette asks the voice. *What's going on?*

I'm Lara, the voice answers, a sob catching in her voice. *You don't know me but I've been here since you were six-years-old, when Grandfather started his games.* Bitterness overtakes grief in the voice.

What games? Annette asks, her inner voice breathless with fear. *Who is this talking to me?* she wonders. *What's going on? Am I going crazy?*

No you are not crazy! I'm Lara! I've been here for years. I take all the bad things and you don't know about them, the voice explains bitterly. *And there have been a lot of bad things. If I weren't here, you would be crazy!* the voice hisses.

What bad things? What games? Annette asks. She's sitting now on one of the chairs facing Abuela's coffin. Someone has helped her steady herself into this chair. Abuela's face is so soft as she lies there, face up on the pillow, eyes closed, looking as though she's sleeping peacefully.

Only thing is Abuela never slept on her back in a pose like that, hands crossed neatly over her chest, a black rosary wound between them. No, Abuela's hands were always busy—cooking, cleaning, wiping Annette's tears when she fell, holding her while she told stories of days gone by, stories of long ago when Abuela was young and beautiful.

Her skin is still so soft! Annette thinks as she gazes at her with tear-filled eyes.

Grandfather's games, where he forced his fingers inside me and told me I'm a cunt and a whore and that I like it! And after, when he'd choke me and tell me never to tell anyone or he'd kill me just like that. And Uncle too, pulling out his dick and making me touch it. You never knew about those things, I never let you know!

The voice trails off bitterly.

Who are you? Annette asks again, feeling another swoon overtake her. Gripping the chair Annette clings to consciousness as she suddenly begins to feel and see the things Lara has been describing. It's like a full sensory film; smells, sights, sensations, sounds all there, but it's also distant, unreal and totally disgusting!

Did these things really happen? To me? Or to you? And who are you?

4

I'm Lara, and yes, they are real. I was raped, too! Lara continues, unable any longer at this time of overwhelming grief over Abuela's death to contain and sequester from Annette the traumas she has endured. *That happened this year, while Abuela was dying! The bastard ripped off my clothes and raped me! Called me a whore and threw me naked out of his house when he was finished with me! I dressed out in the bushes and walked back home crying the whole way. You didn't know about that! I'm Lara, the one who takes all the bad. You just go blank and never know anything about it, but now it's time for you to know, too!*

Sickeningly, the rape plays like a movie in Annette's head, full sensory again, but distant as well, like a real live horror movie. *These things are real? They happened to you? To me? To us?* Annette asks, horror filling her inner voice.

No, to me! Lara hisses as the priest begins the prayers. *You weren't there. I never let you be there!*

Is there anyone else or just us? Annette asks. *Annasita,* the voice answers turning tender suddenly. *She isn't old like us; she is just five years old and innocent. She has no idea any of this happened!* Lara explains and as she says it Annette suddenly has a vision of a completely innocent little girl, the one who Abuela read to and made cookies with, the one who ran down to the swing set not knowing that Grandfather would soon follow along with his sick games. *Annasita!*

Oh Dio! Annette cries internally as tears course down her face, and she doubles over sobbing. *Dio mio! Save me God! Save me from this horror! Take me with Abuela! Take me too!* Suddenly Annette finds herself sobbing over Abuela's coffin, clutching it desperately while crying hysterically and calling aloud, "Dio! Take me too! I want to die, too!"

Papa's arthritic arms pull Annette off the coffin and wrap themselves gently and protectively around her. "Come, let's go outside for some air," he says quietly pulling her close and helping her make

her way down the cold marble church aisle, past the saints with their sorrowful faces lit in candlelight and the statue of the Virgin alit with tiny candles at her feet, and the holy water. They pass under the crucifixion, out into the sunlight.

"Annette, honey what's overtaken you? What's going on?" Papa asks, his face wrinkled in concern.

"I don't know!" Annette wails blankly. How to explain the inner voice? How can she tell him about Lara and about Grandfather's sick games, Uncle's molesting and the rape. *Can it be true?* "I miss her so much!" Annette lies with the truth. "I wish I could be with her!"

"Don't say such things!" Papa admonishes. "Come drink some fruit juice," he orders as he guides her across the playa to the fruit vendor. "You need to eat something!"

No, I need to die! Annette thinks, but she takes the cup of fresh juice and sips it slowly.

You can never tell anyone what I told you! Lara suddenly warns. *Grandfather and Uncle will kill me! You can never tell!*

Then the voice is silent. Annette shivers in fear and Papa takes off his jacket and wraps it around her.

Annette doesn't hear from Lara again until sixteen years later when she's living in Milwaukee and the doctor tells her she's not pregnant and that there will be no baby—not now, not ever. But that's jumping ahead of our story. Perhaps it's better to first go back to the tiny village of Arresto, perched on the cliffs overlooking the oceans surrounding Puerto Rico, back to where it all started.

Chapter One
Mama

Breathless under the blazing hot sun, twelve-year-old Annette with her lithe sun-tanned body clad in an airy white cotton sundress and shod with red leather sandals, pumps her bicycle up the gravel road toward home. The air is crackly with heat and the cool ocean beaches are left far below. Her brightly painted orange cinderblock house with the blue shutters situated at the top of the hill overlooking the jungle on one side and the barrio on the other comes slowly into view.

Alongside the road, disappearing below, is the endless blue ocean, waves rolling in ceaselessly, carrying in the driftwood, smooth pieces of colored glass, seashells and the debris of other peoples lives who have lived far from here.

Annette finally makes it to the summit where it's flat and she coasts now, taking in the ocean view below. Here, high on the hill, the cool ocean breezes blow softly through the sweaty tendrils of her dark hair providing welcome relief as she lazily pedals the short, flat distance left to arrive at the home Papa built with his own hands nine years ago. Leaving her bicycle leaning against the orange painted wall inside their carport, Annette pulls the wood screen-door open and enters.

"Papa?" she asks, as she startles to see him leaning over the kitchen table, home far too early from work. "Why are you home now?" she asks, as she notices his weary and crestfallen face. *Something's wrong!*

Running his hands through his thick curly hair, Papa looks up into Annette's face, pain etched across his as he answers, "Your Mama left today." Then he stands wearily, and as does he pushes the kitchen chair back across the floor. It makes a load scraping noise across the tiles, scraping loudly inside her skull as well.

"What?" Annette asks.

"She left for New York and she's not coming back," Papa answers, his voice flat and his face a mask of pain. Annette's two younger sisters, Maria and Linda enter from the living room, their tear-streaked faces confirming the reality of Papa's words as what's happened begins to sink in for Annette as well.

"Mama left us? And she's not coming back?" Annette repeats, trying to grasp the evanescent words that disappear into the overheated air as soon as they are spoken. "How? She didn't even tell us goodbye!"

"She's gone," Papa answers and turns to go lie down, alone and mute in the darkness of his bedroom.

In the following days Papa gets up for work, but he's not himself. His face is frozen into a wooden grimace. He walks stiffly and is in constant pain.

Annette's taken over as cook for the family in Mama's absence. Papa's plate is always still full when he pushes himself away from the table and goes to sit in the shade of the carport placing his lawn chair just inside the shade. He sits there until sunset, staring out at the jungle leaves and looking down over the barrio. And after a couple of hours sitting silently and staring blankly, Papa goes to bed.

It's the same each night. He doesn't say anything these days, doesn't check to see if Linda and Maria did their homework, doesn't ask about who is getting the groceries, doing the wash or cleaning their house. And now his arthritis has spread, the pain has gone into his hands and legs and on weekends he lays in bed all day long except to get up and swallow some more painkillers. And in the evening he sits in his chair staring incomprehensibly outward.

Maybe he's waiting for Mama to return? Annette thinks, harboring a secret fantasy that maybe she'll come back.

These days Annette comes home early from school, no longer lingering to flirt with Marcos, the boy that all the girls adore. Marcos used to admire her and bring her small gifts, but now she doesn't pay him any attention.

I've got no time for silly things like boys and love! Annette chides herself as she hurries home from school. *I've got to run to the grocery store before it closes and buy supplies for dinner!* When Papa comes home she follows him into his dark room and picks up his work clothes left in a pile on the floor and does the wash. She hangs his clothes to dry in the hot sun. They flap helplessly in the light breezes of the afternoon as she tries to do her schoolwork and make sure her sisters study as well. And interrupting her homework, she sweeps, scrubs and cooks, trying to keep the family running the way Mama did before she ran away.

At the end of the school year Annette's grades have plummeted and she's no longer the top student she used to be. "I tried," she tells Papa, tears filling her eyes, when she hands him her failing report card.

"You need to study hard, go to university or technical school—learn to be a professional!" he answers, as he numbly drops the paper on the table and stares out the window. His pain has grown worse. Now he takes prescription medicines. The doctor has diagnosed rheumatoid arthritis and designated him an invalid. Soon Papa will quit his work at the prison facility and go on disability. Annette lies in bed at night and wonders how they'll pay the bills on his reduced paycheck.

What she doesn't realize is that Mama's walking out on the family is not the worst of it. Annette's life came crashing down long ago—she just doesn't know about it. Only Lara knows about that.

Anne Speckhard

"Grandfather! I don't have to pee!" Annasita says, laughter breaking her voice as she twists away. But Grandfather's hands are firm.

"No Annasita, lay still while I teach you this game," he commands. His eyes are cold and his breath is coming in short panting gasps.

Grandfather takes Annasita's hand forcing it deep inside his pants telling her to hold what seems like a creepy, hardened rod of flesh as he begins groping her bottom with his other hand. Annasita's heart races as she tries to make sense of his hardened flesh and his fingers searching and pushing "down there' as she squirms unsuccessfully to free herself from his steely grip.

"That hurts!" she cries, tears of fear and pain welling up in her eyes and her face covered with the pain of betrayal.

"Hold still!" Grandfather commands. "This is a *good* game! You're going to like it after I teach you," he says as he pushes her roughly back into position. With his hand, he pumps Annasita's small hand up and down along his hardened penis.

But she doesn't like it and it's not a fun game! And he's not the Grandfather she knows. He's transformed into someone else— rough, invasive and terrifying. And his now husky voice holds none of his usual tenderness. Annasita wants to escape but she can barely move. Her breath is short too now, caught down in her chest. *What is he doing? When will he stop?*

Suddenly his finger pushes deep inside. The pain is unbelievable. Shocked Annasita's eyes roll up in her head. She loses all consciousness of what's going on.

When it's over, she's back in the house and her bottom hurts but she doesn't remember anything after the swinging. She senses that something *bad* happened outside in the backyard, and Annasita trembles thinking about it but no memory comes to mind. She just knows that she doesn't want to go near Grandfather or the tire swing anymore, but she doesn't know why.

* * *

Lara, on the other hand, remembers it. Indeed she has a photographic memory and can replay things in her head like a video. "I was there every time he played this game," she tells me years later in the Milwaukee County Jail.

"How often was that?" I ask.

"Every time we went there, which was everyday," Lara answers, anger overflowing her voice.

"And did he threaten you? Tell you not to tell anyone?"

"He choked me," Lara recalls remembering Grandfather's hands around her neck.

* * *

First there was the overwhelming pain, like he was ripping her insides apart and then the pumping—him grinding himself into her aching little hand. Then there was the white horrid goo oozing all over her hand and into the grass. Only then he lets go of her. And then he takes his starched white cotton handkerchief out of his workpants pocket—the one that Abuela washes and irons for him. He takes it and first wipes himself off careful not to let any of the white ooze touch her body or clothes. And then he wipes her hand roughly, making sure there is nothing left on her from their time together. Nothing but the horror, the shame and dread—the things no white handkerchief will ever wipe off her little body now defiled by his sick games.

"You played *good!*" Grandfather croons. His voice is tender again, but his breath still catches strangely.

"This game is a *secret!*" he adds stuffing the sullied white kerchief back into his pocket and suddenly he wraps his big gnarly hands around her willowy fragile neck, his thumbs pressing hard on her windpipe. "You don't tell anyone about this game," he growls, his eyes suddenly piercing and his voice cold as ice, "or I'll choke you like this and I'll kill you!" he growls. She stares in horror at his

face as he suddenly pushes even harder – his rough hands choke off her windpipe. "I'll kill you like this!" he threatens, "Don't ever tell anyone, my Annasita!"

Lara struggles to breathe, but there is no air – his hands are tight around her throat. There is no escape. Grandfather holds her neck hard till the last minute, just before she dies. Sometimes when he lets go, she wishes she had died but today she's just happy he let go.

"Go inside and get your lunch," Grandfather says.

Abuela has gone to town shopping and she left a lunch for both of them laid out on the table. Freed from his iron grip Lara stands up shakily on trembling legs, the ache in her crotch causing her to double over when she stands. But freed now, she understands she should run and she does, running fast through the pain to the house where she tries to forget.

In time Annasita returns and Lara doesn't tell her what happened. Grandfather said he'd kill her if she tells, so best to just keep quiet, not tell anyone—not even Annette.

* * *

Abuela shops everyday and as soon as the door swings shut behind her and as she walks slowly up their driveway carrying her shopping basket in hand, Grandfather takes Annasita's hand firmly in his own and leads her out to the tire swing. Annasita never remembers what happens there and forgetting her anxiety that something is wrong, she is happy that Grandfather wants to play. She laughs looking up at him skipping along to the tire swing expecting all to go well.

"Let's go higher than ever today!" she begs as Grandfather places her firmly across his lap, her legs spread open around him. He pumps the swing into motion and suddenly they are flying and as the pokey thing in Grandfather's pants begins invading her crotch, Annasita is gone.

Lara's here now and Grandfather has opened his pants. His penis is rubbing between her legs and she feels his fingers groping her as they mount higher and higher into the sky. Grandfather pushes Lara's hand down forcing her to pump his hardened self as he pumps the swing.

Lara hates him. *He's a vile man!* When the sticky white ooze squeezes into her hand she looks at him with hatred. His face is soft now and he's lost in his after-sex trance. *He's so dirty!* she thinks. The swing has slowed to a stop and now after cleaning his and her hands with his handkerchief he wraps both his hands around her neck again and repeats the now familiar threats, "This is Grandfather's special game, Annasita," he says. Then as he cuts off her airway and adds, "I'll kill you, just like this if you ever tell anyone!"

Lara struggles for air, scared he won't let go. He waits until the last minute when she's about to faint, like always. Then his fingers release their pressure and he let's her run back inside to their lunch that Abuela unfailingly has left out for them.

Lara runs to the house pretending she's in a race and she's the fastest girl in school. No one can catch her—especially not Grandfather, *disgusting old man!* By the time she's back at the house Lara is gone and Annasita gasps for air and wonders why Grandfather never runs along and why he can't keep up? Lunch is on the table and she sits and takes a burrito before Grandfather comes to join her.

* * *

Grandfather's game is still scary, but it doesn't hurt all the time anymore. He's changed it. They lie together on the grass now. He rubs himself now along her bottom and watches Lara's response, while using the other hand to choke her.

"I'll kill you," he snarls as he pushes hard down on her, rubbing back and forth, "I'll kill you just like this if you ever tell," he repeats squeezing her neck hard, crushing her throat while he pleasures her with his hand and "that vile thing" while rubbing himself against

her until they both come in ragged orgasms. His voice tightens when he's almost finished and while Lara knows he will kill her if he she ever tells, she also now knows that he'll let go just before she's going to faint and just after she orgasms. As she struggles near death—pain, fear and shivers run through her body overwhelming her with terror *and* pleasure. He laughs when she comes and mocks her in a lewd voice.

"There you go, you little whore! You like it!" he says, his eyes wide, as he too finishes.

She hates him, but the shivering part is good—a rush of white heat rushing up inside her body warming her face, arms, legs and head. As soon as the white ooze comes he lets her go and then after he cleans her, she runs—fast—back to the house where she lets Annasita come out again, blissful stupid Annasita who has no idea that Grandfather is a pervert and that he's been hurting her like this every single day for the last two years.

Annasita's not a whore, but Lara is a full-fledged fucking whore, just like Grandfather tells her every single day now.

CHAPTER THREE
UNCLE CARLOS

Annasita draws big squares of pink and green in chalk on the patio. She's making hopscotch like they make at school. The sun is hot overhead and something smells—like whiskey.

"Come in here," Uncle Carlos calls as he steps outside the door and roughly takes Annasita's hand and pulls her into the house.[7] He reeks of alcohol. "Forget that game," he says, his words slurring one into the other. "I've got a much better one."

He pulls her inside into the living room. Abuela is doing her shopping and Grandfather went into town today. They are alone. Annasita looks into his face and feels frightened by his cold drunken eyes assessing her. Fear and confusion overtake her as she pulls her little arm away, struggling to break from his firm grip, confused over what he wants from her.

But Lara knows what's going to happen even before it begins. Pushing Annasita out of harm's way, Lara takes over. *If someone is going to play a dirty sex game with Uncle, it will have to be with me because I am the only whore here,* she thinks to herself.

"You're drunk!" Lara says as Uncle tightens his grip and pulls her close. He tries to kiss her chest while his hands grope inside her shorts pulling them down, taking her underwear with them. Lara pushes him away, but he's stronger. She's ten now and she knows what he's going to do as he pulls open his trousers forcing Lara to hold him while his hands reach for her, his fingers groping and then pushing inside her already wet bottom.

She's aroused despite herself—Grandfather's gift to the whore she's become.

Lara's eyes widen with the pain and pleasure of it; she's used to pain and humiliation by now and she's learned that it feels exciting even when it hurts. Lara watches as Uncle places her hand on him and begins pumping it up and down. He pushes inside her with the other.

"Come on, little whore, make it come!" he pleads as he pumps himself hard squeezing his hand over hers as he does. He rubs her bottom and pushes inside with his free fingers, hurting and pleasuring her alternately.

"You *like* to fuck! A real whorita!" he jeers when she can't hold back any longer and shivers in orgasm. Then finally, he gives up on himself and pushes her away while he refastens his pants. "Whiskey gets in the way," he complains. Then he stumbles over to her, wraps his hands around her neck, squeezing her windpipe hard just like Grandfather and threatens, "You ever tell anyone about this, I'm gonna kill you!"

He squeezes hard until she can't breathe. Lara waits hoping he'll finish like Grandfather does and let her go. "I'm gonna kill you— just like this," he threatens squeezing even harder, closing her windpipe momentarily. And then pushing her away, he stumbles off to his bedroom.

Now Lara has another man in her life. And she's sure she's a whore. Nobody is a bigger whore than her. She even likes it some of the time—when they aren't threatening to kill her.

*   *   *

Lara is eleven now. Uncle has been hurting her off and on whenever he's at the house for over a year now. She doesn't have her period yet. But she knows what that means—the blood—and then you get pregnant if you don't take precautions. So far uncle hasn't

come with her yet. He's always too drunk, and he also hasn't tried to have real sex.

She knows what intercourse is now. The girls in her class whisper about it in the schoolyard and giggle when they point out the older girls—girls who their brothers are 'fucking". "Whores" they call them and laugh while turning their backs on them.

They don't know what it is to be a whore! Lara thinks. When they run back to the school Lara shoves one of the girls hard making her tumble down and scrape her knees, bloodying them on the blacktop. *There stupid girl! Now you have the blood!* Lara thinks, laughing to herself.

Uncle is here again today and Lara knows he'll wait until no one is around and come get her. It's the same every time he's here. He's always drunk, he never comes, and he hurts and pleasures her at the same time, mocking her when she comes. And he always finishes by choking her, calling her a whore, threatening her never to tell.

And she doesn't. Annette has no idea what Uncle does to Lara. Abuela doesn't know and neither does Grandfather. Grandfather still plays *his* games too, choking and pleasuring her, then laughing and calling her dirty names while he comes into his hand.

She's in the bathroom sitting on the toilet tinkling, her shorts around her ankles when Uncle arrives. He doesn't knock on the door. Why would he? "Come on you dirty little whore," he says as she stands up pulling her shorts up around her girlish waist. "Come and get what you know you want."

Lara doesn't want him, but she's so used to it now and she knows he can make her feel good even while causing her pain. Hurt and pleasure are all mixed up. Good and bad no longer make sense. He calls her good when she pleases him; she knows she's bad for all that he does to her.

Maybe today my blood will come and he'll have to stop, Lara thinks. *Otherwise I'll get pregnant! Maybe I'll become like that whore, Juanita, in the 10th grade that all the boys fucked and no one*

knows which one got her pregnant. She has a fat stomach now and even her mother wants to kick her out of the house!* Lara doesn't even have a mother to kick her out. But she knows her father will be angry if she comes home knocked up. *If he knew what a dirty whore I've become!* Lara thinks rolling her eyes.

She follows uncle out to the living room. No one is home so he sits in his usual chair and pulls his dick out of his pants, but this time when he pulls her shorts down around her ankles, he doesn't reach for her as usual. This time he lifts her on his lap and spreads her legs and he pushes his penis up to her vagina rubbing it alongside her clitoris sending tingles of heat through her body. She can feel the heat running up her abdomen, past her breasts and his breath coming hard in her face. It makes her wet down there.

Is it the blood coming? she wonders to herself.

He pushes his penis hard into her and Lara understands now. *He wants to "fuck" me just like those boys "fucked" all those girls they call whores at school,* she thinks knowing she has to make him stop. *He wants to push his dick way up inside me and come and he'll make me pregnant for sure!* She doesn't have the blood yet, but if he fucks her that's what will happen. She learned it in health class and she learned it out on the playground too—just different words and different lessons all with the same outcome. You fuck, you get fucked.

He pushes hard on her vagina but suddenly she's dry and tense and she's not going to let him do it. Lara leans into him bringing her head to Uncle's shoulder and reaching it she bites hard as she can, her teeth sinking down into the flesh of his shoulder biting harder, seeking bone.

Uncles screams in pain as he throws her off. "What are you doing? You dirty bitch!" His dick goes soft as his hand reaches for his bleeding shoulder. "You fucking whore!" he says slapping her across the face, the blood on his hand splattering onto her mouth, smearing across her checks. "Get away from me whorita!" Uncle

cries as he rises on wobbly feet and stumbles off to the kitchen where he pours himself another whiskey and fumbles with his wound.

Lara pulls up her underpants and shorts and runs, this time out to the field where Grandfather plays his game. She runs to the tire but it's hanging empty, no one inside of it now careening up and down in an arc of pleasure. Lara throws herself down on the ground, pushing her blood stained face down into the dirt and falls asleep. Her last thoughts are, *I am a whore, but he hasn't fucked me—not yet!*

Waking, Annette feels her face caked in dirt and wonders why she didn't lay on the grass to rest. *Where is Grandfather? Did they play their special game today? Did they ride the tire swing together?* She can't remember and it's starting to bother her—all the things she can't remember and can't explain to herself. *Maybe I have a bad memory?* She walks back into the house and goes into the bathroom.

Seeing the blood stains on her face she becomes even more confused. Annette flips on the water and takes the soap in her hands splashing water frantically. Clean now, she takes her braid out and straightens her curls once again back into the neat braid Abuela taught her to make. Annette looks again at her reflection in the mirror and smiles thinking to herself, *I'm becoming a pretty little woman now, just like Abuela always says!*

I wonder when my breasts will come and how big they'll be? Annette wonders, as she turns sideways to gaze at her skinny body in the mirror. *I hope they're big enough, like the girls that all the boys like!* She refolds and hangs the towel neatly back on the bar and goes into the kitchen to see if Abuela is back from the market yet.

Chapter Four

Juan

Becoming a woman feels good, Annette thinks as she relaxes in Juan's arms after making love. *Sixteen and a woman!*

"Come to New York with me baby," Juan cajoles as he rolls languidly across the hotel bed, reaching for a cigarette and lighting up. "We'll have a good life there," he promises and exhales smoke across the bed.

"No," Annette answers. "New York is not for me."

Six months of being lovers. It's good between them but not good enough to risk setting up home in New York with Juan. *That's not the lifestyle for me,* Annette thinks to herself as she stands up naked, reaching for her white and red checkered, cotton sundress—the one he bought her in the market. *I don't want to live with a drug dealer, no matter how good life is. It can all come crashing down too fast!* And Annette already knows how that feels. *No thanks to that life!*

"No Juan, it's not for me," she repeats as he blows more smoke her way, his eyes pleading and his smile beckoning. "No," she answers firmly, buttoning up her dress as he lays on the bed still smoking, disappointment clouding his face, as his cigarette smoke wafts to the ceiling.

"You'll regret it," Juan warns, but Annette's face remains firm.

"I love you baby," she calls as she moves quickly to the hotel room door before he can argue anymore. She knows he can charm her with that sweet smile of his. In a few more weeks Juan will leave for New York and Annette knows she can't go with him.

I have to make my own money and make it honestly, Annette thinks as she pulls the door softly closed, leaving him behind. *No more stolen afternoons in hotel rooms paid for by drug money,* she thinks to herself. Papa still wants Annette to go to university and maybe, just maybe, she can do it. Her grades are good again now that she's in high school.

CHAPTER FIVE
RAPE

Annette doesn't drink, but Lara does. Lara is drinking tonight. She needs to drink to "forget" all that *they* did to her—Grandfather and Uncle, how they made her a whore who likes sex and likes it rough.

She's been watching one of the guys at the bar, Paulo, all night and she wants to go home with him.

"So are you drunk yet?" Paulo asks pouring himself some more whiskey and eyeing her lasciviously as she sits across the table from him.

"Don't look at me like that!" Lara says, cocking her drunken head to one side.

"Come out in my car and I'll give you something you like," Paulo says winking and pulling her up from her seat. Out in the car he reaches for Lara and as he kisses her, he pushes his tongue deep into her mouth before starting the car. "We'll have a good time back at my place," he promises laughing.

But when they get to his house it's not a good time at all. Once inside his kitchen, Paulo's winning smile disappears. He pushes her against the kitchen counter kissing her hard, his hands rough as his fingers entangle in her hair and hold her head in place and his legs wrap around hers.

"You don't need this dress," he says ripping the front of her dress down the entire bodice to her waist and continuing to tear it down to the hem where it splits in two. Then he shoves Lara to the floor. "Stop it!" she screams but he has both hands on her now, and he

pushes her down hard and pins her firmly to the cold tiles with his legs and arms.

"You don't need these either," he says, using one hand to rip her panties from her hips, his knee pushing them down to where his foot can catch them and push them off of her feet.

"Stop Paulo!" Lara screams, hot tears coming to her eyes.

"And this either," he says pulling her bra off. His breath is whiskey soaked as he pulls her hair in his hands and forces her to face him. He jams his tongue invading her mouth again as he uses his other hand to open his jeans.

"No!" Lara screams freeing her mouth and fighting with her legs, but it's useless. He's much stronger than her and easily overpowers her attempts to fight. He's got his fingers wound into her hair and pulling it he arches her neck uncomfortably while he shoves himself inside of her. He pumps himself into her hard and long until his release comes and then he pulls out abruptly, and still holding her hair pulls her up to sit beside him and then stand. Releasing her, he picks up her torn dress, low heel shoes, panties and bra and throws them at her.

"Take these and get out of here. I got everything I need from you!" Then rearing up toward her, his fists clenching, Lara sees that he will hit her. She cowers and backs away as he continues to shove her toward the door. "Get out, whore! Get the hell out of here!" he shouts as he opens the door and pushes her through it—naked. It's dark when he slams the door shut and Lara begins to sob, drunk and confused as she pulls on her panties and bra and wraps her torn dress around her. It's a long walk home with his semen still wet between her legs.

CHAPTER SIX
MIGUEL

Juan left for New York and Miguel slipped quietly into his place. There was no more amorous lovemaking, no more romantic hotel rooms, no more dreams of real love anymore. Annette let him do what he wanted with her and she loved him a bit, but it was hard to love anybody when she no longer loved herself, and it was hard to want to make love after what Lara had told and shown her. There was no mother to protect her, no Abuela either now and too many people had used her body. Most of the time when Miguel reached for her, Annette slipped away in her mind. She didn't know it, but Lara was there, taking over, making the relationship sizzle.

"Hit me," Lara would say as he struggled to open the buttons on her dress. "Slap me and call me a dirty bitch!" she taunted as Miguel became inflamed with desire. "Fuck me hard! Choke me and tell me you're going to kill me! Fuck me really hard! I'm a dirty whore!" Lara shouted as he ripped her clothing from her and did just as she told him, pushing his hard self into her wet body and pumping hard into her as he choked the breath and life from her.

"Harder!" Lara would cry, "Choke me harder, so I can't breathe!" Miguel did as she told him until breathless they both crashed intensely into long spasms of pleasure.

"Oh you *are* a dirty bitch!" Miguel would tease afterward as he reached for his cigarettes. "You are one fucked up dirty cunt!"

Lara always got up and drank after they fucked, because that's what it was—fucking. They never made love, just fucked hard. She would drink fast and long swigs of rum and then beg for him to take

her out to the clubs where she would drink more and usually pick a fight with some other "bitch" at the nightclubs, some stupid whore that was throwing herself at a man beneath her.

"Look at yourself, how can you throw yourself at that little prick of a boy?" Lara would taunt and after hurling enough insults she would push and shove the girl until a fight broke out. *It's so satisfying to punish this stupid bitch!* Lara smiled to herself as she punched, kicked and hit the girl over and over again until the girl finally slumped down and called "uncle" or someone pulled her off and pinned her swinging arms to her sides.

On those nights, when Lara picked a fight, she always won. And then she went back home with Miguel and they fucked again, with him calling her dirty names and choking her into near unconsciousness. The orgasms were out of this world. Fucking Miguel was so good!

Annette knew nothing about what Lara and Miguel did. She woke up in the mornings dazed, out of it and confused about what had gone on the night before. Sometimes people would tell her how much she drank or that she was in fight but Annette just laughed it off. *Me in a fight?* She'd think to herself and brush it off as crazy talk. She remembers nothing—a complete blank from the moment Miguel reaches for her to the next morning when she wakes up hung-over in his bed. Sometimes she sees bruises on her neck and her throat feels raspy and painful, but she has no memory to explain it.

It isn't long before Annette's period fails to come and the blue strip on the drugstore pregnancy test turns bright pink. Positive.

"Pregnant? So soon? What about university?" Papa asks shaking his head and then hanging it down into his hands.

"Papa I'm going to marry Miguel," Annette explains. "Don't worry I'm going to go to technical school while the baby is growing inside me. I'll graduate before it's born and then I can become a

bank teller. It's a professional job, Papa." Annette explains hoping he will raise his head from his hands.

Papa looks up and smiles weakly. "Okay Annasita, it's your life now!" he answers. "It's all your life now."

Annasita! Annette thinks to herself. *She's been gone for a very long time, hasn't she?*

CHAPTER SEVEN

CARMELITA AND PABLO

The baby is born; a little girl and they baptize her Carmelita—Abuela's name. Annette graduates from the technical institute just in time and takes a job as the manager of a bakery while her younger sister Maria[8] comes to babysit.

Annette pushes Miguel away now most of the time when he comes for her and there are fewer mornings when she wakes up confused and disoriented about what happened the night before. No more unexplained bruises and sore places on her body. Yet there are still some nights she agrees to make love and those nights she doesn't remember anything and sometimes she feels hung-over after. And on those mornings, Maria is still at the house complaining about babysitting for too long.

Another pregnancy comes, this time with bleeding from beginning to end. Annette doesn't let Miguel touch her during this pregnancy and he goes out a lot alone drinking and partying. *Who knows who he's been with when he stumbles home early in the mornings?* Annette asks herself but not him. She's too busy with bottles, diapers and work to worry too much about it.

Annette doesn't know this Miguel, the partier who doesn't give a crap about her and the babies. They argue daily now. The day the next baby is born they are arguing, when Annette's water suddenly breaks.

"Take me to the hospital!" she says her face suddenly ashen white. At the hospital the baby is already pushing to be released but when they put Annette up in stirrups on the clean white sheets she panics

and for some reason he gets stuck, caught in the birth canal—caught between life and death. The doctor calls the medics and three huge men gather around her and when the doctor gives the signal they all bear down on Annette's belly as she screams and pushes along with them. Finally the baby is born, deep blue and with the cord wrapped multiple times around his neck. He's a beautiful, dark haired baby boy, but barely alive.

Annette watches as the doctors rush to resuscitate him, forgetting entirely about her. Her body keeps pushing as the placenta slithers out between her legs staining the white sheets with a pool of deep red blood. Her son, Pablo, slowly begins to breathe but his APGAR scores remain low and as it turns out, he will forever be damaged, becoming a hyperactive schoolboy unable to control himself and slow to learn.

Annette's doctor gives her shots of Depo Provera when she returns to his office for her six-week postpartum check up. "This should keep you from becoming pregnant," he explains but Annette doesn't hear him because she's not present. She also doesn't hear him explain that for this method of birth control to be effective, she needs to return for additional shots every thirteen weeks or so.

As far as Annette is concerned, she has complete amnesia of the office visit. Annette disappears for anything to do with examining her "down there" and unbeknownst to her, Lara appears. But Lara could care less about birth control or fucking stupid doctors who think they know everything and can stick their hands and instruments inside a woman.

Who the fuck does he think he is? Lara asks herself as he finishes his examination. *I wonder what he'd say if I asked him to fuck me here, hard, right now, on this table? Oh, he's just a pussy and he'd run crying to Mama!* Lara thinks snickering to herself as she rips the paper gown off of her body before the doctor has even made it out the door.

"See you, doc, until next time!" she calls out to him as she ris-es, buck naked off the table, following him to the door to take her clothes down from the hook.   He blushes as he stumbles out the door.

CHAPTER EIGHT

ELISE

The next pregnancy is a girl and she comes into the world more easily. As the doctor is helping deliver the placenta, he offers Annette a tubal ligation.

"It's easy to do now, when you've just given birth," he explains but Annette doesn't hear him. It's all a fog—something about preventing the next baby and she nods her assent, even signs a form the nurse gives her as she slips away when he begins probing inside her.

Lara takes over while they are messing around "down there". And Lara could care less if they cut Annette's tubes and render her sterile. She thinks all male gynecologists are sick to spend their days sticking instruments inside women. *Fucked up doctors who like causing women pain!* She thinks as she too fades in and out of awareness. *Let him cut whatever he wants—the sadist!*

Baby Elise grows up in a world of her parents shouting at each other. Annette works days and comes home tired and yells at Miguel until he gets fed up and leaves for town, angrily slamming the door behind him.

Not wanting any more babies and not understanding that there won't be anymore anyway, Annette pushes Miguel away now when he reaches for her. There are no more hot nights between Lara and Miguel, and no more confused mornings when Annette doesn't understand what happened the night before. There's only diapers and baby food and as the children grow older, school and homework to think about.

And Annette realizes Pablo needs a better school. There are no special needs programs in their village and he is never going to make it here. Annette's sister, Linda, has moved to Milwaukee, a city in the northern state of Wisconsin.

"Come and live with me," she tells Annette. "There are many factories here and I'm sure you can get a job, even if you don't speak English. I'll help you find a good public school. They have excellent programs for learning disabilities here and Pablo will do so much better. Come, Annette, I miss you," Linda cajoles her over the phone line.

Annette thinks it over and decides it's for the best. Miguel is not much of a father. Papa is so weak he can't help, and Maria is married with children of her own now. There's no good reason to stay here.

"I'm leaving you and taking the children with me," Annette announces to Miguel one night.

"I won't give you a divorce," Miguel counters, anger blazing in his eyes.

"It doesn't matter, I'm still leaving. I bought my tickets for Milwaukee. I'm taking the children with me to live with Linda and we leave next Wednesday. Divorce or not, I'm leaving," Annette tells him.

Unable to speak, Miguel just spins on his heels heading for the door—his usual escape back to the bars and the town whores, someone to spend the night with who will pretend to care about him, pretend as long as his money doesn't run out.

To hell with her! Miguel thinks. *Let them go to Milwaukee and find out how it is to freeze in the snow and ice with no Miguel to pay the bills! To hell with them all!*

CHAPTER NINE

MILWAUKEE

Linda meets Annette and the children at the Mitchell Airport in South Milwaukee and helps to gather up their things from the baggage carousel loading them up on a metal trolley. As they head for the parking lot and the glass doors slide open Annette feels a blast of the icy, Wisconsin winter air.

"Dio, it's cold!" Annette says as Linda rushes her and the children across the ice and snow covered street into the parking lot and into her car. Annette feels the artic cold surrounding her body and penetrating into her muscles and organs. *It can't really be that cold here!* She gasps watching her breath condense as she speaks. Looking around her, she notices that all the other travellers are sensibly bundled up in heavy snow parkas, thick knit hats, rubber boots, scarves and mittens. All she and the children have are thin cotton coats and their Puerto Rican sandals.

* * *

Linda helps Annette find a public school, one with a good special needs program for Pablo, and together they enroll the children. Annette understands nothing as Linda efficiently fills out the forms and gives proof of residence. Next Linda takes Annette to the local cheese factory where Annette gets a job on the assembly line, working late shift.

"It will be good because you can sleep during the days when they are at school and be up when the kids come home from school. You can work when they are sleeping. You just need to find a sitter," Linda explains.

After a few months Linda helps Annette find a small apartment in the poor section of the city and Annette settles into her own place with the children. A neighbor lady, Juanita, also from Puerto Rico agrees to babysit nights, sleeping over while Annette goes to the factory to work. *Carmelita is ten now and soon will be able to take over,* Annette thinks as she hands over a good portion of her hard won paycheck to Juanita, but glad that her children are protected while she's at work, she pays without complaints.

* * *

It's only a matter of months before Annette meets Ramón.⁹ She's crossing the street to pick up some groceries at the local Mercado and there he is smiling at her, a big handsome grin.

"You're lookin' good!" he says as she walks by. Annette ignores him, but he follows her into the market, waits for her to check out and then picks up her bags to help carry them home.

"Only this far," Annette says when they get to her doorstep. "I can take them from here."

Ramón asks for her phone number and because his smile is disarming and he seems gentle, she gives it to him. They begin dating immediately.

Ramón doesn't make many physical demands, at least in the beginning, so Annette doesn't worry with him. He seems like a genuine romantic, actually interested in her. Finally, confused that he isn't all over her like Juan and Miguel were, Annette finds herself reaching for him, kissing him. And she stays present at first, making love with him the way she did with Juan. But overtime as things heat up, Annette finds she can't handle it and slips away in her mind when Ramón reaches for her.

In those times Lara emerges and just like before she eggs Ramón on, asking him to call her a bitch and to choke her. Confused, Ramón refuses but he does enjoy the new unleashed Annette, the woman

who suddenly is a tiger in bed. And together after making love, he joins her to drink and dance together at the bars.

For Ramón, it's confusing how she can change so suddenly and she always picks fights at the bars with other women, calling them stupid whores and punching them, but he attributes Annette's change in personality to the whiskey. He has no idea that Annette is nowhere to be seen at those times and has complete amnesia for their nights out. He's doesn't realize he's with Lara, not Annette.

He does notice that Annette drinks an awful lot when they go out to the bars dancing, but she always comes home hot and ready to have another go. He likes that. Annette is a nice mother, good woman and super sexy. He doesn't understand the sudden switches in her personality, but it doesn't trouble him. He's got enough to worry about with the bad economy and making sure he doesn't lose his landscaping job and papers for living here.

All women are moody! He thinks to himself whenever she throws him for a loop. *No sense trying to figure them out!*

CHAPTER TEN

ASSAULT

The biggest confusion for Ramón, comes late one night when he's passing by Annette's place on foot. It's past eleven and Annette is usually at work on the evening shift this time of night, but he sees a well-built man heading for her doorstep. Ramón sees the man open her door and without ringing the bell, enter her house.

What's this? She's got another lover? Ramón thinks incensed at the thought. *We'll just see about that!* Ramón doubles his stride as he lopes up the sidewalk and bounds up the three steps to Annette's unlocked door, pushing it open.

But the scene inside is not at all what he's expecting. The "lover" who has shed his coat and is dressed in blue jeans and a cotton shirt is struggling with Annette's ten-year-old daughter Carmelita, who is crying softly, "No! Let me go!"

He's got Carmelita's underpants pulled down to her ankles and her nightgown pushed up exposing her thin undeveloped chest and his jeans are already unbuckled.

He's *trying to rape her! A ten-year-old girl!* Ramón realizes and a wave of anger rushes over him.

"Bastard!" Ramón yells and jumps in between the man and Carmelita. Ramón swings his fist and gets the first hit. Bam, he hits the intruder again, and then lifts his leg to kick him, swinging the man off his balance as he drops to the floor. Carmelita screams and cowers in the corner, crying as Ramón pummels him with more punches and kicks, screaming all the time, "She's a little girl! You bastard!"

The man ducking and trying to avoid Ramón's punches scoots himself across the floor, rises and flees out the still open front door as Ramón shouts behind him, "Get the hell out of here!"

Then turning to console Carmelita, Ramón hears the sirens. The police arrive as Ramón tries to calm Carmelita who is now sobbing hysterically. The other children have woken and they are crying too.

"You're not their father?" the police ask as he describes to them what's just happened.

"No, I was just in the neighborhood. I go out with their mother," he explains. "I know the kids well."

"There's no babysitter?" they ask.

"She's here," Ramón points indicating Juanita who is back now. Knowing she was wrong to have left the children alone to return home to do her laundry, Juanita is afraid of the police and doesn't explain that she was on duty but left the children alone for a few hours.

No babysitter, the policeman notes on his pad. *No parent present.* After he finishes questioning everyone, he calls Child Protective Services and within an hour a social worker arrives with a car. She helps the children dress, preparing to take them away with her.

"Here, tell their mother to call this number when she returns home from work," the social worker says, handing Ramón her card. The children are scared and crying but there's nothing Ramón can do. He's not their father. He can't reach Annette either while she's on the assembly line. He just has to wait.

CHAPTER ELEVEN

LOSING THE CHILDREN

Ramón stays in the empty house until Annette arrives.

"Why are you here? Where are the children?" Annette asks in alarm when she returns home early in the morning.

"Your babysitter is a liar," he tells her, explaining what happened—that the children had been left alone in an unlocked home. "And that bastard child molester ran away. I gave him a good beating though. I don't think he'll return here," Ramón says proudly, but he scowls thinking about how the intruder got away just before the police arrived.

Fear filling her face, Annette takes the card and dials the number on it, her hands shaking as she enters the numbers.

"I can't see Pablo and Elise until the court date, and it's not fixed yet," she says after she hangs up the phone, her face white from shock. "They are each being placed in a separate home, and they won't let me see them! I have to go to the hospital now to help with Carmelita! But I can only see her while they do her medical examination and then I have to leave. Oh Dio, how can they take my babies from me?"

Annette arrives at the hospital and finds Carmelita in the emergency ward with the sexual assault team.

"Baby!" Annette calls out as she wraps her arms tightly around little Carmelita's thin body. Carmelita wraps her arms tightly around Annette's neck and sobs into her chest. They hold each other close until the nurse arrives.

"Mrs. Morales Rodriguez, we need you to sign these forms and explain to your daughter that the doctor is just going to check if the assailant did any damage. It won't hurt at all. We are very gentle here," the nurse explains, handing Annette a clipboard and a pen.

Reluctantly unwrapping her arms from around her daughter's shivering body, Annette takes the clipboard and then in Spanish tells Carmelita what to expect. "I'm going to stay right here beside you baby and hold your hand," Annette tells her.

When the doctor arrives she asks Carmelita, "Scoot down here sweetie, to the end of the table and let's put your legs up here," she says indicating the stirrups. "I'm just going to take a look," she explains gently. "I'm not going to hurt you."

Annette translates and Carmelita hesitatingly takes the position. The doctor gently opens the girl's labia, examines her vaginal opening and seeing her hymen still intact and that no semen or lacerations are present, that no rape has occurred, she finishes the exam.

"It all looks fine," she says removing her gloves. "You can sit up now," she directs Carmelita and throwing her latex gloves into the bin, she writes a few notes on the chart and exits.

"You can get dressed now," the nurse instructs and Annette gently helps her daughter put on the mix-match of clothes the social worker selected from home. As Annette finishes dressing her daughter, the social worker steps in and announces, "That will be all for now, Mrs. Morales Rodriguez. Thank you for coming in to help out with the examination of your daughter. We'll be taking her now to her foster home and as soon as the court date is set you will learn about visitation and all the rest. You may leave now," the woman states in a business like manner as she takes Carmelita firmly by the hand.

"Mama!" Carmelita protests, but Annette is restrained by the policeman who has suddenly appeared in the examining area, interjecting his body between Annette and the social worker leading her crying daughter away down a hallway into a waiting vehicle.

"Mama, don't let them take me!" Carmelita turns back calling out to her mother, but Annette can see it's impossible to intervene. The policeman won't let her take a step in that direction.

"We have to wait for the police to decide when I can come to get you, honey!" Annette calls after her. "I can't do anything until then! It will be okay!" Tears well up in her eyes and stumbling as they splatter down her cheeks, Annette makes her way out of the emergency ward into the waiting area where Ramón is sitting sipping a coffee out of a cardboard cup. Falling into his grasp, she clings to his arm and sobs as together they walk back to his car.

* * *

Where are they staying? Are they eating? Sleeping? How are they doing without me? How is Carmelita dealing with what happened to her? These thoughts go round and round in Annette's mind keeping her awake after she returns home from work in the mornings as she tosses and turns in her bed. *Where are they? Why couldn't they keep them together? What is little Elise thinking about, all alone? How about Pablo?* Her sleep ruined, Annette climbs out of bed and sobs into her hands. *What is life without my children?*

Annette fantasizes about showing up at school and trying to take the children with her, but *where could I run with them? If I get caught they'll take them away forever!* she muses.

The loneliness is unbearable and Annette begins to avoid being at home alone. She takes a second job during the days—she can't sleep anyway—to avoid being at home without them.

Ramón comes more often now and holds Annette while she cries, trying to console her, but what can he say to a mother who has lost her children? After two weeks of waiting to hear from the court with nothing, no sign of hope, Ramón moves in and Annette is glad to have someone near when she tries to sleep but finds it elusive, no matter how exhausted she becomes.

The court meets only after a month and at that hearing, the judge orders Annette to take parenting classes, change her work schedule and get another babysitter. Annette does everything he orders but the separation wears on, continuing for three long anxiety-filled months.

* * *

When the children are finally allowed to come home they are anxious and clingy. Elise follows Annette around and cries if she leaves the room. And Carmelita is afraid after dark and doesn't want Annette to leave the house at all – even to go across the block to get groceries. Annette has new daytime hours now. At night all three of her children pile into her bed sleeping close and clinging to her like baby mammals.

Annette is happy to see them but worn out with her own emotions. *Can they be taken away again?* she asks herself in the middle of the night when she tires of all the children flopping their arms and legs around and laying on top of her. Slowly she extricates herself to go sleep with Ramón in the other room. But before she leaves she looks at them lying so innocently together asleep in the bed.

How bad is the damage for Carmelita? Annette wonders as she watches her ten-year-old daughter moan and thrash in her sleep, probably reliving the episode. Is there anyway to restore her innocence?

Will I ever be the same? Annette thinks looking at them. It was hard losing Mama when she left, but losing her own children was much worse. *How could she ever leave us?* Annette thinks, her heart breaking at the thought of ever losing her children again. *I won't let anyone take them from me ever again!* Annette vows to herself.

CHAPTER TWELVE

ANOTHER BABY

"So you want to make another baby?" Ramón says, smiling and looking up at the ceiling after making love.

"I don't want to ever lose my babies again," Annette says curling up in the crook of his arm. "Losing them made me realize I want one more," she says rubbing the smooth naked skin of his belly. "I want a baby with you, Ramón."

Annette doesn't realize exactly why she wants another baby. But on some level she recognizes how deeply recent events have affected her, that Ramón's kindness had touched her deeply and that carrying another baby inside of her seems safe. *No one can take that baby away, can they?* She just feels certain that another pregnancy makes sense on so many levels, creating safety and calm in her mind.

"Yes, I want another baby!" Annette repeats hugging him close.

Ramón agrees and within months Annette misses her period.

What's wrong with these tests? I know I'm pregnant! Annette thinks to herself as she stares at yet another strip that fails to turn bright pink after she holds it in her urine stream. *My breasts are sore, my belly is big and I feel sick in the mornings—it's all the signs!* She thinks to herself as she drops the strip into the trash.

Annette tells Ramón that she's pregnant and continues on "as if" while she waits for one of the tests to confirm what she already knows. As her belly continues to swell she wears Ramón's baggy jeans and loose sweaters and the neighbors soon notice as well that she is pregnant. She can't hide it from them anymore so she smiles

and clasps her hands to her belly when their eyes fall to it and smiles back knowingly.

This goes on for months as Annette begins to buy things for the new baby: some clothes, a car seat and a few soft baby blankets. Running her hands over her new purchases piled up in the corner of her bedroom she feels excited for when the baby will be born. The only trouble is that there is no baby.

Annette has no idea, but her pregnancy and all of its signs are one hundred percent psychological.[10] When she figures she must be in her fourth month she goes to the doctor for a laboratory pregnancy test and but the nurse informs her that she is not pregnant. Unable to believe it, Annette just carries on in her own world and Ramón, never having gone through a pregnancy before, has no idea.

Lara however has a harder time keeping up the fantasy. At first she is not sure. But unlike Annette, Lara can see everything and suffers no amnesia for Annette's life and is therefore more rooted in facing life's problems. It's just a matter of paying attention for her and as she begins to listen in, she realizes there is no way that Annette is pregnant—things just don't add up. So finally when another Friday night rolls around and she wants to get drunk, Lara finds it hard to stay "inside".

For Lara, it's hard to hold the memories of so much pain without going out and tying one on once in awhile and picking a fight as well. Lara adores the way it feels when she finds another woman to punish for her stupidity, to punch her and vent all her rage for all the times Lara was naïve and got hurt until someone finally pulls Lara off, making her stop.

Finally in the six month of pregnancy, Lara, realizing that there is no pregnancy (although Annette persists to hope and believe she is pregnant) breaks through on a Friday night to go out to the bars. There Alicia[11], a friend of Annette's, is shocked to see Lara drinking repeated rounds of shots while pregnant. The next day she angrily stops Annette on the street to confront her.

"How can you drink shots when you are pregnant? It's going to hurt the baby!" Alicia exclaims, accusation gleaming in her eyes.

"I, ugh, miscarried. Two weeks ago," Annette stammers out in confusion hurrying to come up with an explanation. As she was beginning to doubt the truth of this pregnancy it seems like the right thing to say. "I was so upset over losing the baby. That's why I was drinking!"

Alicia glances accusingly down at Annette's still protruding belly, her eyes still afire.

"I haven't lost the weight yet, Alicia, and it's okay because I'm going to try to get pregnant again as soon as possible," Annette explains, calming her friend's ire.

Annette has heard so many stories supposedly about herself of drinking, dancing, taking rounds of shots and most disturbing of all, picking fights with other women at bars. By now, Annette has a pretty good guess about the unaccounted times in her life—the blank spaces where she had no memory whatsoever—that Lara has probably been out. And if it's a weekend, Lara has been drinking. Annette knows very little about Lara except the stories she hears the next day about events for which she has complete amnesia. And one thing is very clear to Annette: Lara likes to drink.

Lying to Alicia about the miscarriage causes Annette some discomfort, but Annette never allows herself to think much about heavy problems—in this case the pregnancy that didn't ever show up on the drugstore pregnancy tests or in the doctor's office. Annette is convinced she is pregnant even when the lab tests fail to confirm. She has all the signs and by now, on her fourth child, she is sure. It is only Lara who disbelieves. Though the months wear on and there is still no confirmation, Annette has no room in her mind for anxious news like that. Though she's not aware why she fails to process reality as other people do, the truth is that it's Lara's job to hold the pain, or in this case the discomfort of a pregnancy that keeps failing to be confirmed.

When her pregnancy doesn't advance as it should and isn't confirmed by the doctors, Annette decides that she must have indeed miscarried but she isn't sure when—again a big blank space. But in no time at all she is sure that she is pregnant again and as her life is already very confused in terms of missing time, it doesn't seem odd to Annette that she isn't sure when one pregnancy ended and the next began, or that she has no memory of when she had conceived again. So telling Alicia she miscarried seems true. She tells Ramón vaguely about the miscarriage and soon after that she's become pregnant again and explains to him that she isn't sure how far along she is but everything seems good. He doesn't worry himself about the due date, trusting Annette will let him know when it's time to be ready.

The only thing he says when Annette mentions a miscarriage and wanting to conceive again is to ask in regard to his recent job loss, "Maybe we should wait to try again? I think I'll pick up another job soon, but maybe now it's not the right time?"

Annette ignores his concern and as her psychological pregnancy didn't require too much of his involvement and she never "remembers" sex with him anyway, in her mind she is soon pregnant again. As for his temporary unemployment Annette is also not overly concerned. Ramón works in landscaping and the big firms are always picking up responsible workers like him who are willing to do manual labor at minimum wage without asking for overtime. And she still has her factory job.

This cycle of a false pregnancy and miscarriage repeats itself yet another time and finally on the third "pregnancy" Annette is starting to get concerned. She make yet another appointment with her doctor, this time to ask why her pregnancies never show on the lab reports and to discuss her concerns about her fertility.

CHAPTER THIRTEEN
SHOCKINGLY BAD NEWS

"Not only are you not pregnant," the doctor says in a stern voices as he peels off the latex gloves worn to vaginally examine Annette and tosses them in the trash can, "but you never will be. Your sonogram shows you had your tubes tied after your last pregnancy and you are not pregnant now. You can never become pregnant again."

Annette stares in amazement at the doctor as he delivers this shocking news.

"No, that was only temporary after Elise was born, like the Depo Provera!" Annette gasps in disbelief.

The room is becoming distorted as she struggles to stay present. It feels like the walls are closing in on her and the ceiling is at a funny angle.

"No it's permanent," the doctor explains matter-of-factly. "Unless you can afford a lot of very costly medical procedures then you can't reverse it. But your tubes are cut and tied and there is no way you will ever become pregnant again without a surgical procedure to undo your sterilization or if you can afford it, in vitro fertilization."

"But what about all the signs of pregnancy?" Annette protests, hot tears burning as they well up in her eyes. "My breasts are tender just like when I was pregnant before and I haven't had my period for months! And my belly is big, look!" she says pointing to her swollen belly.

"It's a psychological pregnancy," the doctor explains dispassionately. "You want to be pregnant so badly, your body manufactures

all the signs. But I can assure you that you are not pregnant now, and you will never be again!"

Hot tears trickle down her cheeks as Annette feels the floor rise up to swallow her. And within moments she is gone. Lara takes over.

"Are you sure about all of this?" Lara asks, her voice icy cold. "I don't remember giving permission for such a procedure!" she states, chipping out the frosty words from the frozen glacier of her mounting rage. "How could a doctor sterilize me without my permission?"

"It's common to tie the tubes after multiple births while still in labor and delivery—it's easier to do it then. Perhaps you were tired and don't remember giving your permission," the doctor explains, weariness creeping into his voice. *At this low-income clinic there are too many illiterate women and poor English speakers. It's a wonder they understand half of what goes on!* the doctor thinks to himself as he shakes his head. It's a constant source of tension for him—how to explain medical procedures and make sure he's getting a fully informed consent. *Perhaps it's the same in the clinic in Puerto Rico where you had your tubes tied!* the doctor reflects sadly. *Your doctor probably thought he was doing you a favor after three children born in less than four years time! Why do you want another one now, anyway? You will soon be thirty-five years old and you're struggling to make ends meet as it is!* But he keeps silent as he returns Annette's chart to the door before exiting the room.

Lara gets up off the examining table and angrily puts on her clothes as she thinks over what the doctor has just said. *Annette won't be able to handle this news. She is counting on this baby. But she has to face the truth and tell Ramón too! No more pretend pregnancy!* Lara's primary emotion is anger. She rarely feels much else, perhaps disgust as her secondary feeling. But when it comes to Annette her emotions are more complete and at this moment she feels a swell of protective concern welling up inside. *This one isn't going to be easy to solve!* she thinks to herself.

* * *

Annette is not accustomed to hearing from Lara. The only time Lara has spoken to her was at Abuela's funeral but now she is a near constant voice in Annette's head – harassing her about her pregnancy. It happens the first time just after she exits from the low-income clinic.

You're not pregnant! Lara hisses inside Annette's head. *And you never will be! Didn't you hear him say so?*

I'm six months pregnant and it just doesn't show in the lab tests, I don't know why! Annette answers, doubt casting a chill throughout her body. *Why are you here? Go away!*

It doesn't show in the blood work because you are not pregnant! Lara insists. *You have to stop believing this fantasy. It's not true! Your tubes are tied and you are never going to be pregnant! Didn't you hear him? You are sterilized! Sterile! Infertile! You are not pregnant now and you never will be again!*

Stop! Stop talking to me! Go away! Leave me alone! Annette cries as she runs down the street, tears blinding her eyes as she tries to run away from the voice in her head. But there is no escaping and Lara is relentless pounding away at the truth.

* * *

You have to tell him! He thinks there is going to be a baby and there isn't going to be one! Lara's words intrude into Annette's consciousness as she does the washing later that day. *A baby has a due date. When is yours? When is this false pregnancy going to end?*

Leave me alone! Go away! No one needs you here! Annette answers as hot tears fill her eyes dropping down onto the children's clothes that she's pushing into the washing machine. Annette pours a cup of Tide into the washer and turns the cycle to wash and wear as she tries to push Lara's voice out of her awareness. Pablo's jeans have mud on the knees from playing football and Ramón's work clothes are always stained as well. *They need a bit more detergent,*

she thinks to herself as she adds some more Tide and flaps the washer shut.

* * *

You can't be pregnant forever! A pregnancy is only nine months, Annette! Lara shouts inside her head later that day. *And you can't keep telling him you had a miscarriage. He's going to figure it out sooner or later! You have to tell him!*

But like all emotionally overwhelming and painful things in her life, Annette is not present for them and it's Lara who has to face the painful problem—alone. It's one thing to endure molestation, threats to her life, rape, sex with Miguel and Ramón, *but what can I do to make a false pregnancy real? There is no solution for that! And if Annette doesn't wake up soon her whole life will fall apart and she needs Ramón. Ramón is good for Annette,* Lara thinks to herself. *I must find a solution!*

CHAPTER FOURTEEN
AN EVIL PLAN

Annette finds that reading a book is an effective way to block out Lara's insistent badgering. If she can just concentrate enough on the book and lose herself in the characters she can escape and doesn't hear Lara at all. But it doesn't always work. And Annette finds that as she tries to close Lara out of her mind she suffers horrendous headaches.

What are you going to do, just sit there and read books all the time? Don't you realize it's time for the baby to be born? You can't keep pretending forever! You've got to either tell him or do something! Lara shouts inside Annette's head.

Leave me alone! Annette begs, rubbing her head from the pain of it. And going back to the doctor to ask for a painkiller she finds herself knowingly lying to Ramón for the first time. The truth, that there is no pregnancy, is beginning to break through and she can't bear it and she cannot bear to tell him either.

But since Annette is confused and still lying to *herself* half the time it feels right to tell him what she wishes to be the truth, "The doctor says I need another sonogram." When he offers to drive her to the clinic, she tells him, "It shouldn't take long." And she leaves him waiting in the car as she disappears inside to ask for more painkillers.

When Annette returns with the prescription for a stronger headache medication—this time with codeine, she tells him, "Everything is good, the baby looks fine."

Unable to face the truth herself, Annette still mostly believes what she's telling him. *The baby is fine. Everything is good. The baby will be here soon,* she reassures herself, willing by sheer force any doubt out of her mind.

* * *

Don't you realize? He's going to leave you when he finds out. You keep taking him to all these doctor appointments telling him it's another sonogram or baby examination. He's really excited about this baby! He's not going to accept it when you tell him the truth. And if you can't tell him the truth, you need to find a baby!

That's impossible! Annette answers despite herself. *Why won't Lara leave her alone?*

That's it! Lara suddenly exclaims, her voice happy for once. *We'll find a pregnant woman about to have her baby, trick her into coming home with us, and cut her baby out of her! You can say you gave birth at home and I'll get rid of her body. Then Ramón will think it's yours. Problem solved!* Lara proposes jubilantly.

That's sick! Annette answers revulsion filling her stomach at the thought and realizing Lara means it she adds, *No, I'll never agree to do that!*

And what's your solution? Pretend to be pregnant forever? It's been nine months already! People are beginning to ask questions! Lara taunts, bitterness laced back into her voice.

Go away! Annette answers.

If you don't take care of it, I will! Lara threatens but Annette is already taking the extra-strength painkillers the doctor gave her and has put her nose back in her book, blocking Lara out.

* * *

The next weeks are a living hell listening to Lara continually propose murder.

It's the perfect crime! she tells Annette excitedly. *I watched how to do a Caesarian on the Discovery Channel and now, I know how to do it! I'll get a woman about to give birth to come home with me and when I take her baby out, you call 911 and tell them you have given birth to a baby at home! I'll take her body and hide it and later I'll tie it with cement blocks and put it in Lake Michigan not far from here. I know a very secluded spot and if she is weighted down with stones, her body will sink to the bottom and no one will ever find her,* Lara explains excitedly. *Everyone thinks you are pregnant so no one will suspect it's not yours. Ramón will be happy and so will you!*

You're sick! I'll never do that! Annette answers trying again to block Lara out. She can't hear Lara when she is sleeping so Annette takes more painkillers and sleeps and reads as much as she can. Ramón thinks she is sleeping more due to the baby.

I think I'm losing my mind! Annette thinks to herself in a rare moment of respite. *No one would ever believe me if I told them what I am going through!*

CHAPTER FIFTEEN
LURING HER VICTIM

Ever since alighting on the idea of committing murder to abduct a "nearly born" fetal child from its mother's womb, Lara has been plotting about how to carry out her plan. Engaging her photographic memory, Lara replays in her mind over and over again, the Discovery Channel television show outlining how a Caesarean is performed. She studies the details until after "watching" it for the fifteenth time, Lara is confident that she knows where and how to cut through the skin and muscles to get to the uterus, and then how to cut through the uterine wall to release the newborn from it's mother's body without causing any harm to the baby.

The mother of course dies in this scenario. And coldheartedly, Lara feels nothing for her. Perhaps because "Lara" is not actually her own person but emerged in early childhood as a personality split out of only a portion of her mind, coming into being for a specific task: to endure and then sequester the horror of nearly daily ongoing sexual assault to the young child that Annette was; Lara, like all psychopaths, completely lacks any human feeling or empathy for others. She also feels no fear, guilt, or shame and is able to withstand, what would be excruciating physical and emotional pain for others. Lara just needs to get out to drink and fight every once in awhile in order to vent the anger that bubbles up inside. Other than that she feels very little.

Lara is functioning as a classic psychopathic narcissist, cold and unfeeling toward others and with only her own (and Annette's) interests in mind. Indeed Lara's function, the whole reason for their

split mind, is so that Lara can hold the pain and emerge whenever Annette's emotional life is in overload. And one of those times is now.

How can she tell Ramón that the last two pregnancies have been figments of her imagination and that this one too is only a psychological pregnancy? And how can that be, when it feels so real to her? How can she face this pain herself, much less share it with Ramón who is already so excited about this new baby? And is Lara right? Will Ramón leave her if there is no baby? These are the questions that plague Annette whenever she allows the truth of her situation to penetrate into awareness, but mostly she blocks it all out, even when Lara shouts at her to face reality. And when Lara begins to realize that Annette never will – Lara, unbeknownst to Annette begins making plans in the background to fix everything.

Lara has readied her tools: a baseball bat to bludgeon her victim with once she had lured her home, plastic gloves to wear while cutting her victim and cleaning up the mess, a small sharp X-Acto knife with which to perform the surgery and a plan of how to dispose of her body. Lara plots to find a nearly term young pregnant female home and then knock her unconscious with the baseball bat, cut the baby from her womb, call 911 to inform them that she has given birth at home and later to dispose of the body after wrapping it up in tarp tied with cement blocks into Lake Michigan at a secluded area she has located where people rarely go.

In Lara's "mind" it's a perfect crime. But what she fails to realize is that crimes rarely are enacted as smoothly as one plans them and this one is no exception.

* * *

Lara has just passed the local low-income clinic. She knows there are likely to be many candidates here, and yes—soon she spots one walking along the street toward the bus stop. Sidling up to twenty-three year old Eva Alvarez Mendoza, Lara eyes her victim carefully. Petite—she will be easy to overcome; Hispanic—the baby will look

like Annette and maybe the police will not search for her body the same way they might for a "white" woman's; pregnant—she looks like she's due any day now and she's alone. Lara rolls down the window on the passenger side of the car and leaning over to speak to her chosen victim she asks in Spanish, "You look *really* pregnant; would you like a ride? I can drop you along the way if you like?"

"Oh, thank you!" Eva answers, smiling sweetly. "I have a prescription I need to get filled at the Walgreens. Are you going that way?" Eva asks, indicating further up the street in the direction Lara is headed.

"Yes, of course, I can drop you there," Lara answers smiling brightly. "Hop in!"

Eva opens the door and slowly lumbers into the front seat placing her hands on her belly as she smiles thankfully to Lara. "I just have to get this prescription filled and then I'm going home to rest!" she explains.

"I need something at the Walgreens, too. We can go together," Lara answers, asking Eva how far along she is and when her due date is.

"I already had cramps this morning!" Eva answers, smiling brightly. "The doctor says it can be anytime now!"

It turns out that Eva doesn't speak English well so that when the two arrive in the drugstore Eva asks Lara to speak to the pharmacist for her. Trying to shield her face from the security cameras by keeping her head down, Lara does her best to translate Eva's questions to the pharmacist and then after obtaining the needed answers, she invites Eva home with her.

"Listen, I have some baby things at home that we are not using. They are brand new: a baby seat, some blankets and some baby clothes. Would you like to have them? We can stop by my house pick them up and then I'll drop you home, if you like?" Lara offers.

Unsuspecting, Eva agrees.

Once inside the house Eva begs Lara to use the toilet. "I have to use the bathroom!" Eva says hugging her swollen belly. "I have to go all the time nowadays!"

"Sure, it's right there," Lara answers pointing to the bathroom door. "Eva doesn't notice the baseball bat or plastic gloves sitting out on the counter and once inside the bathroom has no idea that Lara has positioned herself outside the door ready to attack.

Bam! The bat hits Eva's head hard, thudding on her skull as she emerges from the bathroom but it's not enough of an impact to knock her out. Stunned by the blow and lifting her arms to protect her head Eva spins slowly in Lara's direction shocked to see her raising the bat again and raining down more blows bludgeoning poor Eva as she falls to her knees screaming, "What are you doing?"

Lara hits her again, striking Eva's head so hard that she collapses completely to the floor, but Lara sees she's still conscious! Throwing the bat to the floor, Lara leaps on Eva's pregnant body and straddling her huge belly, she instinctively repeats what was done to her repeatedly as a child. She places her hands roughly around Eva's neck and squeezes hard. Eva struggles but she's no match for Lara. Lara has too much experience with choking. She knows how to do it expertly. And as Eva's hands and legs flail trying to throw Lara off of her, Lara pins Eva's arms down with her knees and gradually she overwhelms her, strangling the last breathes of life out of her. Lara stands and reaches for duct tape she has left on the counter and using her X-Acto knife she cuts small pieces and places them over Eva's eyes and mouth, and then cuts larger strips she uses to bind Eva's arms and legs together. Then taking a plastic bag, Lara ties it over Eva's head, cinching it tightly around her neck.

Then Lara panics. There's blood smeared on the floor from Eva's head wound and her purse is strewn open on the floor. Forgetting all she learned about the Caesarean section and the need to act fast to remove the baby from his now lifeless mother, Lara runs for a wet towel to wipe the floor and she gather's Eva's purse and personal

items and runs outside pushing them deep into the trashcan, lifting some trash to cover them. Then Lara runs back inside, and recovering her focus, she takes the gloves and quickly places them on her hands, grabs the knife and pulling the lifeless Eva's blouse up over her face and her pants and purple panties down to her ankles. Then she hurriedly plunges the knife into Eva's belly, cutting into her the same way she saw on the film. It takes longer than she expects but as Lara pushes the knife in deeper, spreading Eva's flesh she sees first the coils of colon doubling back upon themselves and below that, the uterus.

Lara cuts carefully into the uterus, gently releasing the beautiful baby boy from inside his mother's womb. He slips out onto the floor, blue and unresponsive. *He's dead! All this for nothing! This has gone all wrong! I took too long! He hasn't had any oxygen since I strangled his mother!* Lara thinks as her mind races ahead to what to do next. *Hurry!* she says to herself. *You've got to hide the body and call 911 and tell them the baby has died!*

Quickly Lara pulls Eva by her feet down the hallway, opens the door and drags her lifeless body down the stairs, bumping her head on each step as she drags her into the unfinished basement below. Hurriedly looking around, Lara sees a plastic tarp and some used grocery bags. She picks them up and covers Eva's body with them. Then quickly she runs upstairs and gets a wet towel and washes down the floor and the steps. Running back down the stairs Lara uncovers Eva's body and taking her still gloved hand covers it in Eva's blood and then takes it to smear between her own legs as she removes her own panties. Lara throws the tarp over Eva's body again and takes the towel to the sink to wash it.

As she runs back up the stairs she checks to see if she's left any bloodstains and the same with the hallway. There's blood on the living room carpet near the bathroom, where the baby is lying dead in a small pool of blood that is coagulating around the placenta. Carefully Lara peels her latex gloves off and runs them out to the garbage

bin thrusting them deep down next to Eva's things and checks again to be sure the other bags are covering them before she returns the lid.

Then Lara rejoins the baby boy, lifeless on the linoleum where his mother has just been murdered. Distraught, not over the murder of his mother but that she failed to keep the baby alive, she is still hoping against hope that perhaps he can somehow be revived and knowing this will at least solve Annette's problem of her failure to produce a baby, Lara places her 911 call.

"911 operator. Where is your emergency?" a brisk female voice asks.

CHAPTER SIXTEEN
A BABY IS BORN

It's October 6, 2011 when the emergency 911 operator receives the late afternoon call.

"I need an ambulance!" Lara answers, her voice filled with distress.

"Okay, stay on the line with me. Don't hang up," the operator instructs her voice softening. Some beeps occur, then the phone line is transferred to the medical emergencies operator: "What is the address of the emergency?" the new operator asks.[12]

Lara mumbles, inaudibly.

"Hello? What is the address of the emergency?" The operator repeats concerned that the caller may not be able to tell her where to send the ambulance. In that case the call will be traced.

"1627 South 7th Street," Lara answers, her voice now audible, her accent Hispanic.

The operator repeats the address wrongly and Lara corrects her.

"South 7th?" the operator asks to be sure.

"Yes," Lara answers obviously relieved to be understood.

"1627 South 7th?" the operator repeats.

"Yes," Lara tells her.

"What is your phone number?" Lara provides it.

"And what is wrong?" the operator asks.

"I don't know, I was—I was pregnant. And [there was] born, one baby boy, in my house," Lara explains tearfully through a thick

Hispanic accent. She is obviously very distraught, although Lara normally feels nothing.

"Ma'am, ma'am, try and calm down! Take a deep breath. I can't understand you very well. What's wrong?" the operator asks again trying to clarify the situation for which she will soon dispatch a crew.

"I don't know! I was pregnant and [there was] born one baby in my house! Maybe it's dead?!" Lara explains.

"Okay, you were pregnant?" the operator asks beginning to grasp the situation a bit. *It's a late miscarriage? A stillbirth?* she muses as she waits for the reply.

"I don't know! I don't know I was pregnant!" Lara cries into the phone line.

"Oh. You *didn't know* you were pregnant?" the operator clarifies correcting Lara's English.

"Yes!" Lara cries, explaining, "How much I was, I born a baby! And maybe it's dead!"

"Okay, Ma'am you said you were pregnant and you had a baby?" the operator clarifies again, frustration rising in her voice as she tries in vain to grasp the nature of the emergency to which she is about to dispatch a crew.

"I don't know, I was pregnant!" Lara repeats, lying.

"Okay, is there is a baby?" the operator asks getting down to the basic needs of the situation.

"Yes, on my floor and maybe it's dead!" Lara answers.

"*Where* is the baby?" the operator asks trying to visualize the scene through what she is being told over the phone line.

"On the floor," the forlorn voice answers.

"The baby is on the floor?"

"Yes."

"Just one baby?"

"Yes. One baby. He's not breathing."

"The baby just came out of you *now?*" the operator asks.

The Hispanic woman sobs, "Yes!"

"Is the baby breathing?"

"No."

"Okay. And it just came out of you now?"

Lara hesitates before lying again; a sob catches in her throat. "Yes."

"Ma'am, the baby just came out of you now?" the operator confirms as she begins to activate the ambulance dispatch team.

"Again there is a brief hesitation and Lara repeats her lie, "Yes."

"Okay, ma'am, I need you to stay on the line." the operator instructs and already the sirens of the ambulance squeal out of the hospital parking lot along with two police patrol cars speeding on the way to the scene. The operator keeps her caller on the line, questioning her about her own condition and if the doors to the house are locked until the police and crew arrive and take over.

Putting the phone back on the receiver the operator shudders. *A dead baby!* the operator thinks sadly to herself. *I like it better when the woman calling is still in labor and the ambulance arrives in time to ensure a healthy, live birth!* she thinks as she ponders the last disturbing call and waits again perched between boredom and anxiety for the next call of her day.

CHAPTER SEVENTEEN
WAKING UP TO DEATH

When Ramón receives the call from the neighbors that there is an ambulance at his home and that they are taking Annette to the hospital after giving birth at home to their stillborn baby boy, he immediately asks a friend, "Juan[13], can you drive me home? Annette just gave birth at home!" Arriving before the children return home from school, Ramón meets the police at his house. They explain that they are waiting for the coroner to come make out the death certificate for his stillborn son.

One of the rescue workers shows Ramón his newborn son and soon after the kids arrive home. Ramón and the kids cry as everyone takes turns holding the newborn baby boy wrapped up in the soft blanket from the layette Annette had ready waiting for his birth. Having photographed his dead son before the emergency workers took him away, Ramón posts pictures on his Facebook page writing, "My dark haired baby boy was born last night but died at the hour of birth. He was going to be so beautiful! My woman is devastated about him and won't stop crying."[14]

* * *

When the ambulance arrives at the hospital and the medics wheel Lara into the emergency room, Lara waits until they are occupied with other cases and then stands up from her hospital bed and walks out to the nursing stand to sign herself out. "I'm fine. I just want to go home," she explains to the nurses refusing any further medical attention. Then she goes to the street to call Ramón.

"Ramón, I'm at the hospital," Lara tearfully explains. "Can you come and get me?"

"Annette! Are you alright?" Ramón asks.

"Yes, I'm okay," Annette answers as Lara fades out and Annette emerges back into awareness. Blinking in the bright October sunlight, confused, Annette suddenly feels a growing horror that grips at her heart. *Why am I here? What has she done?* Annette begins to ask herself.

* * *

Returning now with Annette from the hospital, where he thinks she's just been examined and cared for after giving birth to their stillborn son, he opens the car door carefully and helps her out of the car. Ramón puts his arm protectively around Annette as they enter their living room.

There is still a large bloodstain on the carpet near the hallway, where Lara murdered Eva. Seeing it, Annette loses her strength, gasping in terror.

"What happened here?" Annette asks breathlessly staring at the bloodstained carpet.

"Annette, darling, you had the baby on the floor over there, that's your blood and the water from the birth," Ramón explains comfortingly, pulling his arm closer around his confused partner.

She's sick with grief, and shock! he thinks as he guides her across the room, steering her away from the bloodstained carpet.

"Baby, what baby?" Annette asks, horror tingeing her voice.

"Our baby!" Ramón answers, grief filling his.

"Oh Dio! No!" Annette moans and drops to the floor.

"Come on darling, let's put you to bed," Ramón answers but Annette slowly rises.

"Where are my children? Come it's bedtime," she says to the children who have gingerly gathered around, frightened to see their mother in such a state of shock.

"The baby was so beautiful, Mama!" Elise says as Annette shepherds her into her bedroom and concentrates on taking her little dress off and helping her into her nightgown.

"Come, brush your teeth," Annette says and calls to Pablo and Carmelita to get ready for bed as well.

After a half hour, all the children are in bed and Ramón helps Annette get ready for sleep as well. "Come, baby let me hold you. You look so weak," Ramón says as he pulls the covers back and helps Annette to climb into their bed. "We'll have another, don't worry!" he says stroking her hair. A stifled sob rises in Annette's throat as she pushes her face down into the pillow.

No never! Annette moans internally. *What has she done?* Annette asks herself, horror filling her mind as she begins to realize the truth of what must have happened right here in this house. *Oh Dio! Make me sleep and never wake up!* Annette prays as consciousness fades and the darkness overtakes her.

CHAPTER EIGHTEEN
EVIDENCE OF A CRIME

Neils Farr, the county medical examiner[15] whistles softly under his breath as his latex fingers pull off snippets of the tissue around the fetal boy he is examining. *Placenta – okay that's normal, but torn up uterine and fallopian tube tissue? That's not normal for childbirth. This woman's internal organs have either torn apart as she gave birth, or someone's cut her! This looks like a botched C-section, not a vaginal birth. Could it be she was trying to self-induce a late abortion? Something is really wrong here!*

Neils walks to the phone and places a call to the Milwaukee police. "You better ask Mrs. Morales Rodriguez to come back to the hospital. There's uterine and fallopian tube tissue on this baby. That makes no sense. She's either cut herself internally during the birth, been cut by someone else or her internal organs have torn loose with the birth. She may be dangerously hemorrhaging. You better get her back to the hospital stat. She needs a vaginal examination and a vaginal sonogram immediately."

The dispatcher immediately sends a patrol car and two officers to Annette Morales Rodriguez's house while the medical examiner's office places a call to her as well.[16]

* * *

Annette is sitting in her faded bathrobe and still has her fingers wrapped around her coffee mug when the phone rings. "Mrs. Morales Rodriguez?" the woman's voice asks. "This is the medical examiner's office calling," she explains.

"Si," Annette answers, the coffee not yet coursing through her veins and last night's shock still leaving her with a dulled mind.

"The medical examiner has examined your baby son and he's recommending that you return *immediately* to the hospital for another examination. He says it's a matter of life and death and you should go *right away* to the hospital. Do you understand?"[17]

"Yes," Annette answers in heavily accented English. "Yes, I understand."

"Since this could be a medical emergency, we are sending a patrol car to escort you to the hospital," the woman explains. "They should be there any minute now. Can you get ready to leave?"

"Yes," Annette answers as her fingers suddenly release her coffee mug and it half falls harshly rattling against the Formica table as she hangs up the phone.

"What's wrong?" Ramón asks, startled by her reaction.

"I have to go back to the hospital! They say it's an emergency and they are sending a police car to escort us. Can you drive me there?"

"Of course, porbrecita! I will drive you and stay the whole time! Hurry gather your things!" Ramón answers. The doorbell rings and he goes to the door as Annette shuffles down the hall to hurriedly change into a pair of slacks and a blouse and grab her purse.

"I have to return to the hospital," she explains to Carmelita as she passes her room. "Can you feed the others breakfast and keep an eye on them until I return home? I'll call Ella[18] to come take them if it takes too long," she adds, referring to the neighbor who babysits Pablo and Elise.

"Sure Mama," Carmelita answers from her bed, her eyes still sticky with sleep. "You going to be okay?"

"Yes, I hope so!" Annette answers as she hurries to the door. The two police officers are standing there in their dark blue uniforms,

silver badges pinned to their chests and radios and pistols strapped around their waists.

"This way ma'am," Officer Patrick Elm[19] says, guiding Annette to Ramón's waiting car. Officer Robert Velez who speaks Spanish, translates and opens the door for her and she slips in. He closes the door behind. "We will follow close behind your car," he instructs and switching on their police lights the pair of cars speed through the Milwaukee rush hour traffic, the other cars pulling to the side to make way.

At Saint Francis Hospital they are met by an aide who takes them up to the fourth floor to the labor and delivery department. There they check in with a nurse's aide who escorts Annette into a small examining room, instructing her to remove her pants and underwear and put on a paper gown and then wait for the doctor while seated on the examining table. Annette does as she's told while Ramón and the two policemen stand waiting outside the door.

Annette's hands shake as she pulls down her pants and removes her underpants, hanging them both neatly over the hook on the back of the door. *What has she done? What will happen to me now?* Annette asks herself anxiously as she seats herself on the examining table. Within minutes, a nurse and doctor knock and enter and Annette notices that the policemen are still standing guard outside her door. Her hands and legs tremble as she looks at the female doctor who has begun speaking to her.[20]

"Can you scoot down a bit and put your legs up here in the stirrups? And let's lift your blouse up to here" the nurse instructs, indicating pulling her blouse above her bra line, as Annette begins to understand what they will do.

"We are going to do an ultrasound so I'm going to first squirt some of this gel on your belly and then after I'm going to examine internally with the wand, okay?" the doctor asks in a matter of fact voice.

Annette does as she is told and feels the cold gel squirting out on her belly and the slightly pulsing ultrasound probe running over her lower belly. The doctor is fixated on a nearby screen adjusting where she points the probe as she watches the screen. Annette's legs tremble in fear.

"Okay we're going in now," the doctor says switching off the external probe and picking up the wand. Annette takes one look at the wand and understands what she means to do with it and then she's gone.

*   *   *

It's Lara who feels the doctor slowly inserting the wand into Annette's vagina. It's slim and covered in gel so it slips in easily. *Great now the doctors are fucking me too!* Lara thinks watching her.

"I'm going to examine you vaginally as well," the doctor explains after removing the wand. She takes a shiny stainless steel instrument out of a drawer beneath the table Lara is splayed out on and Lara nods knowing what comes next. Annette never stays for these examinations—it's always Lara's job to endure them. *Annette is weak but this is nothing compared to the real thing!* Lara thinks to herself contempt filling her face.

"Okay, I have what I need," the doctor says, backing her stool away from between Annette's open knees and standing. She drops the metal instrument onto a nearby table where it rattles jarringly, and she peels the gloves from her hands and discards them into the trashcan as she goes to the sink to wash. "You can get dressed now," she says, her voice suddenly turned cold. The nurse exits, and it's just Lara and the doctor alone in the room now.

She knows I haven't given birth! Lara thinks, panic suddenly overcoming her. Annette is buried deep in unconsciousness and Lara knows it's now up to her to find a solution.

"Okay, what about the bleeding after birth? When will that stop?" Lara asks aggression filling her voice.

"You have no bleeding!" the doctor answers, surprise and a bit of fear filling her eyes.

"No, I'm bleeding on and off," Lara challenges, "Quite heavily last night after the baby was born dead," she adds.

"There's no bleeding!" the doctor says edging for the door. "You can get dressed now," she repeats as she swings open the door and leaves Lara alone.

Bitch thinks she can out me! Lara thinks as she swings her legs down from the stirrups and stands up from the examining table. *I'll show her!*

Lara strides across the small room and finds what she needs, a small glass slide. She slams it against the counter top breaking it into a sharp diagonal and then taking latex gloves she places them on her hands, picks up the glass shard as she moves into the adjacent toilet room. Standing straddled over the toilet, Lara takes the broken piece of glass and inserts it high into her vagina cutting herself. Blood pours out as the pain rips through her. Satisfied Lara removes her gloves, tossing them, and the glass shard into the toilet and flushing it. Taking toilet paper, she wipes the toilet seat clean.

Running back into the examining room with her gown now around her knees and blood streaming between her legs Lara whips the door open and calls down the hall, "Nurse! Nurse! Help I'm bleeding!"

Standing with blood dripping down onto the white tile floor of the examining room Lara watches with satisfaction as the two policemen conferring with the doctor look up abruptly and the doctor and a nurse come running toward her.

"What have you done?" the doctor sternly exclaims looking at the pool of blood on the floor and the blood streaming between Lara's bare thighs. "Give her a heavy pad and a towel and tell her to get dressed," the doctor instructs. Then looking coldly at Lara she tells her, "You need to get dressed and go to the emergency room. The police are waiting outside the door to take you."

"I'm bleeding after your examination!" Lara cries. "Look at all the blood, it started up again, just like after the baby was born!"

"No, you cut yourself," the doctor says backing out the door again, her face filled with disgust. The nurse hands Lara a heavy pad and a towel and exits along with the doctor.

CHAPTER NINETEEN
VAGINAL ASSAULT AND A COERCED CONFESSION

Officer Rodolfo Gomez[21] has been on the beat ten years now, but he's never seen anything like this.

What kind of witch is inside that room? He asks himself just as Annette emerges in her hospital gown, red blood streaking down her inner thighs, crying out that she's bleeding from giving birth!

And now the doctor says she cut herself!

Shit, how can a woman cut her own insides? Gomez asks himself. *Doesn't that gotta hurt like hell? Who is this crazy lady they've been sent to investigate?*

Fucking psychopath is what she is! Why does she have to be one of ours? Giving a bad name to all Hispanics! Gomez calls in to HQ to give Harry Jones[22], his boss the scoop.

"There's no way she's been pregnant," Jones tells him over the phone as they discuss what the doctor said when she briefly conferred with Gomez and his partner out in the hallway. "The hospital director has already reported to us that there's been *no pregnancy and no birth!*" Jones reports. "And the hospital has received a call about a missing persons report, a young Hispanic *pregnant* woman in labor! This is beginning to look like foul play."

"What the hell?" Rodolfo shouts back into the phone.

"It just doesn't add up," Harry answers. "She didn't give birth, now we have a missing pregnant woman in labor. This may be her baby."

"Geezus Christ! Okay I'll keep on her," Gomez answers, hanging up the phone.[23]

In the meantime Lara has cleaned herself up and emerges from the room. Her boyfriend Ramón runs to her, hugging her, asking if she's okay as Gomez stares in disgust at the couple. *Oh God almighty is he in on this too? If they took the baby, where's the mother? Is she still alive?*

"Can you come with us please," Officer Gomez interrupts them, explaining that Annette needs to report to the emergency room before being discharged. Officers Diedrich[24] and Gomez flank Annette who is being hugged by Ramón, as they make their way on foot to the elevator and down to the first floor emergency room.

There, the hospital staff sequesters Annette in a small curtained off cubicle telling her to wait for the doctor to discharge her. Officer Gomez decides it's time for a chat and he enters the room. Ramón has been sent to the waiting area so there's no one present except he and Annette.

"How are you?" he begins kindheartedly speaking in Spanish despite his disgust.

"I'm okay," Lara answers. Annette is far away and totally unaware.

"What's going on?" Gomez inquires after asking her to verify her name.

"I came for an exam and now I'm here," Lara answers nonchalantly. Then perhaps with Annette's anxiety bleeding through to her, Lara adds, "Do you know where my children are?"

Officer Gomez informs her that they are at home and will be taken care of if necessary.

"I'm sorry for what I did," Lara suddenly blurts out and then pointing at Officer Diedrich who is hanging about the doorway she adds, "I don't want to talk in front of her. I don't like her!"

"What are you sorry for?" Gomez prods but at that moment a nurse enters.

"You need to take your pants off. The doctor wants another examination," the nurse announces in a matter-of-fact voice as she hangs Annette's chart on the end of her bed.

"I don't want another examination!" Lara answers, her eyes widening with terror.[25]

"Doctor's orders," the nurse says turning to set up the adjacent table with the instruments needed for Annette's gynecological examination.

"I don't want another exam! Please leave!" Lara repeats and turning to Officer Gomez she explains, "I cut myself, with my fingernails inside latex gloves!" Her face terror-stricken she then pleads, "Do you want me to cooperate?"

"I want the truth," Gomez answers as he suddenly sees his opportunity to crack this case.

"Then tell her to leave," Lara instructs.

Gomez nods and asks the nurse to leave.

"How much time will I serve?" Lara asks.

"I can't give you any time frame until I know what we are talking about," Gomez answers.

"I'll tell you her name – it's Eva Alvarez Mendoza," Lara states.

"Can you make it easy for me and tell me where she is?" he asks.

Nodding, Lara understands that the game is up and this is the only way to ward off another vaginal exam—what feels to her like an assault. Beginning to shake uncontrollably, Lara answers "She's in the basement at the house."

"She's hurt?" Gomez asks taking Lara's hand in his to calm her.

"You can't help her, she's dead," Lara answers thinking, *It's better if I confess. I'll go to prison and Annette will be safe, otherwise they'll blame her.* Apparently Lara is confused, forgetting that their

two selves share the same body. "How long will I have to stay in prison?" Lara asks again, her face filled with anxiety. "How long will I have to serve?"[26]

*   *   *

Officer Gomez doesn't answer. He slips through the curtains and makes a phone call back to the station telling them to send a squad car and detectives to Annette's house, that the missing pregnant woman is apparently dead in her basement.

Meanwhile the nurse reappears with the doctor.

I won't cry! Lara thinks to herself as the doctor probes past her lacerated inner flesh. It hurts like hell but she is determined now to show it – not to the doctor, not to the nurse, not to anybody.

"You've cut yourself pretty badly," she says slipping the instrument out of place and probing with her latex gloved fingers now.

"I just had a baby, I've been bleeding on and off since then!" Lara retorts.

"Okay then. You can get dressed and leave," she answers pulling out from inside her and discarding her gloves as she turns to leave. Lara stands up and pulls her underwear, now heavy with the blood filled pad attached, and her slacks, up around her.

I wish I'd brought a sweater! She thinks to herself as she rubs her hands over her chilly arms. Taking her phone she dials Ella, the babysitter, and explains, "It's more complicated than I thought. Can you keep the kids all day? Ramón will come home soon I think." . . . "Yes I'm okay," she answers before ending the call.

Lara waits as Officer Gomez enters the room again.

"We are going to take you down to the station for questioning, okay?" Lara nods and soon Officer Latanya Diedrich arrives to take her away. Apparently they've explained to Ramón, as he is nowhere to be seen as Lara gets into the police car. Officer Diedrich doesn't put cuffs on Lara and it's a short drive.[27]

At the police station Officer Hutchinson and Gomez escort her into a small cinder block room and seat her at a table. It's cold and Lara rubs her hands over her arms, flipping her hair back over her shoulders, as they begin to explain the procedure. It's something about her rights and they explain that she can have a lawyer. "You understand, right?" Gomez asks speaking in Spanish, rubbing Lara's bare arm as he does. And when she nods he instructs, "Sign here."[28]

Lara signs saying, "I don't want Ramón involved in this because he is innocent. And then I want a lawyer." Then without helping her to understand that she can now contact the lawyer she has just requested, rather than after they question her, they are off, the police asking about how she met Eva, the woman she's just murdered, and how Eva happened to be at their home and how she died.

"She owed me money," Lara lies, her mind racing as she thinks through the best way to present her case. I saw her on the street and asked her for the money. "Then we went to my house and we got in a fight," she explains. "She hit me so I choked her and then her head hit the ground."

"But that doesn't explain the baby. Why did you cut her open and take her baby?" Gomez asks.

"I thought she was dead and I wanted to save the baby," Lara lies.

"You're lying," Gomez challenges. Lara stares him in the eyes and doesn't give a fuck what he thinks.

I'll confess and Annette can go free, Lara thinks as her mind races ahead. *I can rot in fucking prison just as long as Annette goes free!* Lara decides. *It will be like it always is. I'm strong. She's afraid and weak. I can take the bad things.* Slowly she begins to tell them the truth including how she put duct tape over Eva's mouth and eyes, bound her arms and legs, wrapped her head in a plastic bag and cut her baby from her body.

CHAPTER TWENTY
MILWAUKEE COUNTY JAIL

It's all over the news, the story of a dead woman with her fetus cut out of her. Overnight Annette Morales Rodriguez's murder of Eva Alvarez Mendoza has become the talk of the town.

"You should take this case," Patrick Rupich says as he sits for his morning coffee with Bob D'Arruda, one of the leading Milwaukee criminal defense attorneys. "What is your streak now? Three wins out of the last four trials?"

Bob nods. He's confident of his skills at trial, and this case is definitely going to trial. He's begun to get a reputation in Milwaukee as the man to turn to for building some chances into very rough cases. Without a doubt, this case would be very rough.[29]

"It's a really wild case," adds Michael Torphy the third attorney in their team, when called by D'Arruda. Mike has the most experience with the mentally ill; he previously set up and managed an organization safeguarding the disability benefits of mentally ill and he's seen it all. Until now.

"She must be crazy to do such a crime? We'd need to get a psych evaluation, no?" Mike asks over speaker phone.

"It's got to be an insanity case for sure!" Pat adds. "Insane what she did!"

"She hasn't got any money," Pat notes. "We could do it pro-bono but keep that under wraps, make a private arrangement not to charge her. Want me to check it out?"

"I'll do it if we do it as a team," Bob answers, smiling at the prospect of an exciting and headline-grabbing case. Mike agrees and

Bob cuts the line as he smiles at Pat and picks up his briefcase ready for action. Leaving their breakfast, Bob heads out to the Milwaukee County Jail in hopes of picking up one more notch on his belt.

* * *

Annette meanwhile has been booked into her cell. She lies huddled on the narrow hard bunk staring at the cement block walls of the confined space of her tiny, airless cell. Outside the guards patrol by and occasionally glance in the long, glass pane of her cell window. There's no privacy and the light is artificial, provided by the buzzing overhead fluorescent lights. The one small window is covered with clouded Plexiglas.

I'll go crazy in here! Annette thinks to herself and then remembering all that has occurred she adds, *That is, if I'm not crazy already! What has she done? What? How did she do it?*

Lara's voice intrudes into her head trying to explain but Annette blocks her completely. *Don't speak to me. Don't ever come and talk to me again. You are evil!* Annette answers before Lara can say a word. *Go away from me—forever!*

Shocked, Lara retreats. *What have I done?* Lara repeats the question to herself. *I didn't mean for this to happen. I thought I would go to jail and she would go free!* For the first time in her life, Lara feels genuine remorse.

* * *

Annette's jailers let her out of her cell one hour per day. During the hour she is allowed to walk about in the area just outside her cell. Today is a lucky day. The guard has come to take her out once again, this time telling her, "Your lawyer is here."

Annette meets Bob D'Arruda and his translator in a small cement block cell. The fluorescent lights buzz overhead here too, and she has a hard time concentrating as he explains her case and offers his services. He's brought an interpreter, and it's not a matter of language that makes it hard to understand. She just can't stay present

very well. He asks her to sign some papers and after she complies, they get up to leave.

* * *

Waking from a nightmare, Annette shakes herself awake and is terrified to see the walls and fluorescent lights closing in on her. Cowering under the rough jailhouse blanket she stares in incomprehension, slowly reorienting herself. I'm in jail! She did this!

Annette's mind wanders back over the nightmare. *It's her, or not her—Lara—straddled across a woman, strangling her. The woman is struggling, flailing her arms and legs, but Annette—no it's her, Lara—climbs up further on her belly pinning the woman's struggling arms with her knees as she continues to clench her hands around the woman's throat. Slowly the struggle ends. The woman stops breathing and rests. She's dead?!*

Annette awakens fully. Sweat is drenching her body. She throws the blanket to the floor and struggles quickly up from the bed, horrified at her dream!

The reality of what happened! She realizes as she goes to the sink and throws cold water over her face splashing it again and again. *She did this!* Annette thinks as a frozen dread moves down deep into her belly. *She did this! We will be in prison forever!*

Annette's mind wanders further back into the dream. *Lara stands by the bathroom waiting for the woman to emerge. She has the bat held high in her hand and when the woman opens the door and walks back into the hallway, Lara springs, beating her over and over again on the head with the heavy bat as the woman screams in terror until she falls to her knees and then with one more hard hit collapses to the floor. Lara pounces on top of her, strangling her breath from her body.*

"Oh Dio!" Annette calls out, falling to her own knees, her head bowed to the cold cement floor as she sobs. "Dio help me! Help me! What about my children?"

Annette sobs until exhausted with tears, she lies prone on the cold floor, sobbing until she falls once again into a deep sleep.

After some hours, Annette awakes to hearing a *baby crying. It's crying plaintively and loud, keening for its mother.* It's dark now and Annette crawls to her bed and puts her hands to her ears to try to shut out the baby's cries. *But nothing shuts out the baby's sorrowful wails.*

* * *

A few days later, another lawyer, this one named Patrick Rupich, arrives to meet with her, bringing the same male interpreter. Pat is gentle and she likes him. He seems kind and she hopes he can deliver her from this tomb she is suspended in.

Patrick has a DVD with him and he asks her to watch it on the computer he's brought along. It's the video of Lara confessing to the police—in Spanish. Annette watches it as horror fills her belly.

"Do you have anything to tell me about this confession?" Pat asks but Annette cannot answer.

My confession! I didn't do those things! That's not me talking on the video! She wants to shout but how can she explain?

No normal person can understand what goes on inside her head. No one would believe her even if she tried to explain. And how can she speak for Lara? Only Lara can say what she did, Annette thinks as bile rises into her throat and chokes her. Wide-eyed with terror, Annette simply shakes her head no. Pat takes his computer and leaves and the guard locks her back in her cell.

* * *

Enraged, Annette paces back and forth across her cell. *She really did it! And she even confessed! There is no way out of here now!* Annette realizes as she eyes the six feet left to the wall, measuring the distance from there back to the center of her cell. *This is it from*

now on! Annette thinks as the walls and ceiling seem to close in on her.

* * *

It's afternoon and Annette begins to see visions. It's the same always: a woman appears with a knife in her hand and Annette becomes completely terrified. "Guards! Guards!" Annette screams in terror. "There's a woman—a woman with a knife in her hand!" she screams, cowering near the door as the guards come and try to calm her. Sometimes they take her to the dispensary where the jail doctor gives her another dose of something to make her forget and go to sleep.

* * *

Meanwhile, Lara is determined to get out of this place. She has been plotting her escape and has managed to block the door from locking completely. Seeing the guard patrolling past—a female this time, Lara takes her opportunity. Pushing her door open, Lara leaps upon her and throws the guard off balance as she maneuvers the guard into her cell while grabbing the radio from the guard's pants pocket. She throws the radio into the corner of the cell, making it impossible for her to radio for help. The guard, surprised by Lara's sudden attack, now regains her equilibrium and begins to fight back. The two women struggle as Lara tries hard to subdue her, but the guard knows how to fight and she soon gets the upper hand pushing Lara back into the cell as she quickly backs out the door, slams it shut and begins yelling for help.

Five male guards come to the rescue, and Annette is soon manhandled into a straightjacket. From then on she is dressed in a blood red prison uniform a designation of dangerousness and now when she goes from her cell for her one hour of exercise in the hallway, her hands and legs are also manacled. There's no possibility of escape now.

* * *

Annette tries to escape into the concoction of medications the jail doctor gives her but she keeps waking to seeing the woman with the knife and each time she screams hysterically for the guards. Everyone tells her it's just a hallucination, but to Annette the woman seems real and terrifying.

When she can't sleep and the woman is not there terrifying her Annette thinks about the blue color of the sky in summer, the color of green leaves, and the feeling of the sun shining on her shoulders. She remembers the smooth skin of her children, and how she loves to brush their hair and cuddle with them in her bed. She longs to be home again, to cook her own food, care for her children, clean her own house and to be able to walk out the door and see the sun again. *It's so dark and airless here!* she thinks to herself trying to fight the feeling that the walls and ceiling are closing in on her.

CHAPTER TWENTY-ONE
DR. PANKIEWICZ

"Time to talk to the psychiatrist," a male guard says as he opens her cell a few days later. Annette walks behind him with short, manacled steps as he escorts her down the hallway and around the corner to the same room where she met her lawyer. This time she is introduced to the State's psychiatrist, Dr. Pankiewicz, and Christina Green, his interpreter.[30]

Christina is a Hispanic middle-aged woman and seems kindly as she makes the introductions in Spanish. Dr. Pankiewicz is middle-aged with thinning hair and watches her closely as she takes her seat across the table from him. Annette immediately doesn't like him, although she is not sure why. What she doesn't get is that it's Lara who doesn't like him and Lara is, unknown to Annette, giving her a very dark feeling.

The doctor begins with an explanation of his role. "Mrs. Morales Rodriguez, it is important that you understand that I am here working for the State of Wisconsin as a psychiatrist to examine you for psychiatric health and to report back to the court if you meet the criteria of the special plea of not guilty by reason of mental disease or defect. What you tells me here will not be confidential as I will be reporting a summary of our discussion back to the court," he advises and pushes some papers for her to sign across the table. Christina explains that she must give her consent to the psychiatric examination, and Annette reluctantly signs the paper.

The doctor begins by asking her some about her life, her marriage and separation, the birth of her children, her education and

employment history, how she came to Milwaukee, and about her health history—they discuss that she was in a car accident years ago and sustained a head injury that she sometimes takes Tylenol with codeine for, about the voices she has heard in the last year and the hallucinations she has had in the prison.

"Sometimes I see a woman with a knife in her hand and I get desperate and yell for the guards," Annette tells Dr. Pankiewicz, but he doesn't ask much about this woman and Annette doesn't explain to him that she is beginning to realize that it is Lara and that the voices in her head, prior to the crime, were Lara threatening to commit it. She does tell him about the baby crying and when Lara dares to speak in her head during the interview Annette repeats what Lara has said, "I hear a voice telling me to kill the both of you," Annette says testing the waters of how much this doctor can handle to hear.

The doctor seems unimpressed although Christina seems to recoil a bit. He doesn't ask for more details and Annette doesn't think she can tell him about Lara. *He would never believe me if I told him about her,* Annette reflects sadly.

"I heard voices before, too," she tells the doctor. "They were worse when I was upset, but I always tried to distract myself [so as] not to hear them," Annette explains.

"You were pregnant recently?" Dr. Pankiewicz asks, changing the subject.

"Yes, two times," Annette tells him explaining that one of the drug store tests came out negative and one positive, and she believed she was pregnant since her belly was swelling and she had the signs of pregnancy, but then she miscarried both times. She expresses her own and Ramón's sorrow over the miscarriages. She fails to tell him about the last pregnancy, that she thought it was real and even now believes she is still pregnant, and that she didn't hear—refused to hear—what the doctor told her about having had her tubes tied, that only Lara heard and that Annette still refuses to believe it. *The baby*

is still coming, Annette thinks to herself staring off into the distance and unconsciously moving her manacled hands over her belly.

Satisfied that that he knows enough about her background and health history, Dr. Pankiewicz launches into asking her about her confession to the crime of killing Eva Alvarez Mendoza.

"I don't know anything about that," Annette tells him speaking sincerely.

"But you confessed to doing it," the doctor protests.

"I don't remember confessing," Annette tells him. That kicks off a discussion with the doctor insisting that she has confessed, reading her details from her criminal file and asking her why she did what she did. Annette again sincerely tells him that she has no memory of the crime or of confessing to it. Instead of taking her at her word, Dr. Pankiewicz apparently sees this as the usual criminal cry of innocence.

"What I remember is just flashes of memory, not like I was there," Annette explains to him. "I have some memory of picking the girl up and taking her to the Walgreens and offering to have her come home with me to have some baby things. She came home with me, but from that point I have no memory of anything, until some time at jail."

"You don't remember hitting her and choking her as you told the police? Or going to the hospital and being examined?" Dr. Pankiewicz asks her.

"No," Annette tells him. "I've been told that I supposedly killed the girl and tried to have the baby pass as mine, but I have no memory of any of that." Annette looks down in shame and then adds, "I think I am innocent." Looking up at him jotting down his notes, deep sorrow fills her eyes.

The doctor finishes his examination, and Annette is led back to her cell. Some weeks later he finishes his report and submits it to the court stating that some of her symptoms are consistent with psy-

chosis but others are not and that he does not judge her either as incompetent to stand trial or as qualifying for the insanity defense.

Despite recording Annette describing her terrifying hallucinations of seeing a woman wielding a knife in his formal report to the court, Dr. Pankiewicz states:

> Ms. Morales did not reveal or endorse any delusional ideation. She did not appear internally preoccupied or distracted by her reported perceptual disturbances. Her responses were coherent, linear and goal directed. She reported distress and depressed mood over her present circumstances.

Giving his expert opinion Dr. Pankiewicz concludes,

> Based upon my examination as well as a review of collateral records, I did not find evidence to indicate Annette Morales-Rodriguez suffered from a mental disease or defect at the time of her offense on October 6, 2011. Ms. Morales reports a number f subjective symptoms at the time of examination but indicates no recollection of her offense-related behavior. She did not recall making contact with the victim ... Her only recollection is offering Ms. Alvarez Mendoza[31] assistance by giving her a ride to the pharmacy and also offering her baby clothes. Ms. Morales did not indicate she was suffering from any symptom of mental disturbance during the time of her contact with Ms. Alvarez Mendoza that she can remember.
>
> Ms. Morales' reported circumscribed amnesia, beginning shortly after arriving to her own home with Ms. Alvarez Mendoza on October 6, 2011 and ending at some point while in custody at the Milwaukee County Jail, is not consistent with any psychiatric

disorders. Individuals who suffer trauma, even if they perpetrated the trauma, can have more isolated repressed memories, but the specific period of amnesia Ms. Morales reports is very unlikely.

A review of the case materials indicates that Ms. Morales attempted to conceal the homicide of Ms. Alvarez Mendoza and claim that she had a spontaneous birth of a non-breathing infant. She made efforts to conceal Ms. Alvarez Mendoza's body and also to appear as though she had actually spontaneously delivered a child. She then changed her story, indicating Ms. Alvarez Mendoza's death was accidental secondary to a fall during an altercation. She then changed her story again and described a specific plan to search out a pregnant female in a desperate attempt to provide a son for her boyfriend. Ms. Morales demonstrated a clear understanding of the criminality of her behavior when she told authorities she was going to answer questions because she did not want her boyfriend to get in trouble. During interview, she asked police officers how long she would be incarcerated for a homicide. This demonstrates that she had a clear understanding that her behavior was wrongful and illegal.

Ms. Morales also demonstrated other inconsistencies in her statements in an effort to conceal what was actually going on. She had convinced her best friend and boyfriend she was actually pregnant. During examination she claimed she was not pregnant and in fact had offered the victim baby clothes, which Ms. Morales did not believe she needed. I believe this is further demonstration of attempted deception to avoid her culpability for her offense.

I have no doubt that Ms. Morales is presently experiencing substantial distress given her circumstances. Her subjective symptoms are mixed, with respect to being reflective of legitimate mental illness. Whatever the case, there is no evidence to indicate mental illness was an operative factor in her offense related behavior. I therefore believe to a reasonable degree of medical certainty Annette Morales-Rodrigues does not meet the criteria for the special plea of not guilty by reason of mental disease or defect and offer that opinion to the court for its adjudication.

CHAPTER TWENTY-TWO

GETTING INVOLVED

October 11, 2011 – "A Wisconsin woman who already had three children and was desperate to have one with her new boyfriend was today charged with killing a pregnant mother, cutting out her baby and passing off the child as her own." *The Daily Mail, UK* [32]

"This case is unfolding here," Victoria Thorn, a Milwaukee based colleague, e-mails me just before I am scheduled to come to Milwaukee to give a talk at a conference she is organizing. "I think you will find this interesting," she writes, attaching a news article entitled, "Suspect pretended to be pregnant for months, neighbors say."[33]

I open the attachment, registering shock as I read what sounds like a disgusting crime. When I arrive in Milwaukee, Vicki tells me more about it.

"You should get involved in the case. I bet it's abortion related," Vicky advises, knowing I've done research studying women's post-traumatic and sometimes bizarre responses following an abortion.

"I don't know," I answer as my stomach turns at the thought. "Fetal abduction! I suppose if she had been forced into an unwanted abortion at one point in her life, she could have somehow felt cheated of her own baby and twisted that into justifying taking another woman's fetus?" I muse aloud.

"Yes!" Vicki answers. "I think it is all connected. Her boyfriend wanted a son and she supposedly couldn't get pregnant. She randomly chose this woman and brutally bludgeoned her, then called the EMTs saying she'd given birth when the baby wasn't breathing and so on!"

Busied with the affairs of the conference Vicki has organized, we don't discuss the case again, but Vicki's comments linger in my mind as the idea of abducting a live fetus—literally cutting it out of the mother—captures my thoughts, motivating me to Google the story and contact Gitte Laasby, one of the Milwaukee journalists covering it, to ask more.

"This isn't the first case of its kind," Gitte tells me, causing me to gasp in surprise. "There have actually been eleven fetal abductions in the United States. We've been covering the story in the Milwaukee Journal Sentinel." Gitte gives me her newspaper's website to search for their other stories about Annette Morales Rodriguez.[34]

The thought of someone going to the bizarre length of cutting another woman's fetus from her body sticks with me as I fly home to McLean, Virginia, the suburbs of Washington, D.C. where I live.

Eleven fetal abductions! Why would anyone cut a child out of another woman? I ask myself. Why wouldn't she just abduct a newborn? It can't be easier to murder a pregnant woman and try to hide that! There must be something about taking the fetus from another woman's body—some feeling of justification or twisted reason for taking a fetus—and that might be abortion or pregnancy loss related.

When I was completing my doctoral research in the eighties I had studied and interviewed women who had traumatic responses to abortion, and ever since I'd been fascinated by women's varied and sometimes bizarre responses to pregnancy and its termination. I know from my studies that women who humanize the embryo or fetus, and even more so, those who make an emotional relationship to what they see as their "fetal child" often suffer with a pregnancy

termination, experiencing it as a traumatic death event. For them, loss of a pregnancy they have humanized or attached themselves to, even very early on, is subjectively experienced as "the death of my baby"—even if it occurs with an abortion they voluntarily chose.[35]

And I know that although abortion confers reproductive rights to millions of women who would otherwise be saddled with pregnancies they do not wish to carry, not all women *choose* their abortions freely. There are also thousands of women who have abortions *they don't want*. Far more coercive spouses, partners and parents than any of us like to admit demand that their pregnant relative or lover abort a pregnancy despite the wishes of the woman herself.

Lorena Bobbit, whose trial I had served in as a psychological expert in 1993, had undergone a coerced abortion just a year prior to her crime of chopping off her husband's penis after he raped her for the last time. Some speculated that the anniversary reaction of her traumatic abortion may have caused her to "lose it" that day. I didn't necessarily agree with that view given how horribly he had abused her over the years, but I did know that she had proudly announced her pregnancy to her husband, John, only to have him throw the phone book at her and insist that she locate an abortion clinic—a clinic he said "where whores go". Then he drove her there and sat glaring at her to ensure that she consented to and had the abortion he was forcing upon her.

In Lorena Bobbit's case, no one at the abortion clinic checked to see if he was a spouse abuser—which he was—with a record of the police repeatedly being called to their home to break up his brutal beatings. And no one at the clinic understood she was signing her consent under the extreme duress of his demand.

Forced into the abortion of a wanted pregnancy was the ultimate in the many forms of abuse Lorena had endured at her husband's hands, but she was only one of many such women. I know from my research that while abortion frees many women, there are also many women like Lorena Bobbit who are coerced by abusive fam-

ily members. And some may commit crimes when the posttraumatic recall of that abortion intrudes back into their consciousness, filling their minds with overwhelming psychic pain.

Is Annette Morales Rodriguez one of them? I asked myself. *Was she perhaps also forced to abort a wanted pregnancy, and then thought she could take someone else's baby to recover her loss?*

In all the years I'd studied and collected interviews of traumatic reactions to abortion I'd heard a lot of strange stories, including women who returned to abortion clinics late at night banging on the doors crying, "Give me back my baby!" Women who psychotically "heard" their aborted babies crying for months afterward, women who arrived at abortion clinics and requested water that they poured over their bellies to "baptize" the fetus that they then voluntarily aborted and so on. Even Dr. Elizabeth Karlin, an abortion provider in a Wisconsin town not far from where Annette Morale Rodriguez committed her crime, testified about a woman who regressed into baby talk while Dr. Karlin was performing her abortion.

And I know from my research that there are so many women who can't forget their abortions; keeping their "fetal child" psychologically alive long after their physical presence had been removed from their bodies. Such women would describe to me the "child" they would have had as though it was still somehow alive – being able to tell their aborted child's name, "current" age, its gender, what it would have looked like and all kinds of other details. I had labeled that type of a complicated grief reaction as "a preoccupation with the fetal child" and written that women whose grieving over an abortion is a blocked need to come to a congruence between the psychological presence and physical absence of their aborted "child"—grieving their "babies" and letting them go.

Maybe Annette Morales Rodriguez couldn't let her "baby" go and felt that she had to get another one at the same stage of development? I ask myself. *What else could possibly motivate a woman to cut another woman's fetus from her pregnant belly?*

Finding that I cannot dismiss her crime from my thoughts, I decide I have to find out. Searching the news again, I locate the name of one of her attorneys, Patrick Rupich, and call and leave him a message. I tell him that I am an Adjunct Professor of Psychiatry in Georgetown University's Medical School, an expert on adverse psychological reactions to pregnancy loss and that I am interested in her case. "Do you need an expert to conduct her evaluation?" I ask.

Mr. Rupich calls back agreeing that it's an extremely bizarre case. He doesn't know if there is an abortion in her history, but he is open to letting me evaluate her if I'm willing to serve as an expert witness in her case. We discuss my usual fees for forensic work and I agree that given that she is indigent I will serve on the case for a reduced fee, but in that case, I want her to assign to me the right to write up her story. Pat confers with his two other colleagues on the case and they agree. I send them my evaluation consent form with lines added which give me permission to write up her story afterward.

I wait some weeks while Patrick and his colleagues set up the evaluation. Pat sends all the background material he has at his disposal: the police reports, the DVD of her confessing and gruesome pictures of the crime scene, including Eva's cut up body and a few heartbreaking pictures of the newborn baby boy lying dead on the floor. I digest it all as I prepare my questions for the evaluation. Meanwhile Pat sends me many texts, some of them funny while others make me wonder if he's drunk, but as I'm poring over the material I don't have much time to think about it.

Soon I'm on a plane bound for Milwaukee. I don't know what to expect. *Maybe she's just a crazy murderer and she'll be incomprehensible,* I think. *Maybe she's aggressive and I'll be afraid of her?*

What have I gotten myself into? I ask myself as I recoil at the idea of facing her. *Come on you can do it,* I reassure myself. *I've interviewed hundreds of terrorists as well as victims of the Holocaust—they were murderers in one case and extremely traumatic*

stories in another! How bad can this be? I should be able to handle my reactions.

But all the same, I felt queasy about actually meeting her. She is a cold-hearted murderer after all: a woman who had lured another woman into her home, beaten and choked her and then brutally cut out her baby.

"You're going to *evaluate her?*" my former college roommate, Anita, asks at dinner as we gather around her table.

"She's got to be crazy to do a crime like that!" Anita's husband, Jeff, adds, shaking his head.

"Yeah, I guess they don't really need an expert to tell them that," I answer as we finish our meal together. "I head off to the jail first thing in the morning," I later tell Anita as she shows me to her guest room. "I won't be back until dinner time because I expect to do a full day with her today and tomorrow." Anita gives me a hug and looks at me with concern in her eyes and we both head off for bed. Tomorrow, I'll see for myself what kind of woman Annette Morales Rodriguez really is.

CHAPTER TWENTY-THREE
EVALUATING ANNETTE MORALES RODRIGUEZ

Jan. 3, 2012 – "Lawyers for Annette Morales-Rodriguez, charged with killing a pregnant woman and her unborn son during an involuntary Caesarean section birth, have recruited a nationally known psychologist to help them establish an insanity defense. Anne Speckhard, an adjunct professor at Georgetown University in Washington, D.C., was part of the defense team for Lorena Bobbitt, infamous for cutting off her husband's penis. (She was found not guilty by reason of insanity). Speckhard has also testified as an expert in courts around the country and before Congress about posttraumatic stress disorder and worked with international committees on terrorism and its socio-cultural impacts. She has also studied and written about the traumatic stress of abortion, according to her online credentials." *The Milwaukee Journal Sentinel*[36]

The Milwaukee County Jail is not a welcoming place.

We pass into the secure reception area on February 9, 2010. We hand over our IDs and are introduced to the woman at the desk by Annette's attorneys, Patrick Rupich and Michael Torphy.

"You've got to store all your things in the lockers over there," the female jail attendant instructs. Our translator, Christina Green,

obviously experienced with this routine, picks up the two keys proffered by the attendant and, picking up our coats, leads me back outside the security zone to the lockers.

"Here, take a token," she offers, holding out a plastic coin. "We
lock our things in here," she says, explaining how the lockers work.
Then returning with only my briefcase and a pear in my hand (from
Anita's house), the woman at the desk scolds, "You can't take that
pear into the jail."

Suddenly something rankles inside and my inner rebel rises in
response to *the rules*. "I'm hypoglycemic—I have a rather severe
blood sugar disorder," I obstinately inform her, refusing to give up
the pear. "I need the pear."

As the words come out of my mouth I realize I am being a complete pill but something inside just doesn't want to be stripped of
everything I brought with me. And maybe from the stress of surren-
dering control to the jail routines, I sense that my blood sugar *might*
drop precipitously and I will need the pear. I've already been in that
situation before, where I've fainted from low blood sugar, so I dig
in my heels.

"I can't leave the pear here," I say firmly, as the attendant offers
for me to leave it at her desk.

The two attorneys catching my eye, exchange brief wicked smiles
with me as I continue to haggle over the pear, causing the attendant
to call her supervisor. My pear, it turns out, gets passed into the jail
along with me, my computer, mobile phone and camera. *I haven't
surrendered anything but my coat!* I think smugly to myself as we
take the elevator up to the fourth floor.

In the elevator I turn to Christina giggling, "I guess I was a bit of
a pill about the pear, wasn't I?"

She laughs back with eyebrows raised. "You can't bring *anything*
into this jail!"

My worries over facing Annette Morales Rodriguez have intensi-
fied since reading all the news reports over her. A November 15th

article details the prisoner's new designation as a "dangerous" inmate:

> MILWAUKEE- The woman accused of killing another woman and cutting her baby from her womb has attacked a jail guard. Annette Morales-Rodriguez is in the suicide watch unit at the Milwaukee County jail. Monday night, a guard went in to check on her, and Morales-Rodriguez went after her," Annie Scholz of TMJ4news reported on Nov 15, 2011, a month after Annette Morales Rodriguez had been arrested. David Clarke, the Milwaukee County Sheriff explained, "She was able to push the door open and then as this officer was coming over to do the inspection, she grabbed her, pulled her into the cell." Indeed as the guard patrolled the secure area near the cells Morales-Rodriguez, who had rigged the door on her cell so it wouldn't lock, pulled the female guard into her cell, throwing aside her radio and handcuff. A seven- minute struggle ensued after which the officer, taking only minor injuries gained control. "I just want to go home," Morales-Rodriguez was reported as saying at the conclusion of the incident. Now consigned to wear a red uniform designating her as a dangerous inmate, Morales-Rodriguez faces a possible six year sentence for the attack, though she's already looking at a life sentence for the two murders that she was imprisoned for in the first place.[37]

As the elevator creeps slowly up to the fourth floor, I'm feeling a serious sense of anxiety in facing Annette. When I previously worked for the U.S. Department of Defense designing and preparing to pilot test the Detainee Rehabilitation Program in Iraq, a prison specialist warned me about trusting prisoners whom we were attempting to rehabilitate. By way of example, he told about a terror-

ist imprisoned in New York who had made a friendly relationship with his prison guard. The two talked nearly every day and the guard had come to trust the prisoner—until *seven* years into their relationship when the terrorist inexplicably attacked him. Taking a plastic comb the prisoner had whittled into a dagger sharp point, he thrust his weapon deep into the guard's forehead, killing him instantly.

"That's what can happen to you if you ever let your guard down," the specialist had warned. The lesson imparted: you can feel empathy for the prisoners you work with, but you better not be caught off your guard—especially with those who are seasoned killers! His warning remains buzzing about in my head now.

Will she be physically threatening to us? I wonder, recalling how she told Dr. Pankiewicz and Christina Green, the same translator as today, that she heard a voice in her head telling her to kill them both!

The elevator stops and its heavy metal doors slide open. We exit and approach a locked door where we are buzzed in. From there, we take a short walk down the painted white cement block hallway to the guard station. Pat introduces me and explains that I am here to conduct a psychological evaluation of Mrs. Morales Rodriguez and will need a conference room to accommodate the prisoner, our translator and me. Christina Green is well known here and doesn't need an introduction.

"We're short-staffed today, and she needs an escort with her at all times, so it might be awhile before we get her down here," the guard explains.

Patrick nods, "Let's get the room set up first then."

The guard directs us around a corner, down the hall to another guard station where Patrick speaks to the attendant there. As they settle their business, I gaze around at the surrounding cells. There are no bars on these cells. Instead the doors are made of heavy glass with a wooden horizontal beam crossing at waist height, allowing the prisoners to be observed. This appears to be an all-male unit.

Looking in through the glass doors, I can see that the cells are tiny and have windows that are covered in opaque plastic so that they barely let the sunlight in, blocking any view of the outdoors.

As I scan the cells on the wall opposite, I see that one of the prisoners is standing totally naked inside his cell facing us. And he's masturbating! His face contorts in a sexual grimace as he pumps up and down while leaning on the glass door and I notice that thankfully the wooden beam covers his genitals!

I quickly avert my eyes, scanning the other cells as I do. Next to him is a man standing in a straight jacket, also facing outward. He has a hood wrapped over his neck and shoulders and is glassy-eyed, staring forlornly outward seemingly waiting for a helpless eternity to pass.

This place is a hellhole! I think as the guard motions for us to follow her. Further down the hallway she leads us into a small cinderblock, windowless room asking, "Is this too small?"

At first it seems fine, but as we enter I feel my throat constricting. "You think we can get a larger room?" I ask, noting how airless and containing it seems.

I'm really nervous! I note internally to myself. *I can hardly breathe in here!*

Calm down! I tell myself, firmly reining in my emotions. *You have to keep your cool and master your responses or you'll never get through this evaluation!*

Thankfully the guard takes us further down the hall to a larger cinderblock room with a window facing out to the hallway. "This is much better," I say, taking a seat at the long white Formica table, my back to the wall. "I think you should sit here next to me," I tell Christina, "so she will be looking at both of us as you translate."

I begin to place my things on the table for note taking. *The table will serve as a nice protective barrier if she really is dangerous for us,* I think. My throat constricts again, and I force myself to breathe calmly. *You can't afford to get wheezy in here,* I tell myself. Looking

with some panic at the closed in cement walls, I reflect, *I'd never survive prison!*

"I won't be looking at you at all while you translate," I explain to Christina as I distract myself with the business at hand, forcing myself to breathe in calm and exhale stress, inhaling slowly and deeply as I do. "I want to look at Annette when I'm speaking to her—to make eye contact—and also watch her responses as you translate what I'm asking her and what she is saying in reply. I hope it will be okay with you if I basically just listen carefully as you translate, but otherwise ignore you?"

"It's fine," Christina answers. And then she gushes in a complimentary tone of voice, "I'm really thrilled to be working with you Dr. Speckhard! I read your website and you have a lot of fascinating experience in your background!"

I give her a bemused smile in return, feeling a bit embarrassed and tongue-tied momentarily by the strong admiration in her voice. Christina adds, "And you seem like you have a lot of experience working with translators!"

"Yes, I think it's a bit of an art working with a translator," I answer, glad to have the focus off of me. "I have a feeling we will work well together. You seem really warm and that will likely be important in this case."

Now it's Christina's turn to nod and blush.

We don't have much time to continue our preparations as three prison guards suddenly appear in the hallway with Annette in tow. She's dressed in a deep red prison uniform and both her wrists and ankles are shackled. As they seat her across from us, one of the guards bends down and appears to cuff her ankles to the chair. Meanwhile I notice that Annette moves stiffly, her face a mask of terror.

She is wide-eyed, and her face is taut with tension. She gazes in terror at me, and at Christina who she's met previously. Annette she seems calmer looking at Pat, though she doesn't seem to draw

any comfort from his presence. She appears completely terrified, especially of me.

The guards begin to withdraw from the room but before the last one exits, I quickly ask, "Can we unshackle her hands? It may be difficult to express herself that way."

The guard uneasily looks at Annette and then turns his gaze back to us and answers, "No, she has to keep the cuffs on." Then he leaves to stand guard directly outside the open door.

Pat follows him to the door and swings it shut saying, "I'm going to close this for privacy, okay?" Then Pat turns to Annette saying in a very soft and kindly voice, "This is Dr. Speckhard, and you remember Christina Green. I want you to talk freely with Dr. Speckhard and answer all her questions."

Annette is so obviously terrified that I jump in immediately, saying to her in a soft voice, "Listen Annette, I'm here to help you. I have to tell the truth and I have to stay objective, but if I can help you I will, so it's very important you tell me everything you can, okay?"

Wide-eyed she stares at me like a crazed, caged animal as Christina translates my words. Her eyes are so wide they look like saucers and she looks as though she could pounce in self-defense at any moment.

"Are you afraid?" I ask.

Annette nods.

"What are you afraid of?" I ask.

"That you will say that I'm normal and then I will have to stay in here forever," she explains relaxing almost imperceptibly.

"I can't lie," I say, "But if you tell me everything you can, I will try to help you. But you understand that if you are able to mount an insanity defense you won't go free entirely. You will go to the psychiatric hospital instead of prison."

"Yes," she nods, and I see that she is beginning to trust me. I know that I often have this effect on people, and I'm pleased to see it working here too. Patrick leaves and together with Christina we begin our journey of examining Annette's life, mind and crime.

CHAPTER TWENTY-FOUR
PUERTO RICO TO MILWAUKEE

"I was born in Puerto Rico," Annette begins in response to my questions about her life history and early childhood.

My method of psychological evaluation is always to begin with a very detailed childhood and family history, even going back to the grandparental generation in some cases. It takes the pressure off of the subject at hand while we get to know each other and I always find that if I get a good read of the psycho-social, familial and emotional history of my patient I have a good foundation to work from in terms of understanding what motivates them and how they think.

"My mother was a secretary and my father worked in a corrections unit until he became disabled with rheumatoid arthritis at age thirty-three. I was the oldest child; I have two younger sisters."

Her eyes are still big as saucers as she sits uneasily in her chair, arms and legs bound with stainless steel shackles, her heavy deep red, cotton prison uniform covering her body like a bloody stain. She leans forward as she speaks in a soft voice, barely above a whisper, and I find that I need to lean forward to hear her as well. Christina translates nearly simultaneously as I keep my eyes on Annette, watching her micro-facial responses and body language while recording her words on my tablet as she talks.

"Who took care of you while your parents worked?" I ask.

"My grandparents," she answers telling me about her paternal grandparents and the close relationship she had with "Abuela", her grandmother. "We lived with them until I was three years old when my father built a house of our own. But we still went to our grand-

parents during the days for babysitting when our parents were work-ing," she explains. Annette's eyes remain wide and Christina also leans forward as she strains to catch Annette's soft voice. It's slow going, but I can see that between Christina's warmth and my cau-tious slow probing we are beginning to make a connection.

Contrary to what I would have expected, Annette's childhood sounds tender and nurturing, idyllic even, until age ten when she tells us that her mother abruptly left for New York without expla-nation, abandoning the family. "Everything, everything, changed," Annette recalls of that time. "I had to take the role of the mother, cleaning, cooking, etc.," she explains, her eyes still wide but her demeanor relaxing as I push slowly for her to open up, gently asking about that pain. "Emotionally speaking, that never went away. I still have that trauma," she answers.

I ask Annette carefully about her sexual history starting first with "puppy love" and later with more serious affairs. Annette tells me first about Marcos[38], the boy she liked in elementary school who also liked her, and then about Juan, her first real love.

"You slept with him?" I ask, and Annette nods. "It was consensu-al?" I ask, and she nods again smiling at the memory. "No violence involved?" No, Annette reassures me, her first sexual experience was good—it was "making love".

Annette tells me that she and Juan did not stay together because he left for New York while she remained behind. "I didn't want to go with him because he was involved with dealing drugs, and I didn't want that lifestyle," Annette explains. Impressed by her ma-turity at age fifteen, we continue.

Miguel, a bit older than her, was her next lover. Annette con-fesses that she did not love him with the same passion as Juan and was upset to find herself pregnant by him, a contraceptive failure. "I had to face the responsibility of pregnancy," she recalls, explaining how she decided to marry Miguel despite feeling less than a strong relationship with him.

Annette recalls her father being upset that she had "spoiled" her life and educational prospects and reminded her that he had wanted her to get a technical or university education. "But I enrolled in technical college, earning a one-year degree toward becoming a bank teller while I was pregnant," Annette recounts, obviously proud of herself for still carrying out her father's dream. "I graduated when the baby was born and found work in a bakery as its manager."

Annette's second child was planned. She recalls the pregnancy as difficult with "bleeding from beginning to end". And she also recalls medical orders for bed-rest that she could not afford to follow because she needed to work.

The birth of Pablo was difficult. "He was born blue!" Annette recounts, saying Pablo later became a "hyperactive" child and had many educational challenges.

Annette's third pregnancy occurred after the failure of what she refers to as "injections" (which were likely Depo Provera) and ended in a healthy birth of a daughter. Annette explains that her marriage turned sour after the birth of her third child, recalling, "We fought over his drinking and that he was always going out."

Annette explains that it was then that she decided to leave him and join her sister who had moved to Milwaukee, Wisconsin. Annette explains that aside from getting away from Miguel, she wanted to take her children out of the conflicted situation of their constant marital fights and also to obtain public school services for Pablo. When I ask about violence, Annette answers that there was constant verbal conflict but no violence in her marriage.

"He refused to grant me a divorce," Annette says, detailing that she is still technically married to Miguel because she was not able to afford to legally fight him for a divorce. Instead she left Puerto Rico without a divorce and took the children with her, uncontested by Miguel, thereby ending their relationship.

Annette explains how she found a job in a cheese factory working the night shift while living at her sister's until she could afford

her own place. She talks about then meeting Ramón, a smile crossing her face. As I listen, I think Annette sounds pretty self sufficient and mature: working hard to provide for her children, building relationships and setting up her new life pretty quickly to become independent. It isn't easy moving to a new country dealing with a new language and new system—I very well know, having moved many times around the world in my life. Annette sounds a bit undaunted by all the challenges.

I ask many questions about the babysitter who left Annette's kids home alone the night her daughter was assaulted. She explains that the babysitter inexplicably left the children alone, returning home to do chores at her own house and that Carmelita had been sleeping in her nightgown when the stranger entered their home. I'm surprised to learn that Child Protective Services took all three of her children from the home before she returned home and that she was allowed to see only Carmelita—and then only briefly at the Milwaukee hospital, while the doctor performed the rape kit examination for her. "I didn't have my children for three months and for one month I didn't even know where they were!" Annette says.

It's clear that Annette is extremely traumatized by the whole episode. She trembles visibly, stating that she felt scared, desperate and angry mixed with some degree of guilt that she had been at work when someone tried to assault her daughter. After one month and a half of no contact, she was finally allowed visitation and to regain custody. "The court ordered me to change my work shift, change the locks on my doors and hire a different babysitter, and I had to take parenting classes before they would give my children back to me," Annette explains.

After three months the children were finally returned to her and Annette recalls that she and her children were all traumatized by the separation and that her children "were clingy". She tells me that her children kicked Ramón out of her bed and that "for two months they all slept with me," and that, "I needed that too."

Annette breaks into tears when she tells me she was ordered to go with them to family therapy and that her children showed "fears of separation" and "got scared when I left for work" and "they didn't want to get separated from me ever again."

Obviously, due to her present circumstances, the rift and their abandonment has occurred again. Through tear-filled eyes Annette looks at me with the deepest pain filling her face.

CHAPTER TWENTY-FIVE

GETTING TO THE TRUTH

It's past lunchtime, and I'm beginning to feel tired out. We've been going at it since morning with no break—not even for my pear—and soon we must eat and use the restroom, but I'd like to connect the dots. Annette has shared her childhood history and move to the U.S. making everything but the abandonment by her mother and her failed marriage with Miguel out to be pretty good. But I know that can't be the whole story as something led her up to the point where she is now: in a jail cell, dressed in a blood red outfit designating her as a dangerous prisoner.

Up to now, Annette has omitted any mention of the child sexual abuse and the rape she endured in childhood because as far as she's concerned, it didn't happen to her. She knows about it only in an oblique way because Lara shared it at the funeral, but it's like an altered reality—not her own—and besides that, Lara has strictly warned her never to tell anyone about these things.

Yet, somehow, without her telling me, I sense that there's much more. I just don't know how to get to it.

"Weren't you just ten years old when your mother left the family?" I ask. Annette nods. "Did it feel like your past when your daughter's world fell apart a bit like yours when she was assaulted and all of you were so suddenly separated at about the same age?" I ask, knowing that families often mysteriously reenact traumas throughout the generations. Annette nods her head in affirmation.

"Did anyone ever do anything like this to you? Did anyone ever attack you sexually?" I ask, figuring this is the best opening I will get to ask directly about such a sensitive topic.

"No," Annette answers shaking her head. Her eyes are saucers again—the question scares her, I see.

"So you've never been sexually molested or raped?" I ask again, knowing it often takes many passes to get sexual abuse and rape victims to open up about their traumatic experiences. It's common for victims to deny and even to fail to remember rape and childhood sexual assault.

"No," Annette shakes her head again at me, looking at Christina for support. "No, that never happened to me." I feel as though she wants Christina to convince me of the truth of that statement, but I also know when to drop a subject that is becoming too threatening to explore further for the time being.

"You must have been a bit crazed to be separated from your children like that after having made the move all the way from Puerto Rico to try to make a better life for you and for them?" I ask, tacking in another direction.

Annette nods, obviously relieved to change the topic and to be understood, "I was completely crazy from it! I couldn't sleep, I couldn't think. I couldn't handle the loneliness. I didn't want to stay in the house anymore when they weren't there. I took two jobs just [so as] not to be at home! And I was scared because I didn't know if the authorities would ever give them back to me!"

"You had a *real* babysitter? You had hired her?" I ask, wondering what the actual story is behind her babysitter having not been present. That also doesn't add up in my mind—too many unanswered questions and strange events. Maybe she left the children unattended but doesn't want to admit it.

"Yes, I paid her in cash each week," Annette answers. "She was supposed to be in my house, but she went home for some reason."

"You must have been angry at her," I ask.

"Yes," Annette nods, looking down at her hands.

"How did you deal with the emotional stress of being separated from your children?" I ask, trying to get a picture of how she copes.

"I tried to put it out of my mind, to not think about it, to try and forget until the judge told me they could come home again," she answers. I nod and move to the next stage of her life.

"You were trying to get pregnant with Ramón, no?" She nods. "Can you tell me about that?"

"After they took my children, we decided we wanted a baby together," Annette explains. "So I was trying to get pregnant. I thought I was pregnant."

"What happened with that pregnancy?" I ask.

"I don't know. I think I had one miscarriage and then I got pregnant again, and I was pretty far along but when I went to the doctor he told me no, that I was not."

"What made you think you were pregnant?" I ask.

"I stopped getting my period and noticed my breasts and stomach swelling and I felt morning sickness. I'm sure I was pregnant," she states. One drugstore pregnancy test came out positive although three others had been negative, Annette tells me. In August, Annette recalls going to the local low-income clinic to confirm her pregnancy, but was told she was not pregnant.

"You felt pregnant, but the doctor said no?"

"He said it was a psychological pregnancy and that I couldn't be pregnant because I had my tubes tied—that I would never be pregnant," Annette answers, fear filling her face again.

"You didn't know about your tubes?" I ask.

"No, I knew the doctor in Puerto Rico did something after Elise was born but I thought it was like the [Depo Provera] shots—temporary. But he said no, it was permanent and I'd never ever get pregnant again, unless I had a lot of money and did a reverse procedure."

"You were upset?"

"Yes I couldn't think! I was crazy from it and I didn't know what to do, what to tell Ramón. He thought I was pregnant, too."

"What did you do?"

"I tried to put it out of my mind."

"Like when they took your children?" I ask, suddenly seeing the picture of how she copes. She's good at dissociating, or separating painful things from her conscious thoughts. I wonder how dissociative she is and how much ordinary cognitive functions, such as thoughts, feelings, memories, etc., drop out of her mind. "Are you able to do that pretty well?" I ask. "Put things out of your mind that you don't want to think about?"

"Yes, I can forget things that are too difficult to think about," Annette admits.

"Are you spacey sometimes, forgetting that time is passing and sort of wake up, 'out of it' and confused a bit?" I ask trying to judge the extent of it.

"Yes, that happens to me a lot," Annette admits, her voice calm given the gravity of what she is saying.

"You lose time? Don't know what happened when you were 'out of it'?" I ask.

"Yes," Annette concedes, still calm.

"For a long time or just a few minutes? Are we talking small lapses of time or hours or even days?" I ask.

"It's hours or even days sometimes," Annette confesses, her eyes locked with mine.

"And you don't remember what happened during those times?" I ask, amazed that she's admitting this so calmly.

"No, nothing," she divulges.

"Do you ever feel like someone else, or do people tell you that you did things that are uncharacteristic for you during those times?" I ask.

"Yes," Annette answers.

She's admitting to the profile of an extremely dissociative person and usually that only occurs to individuals who were the victims of violent, sexually abusive or extremely chaotic childhoods.

"Annette, are you sure no one ever hurt you as a child? You were never molested or sexually assaulted?" I ask in my gentlest voice, leaning across the table as I explain, "because this type of dissociative phenomena—losing time, having amnesia for long periods of time, feeling like someone else—are usually characteristic for people that have been sexually or violently abused in their childhoods. You weren't molested?"

"I wasn't, but Lara was," Annette answers, her face emotionless.

"What happened to Lara?" I ask, mirroring her lack of emotion and acting totally normal about her admission of another "personality". Inside I'm flabbergasted, but I decide, *I'll react to that later*. Lara, I assume given my experience treating persons with dissociative identity disorder, or multiple personalities, *must be a dissociated part of Annette*. I remind myself to stay with the flow before making advanced presumptions.

"She was molested as a child," Annette says, and her eyes momentarily roll back in her head as her eyelids begin to flutter rapidly. I recognize this also: it's a classic sign of a dissociative disorder (or multiple personalities), a sign that often occurs during a personality "switch". I've treated eleven persons with this very severe disorder and this is exactly what they do when they are about to switch into another personality

"By who?" I ask.

"Grandfather," Annette answers, her eyes wide again, terror overtaking her face.

"At what age?"

"Six years old."

"Until when?" I ask pushing ahead while the going is good, knowing that given how much Annette denied all morning, she can easily lapse right back into denial.

"Twelve," she answers.

"He touched her sexual parts?" I ask, referring to Lara as another person so as to not shut Annette down. I want to stay with her "reality" while she is opening up to me rather than shut her down with my version of the facts.

"Yes," Annette answers, her eyes again rolling up into her head with the rapid eyelid fluttering repeating itself, but again she returns.

"He put his fingers inside her?"

"Yes," she answers. Her eyelids flutter.

"Did he make her touch him also?" I ask.

"Yes."

"Did he put his penis in her mouth or her vagina?" I ask, revolted by the thought of a six-year-old involved in sex acts of this type but knowing it's necessary to ask.

"No, he never did that." Annette answers.

"Are you sure?" I ask.

"Yes."

"Did he threaten to hurt her if she told anyone?"

"Yes, he choked her and told her that he'd kill her," Annette answers, her eyes back in her head again with eyelids fluttering rapidly.

"And what else happened to Lara?" I ask.

"Uncle hurt her too," Annette answers.

"Your mother's brother?"

"Yes."

"He touched her, too?" Annette nods, clearly terrified discussing these things. "Did he put his fingers inside her also?"

"Yes."

"And did he make her touch him?"

"Yes," she answers with her eyes rolled back again in her head and her eyelids fluttering away.

"Did he put his penis inside of her or in her mouth?"

"He tried to put it inside of her but she bit his shoulder and ran away!" Annette answers.

"And that worked? That made him stop?" I ask smiling at some good news and laughing inside at the thought of a spunky kid getting the better of this sick uncle.

"Yes, he was drunk," Annette explains.

"And did he threaten her also?"

"Yes, he choked her and told her he'd kill her if she ever told anyone," Annette answers, eyelids aflutter. I'm amazed actually that she is sharing any of this with me given the threats to her life. It often takes months for adults who were severely sexually abused as children to open up and admit it in therapy.

"How old was Lara when Uncle was doing these things?" I ask.

"From ten to twelve years old,"

"Why did it stop at twelve? Were they afraid of a pregnancy?" I ask.

"No we stopped going there," Annette answers and explains that after her mother left they weren't dropped at her grandparents anymore for babysitting.

"What else happened to Lara? Was she ever raped?" I ask, going for broke now that Annette is answering honestly. Although I notice she is answering in a way that is very emotionally detached from the experiences she is describing—almost as if in a trance; and she is referring to these events as having happened to Lara, not to herself.

"Yes, when she was sixteen," Annette answers and tells me about an older teenage boy who seduced Lara to come drink with him at his home, tore off her clothes, raped and threw her out of the house

naked with her clothes in her hands while telling her she'd just become a whore and was no longer needed.

"Who is Lara?" I ask, pretty much knowing the answer before she explains.

"Lara is the one who takes the bad things," Annette answers softly.

"And how do you know about these things?" I ask, understanding that a dissociative split in Annette's personality occurred at age six when Grandfather started molesting her and that Lara has all the accumulated horror stored in her part of the mind while Annette has partial to complete amnesia for them.

"Lara told me," she answers softly, her eyes filled with infinite sadness.

"When?" I ask softly.

"At Abuela's funeral. She talked in my head. It was the first time I knew she was there. I thought I was going crazy. She told me everything that has happened and she showed me some of it."

"You saw and felt it, or it was like at a distance?" I ask understanding how chronic sexual abuse victims sometimes create a dissociated self in whom they place all the horror and sexual trauma.

"At a distance."

"But you know these things happened to her, and to you?" I ask.

"Yes," Annette answers. "They happened to Lara, but I know about them," she says refusing my interpretation of them happening to both Annette and Lara.

"Is there anyone else?" I ask referring to the potential host of inner personalities she has just begun to open up about.

"Yes, Annasita. She's six years old and she doesn't know about any of this."

"She's the innocent child?"

"Yes."

"Have you ever told anyone about this, about the abuse and these other personalities?" I ask.

"No, no one," she answers, her eyes locking with mine. I feel her trust and know I must not betray it.

"Lara talks to you in your head?" I ask.

"Yes," Annette answers and I notice she seems more present now that we've backed off of talking about the experiences that she only knows from a distance—the things that happened to Lara, not her.

"When?" I ask.

"After the doctor told me that I could never have a baby, she shouted at me and told me how stupid I was that I thought I was pregnant and that I was never going to have a baby, that I had to tell Ramón, and that he was going to leave me!" Annette explains, tears filling and overflowing her eyes.

I take out the tissue packet that I've brought with me just for this purpose and slide it across the table. Annette takes some to wipe her eyes with her shackled hands as we continue. "What else did she say?"

"She mocked me and said I better come up with something soon, if I wasn't going to tell him the truth about the pregnancy and never having a baby," Annette answers her eyes wide with terror and the backward eye roll and eyelid flutter starting again. "And she said I better find a pregnant woman and cut her baby out of her if I wanted to give Ramón a baby."

I gasp internally and ask, "So Lara wanted to get a baby for you?"

A pregnant silence rests between us as I let Annette's words sink in.

"What did you say?" I ask.

"I told her no, that we couldn't ever do that, but she kept shouting at me and telling me that I had to do something, that I was stupid, and that Ramón was going to leave me."

"Did you agree with her?" I ask.

"No, I tried to make her go away! I tried not to listen! I would read books and take aspirin because I'd get a really big headache when I tried to block her out. She kept talking and shouting at me and calling me names and mocking me."

I look at Annette for a few minutes, fully understanding now what we are dealing with. We are all silent and I feel a bit of shock with what she's just admitted. She has a severe dissociative identity disorder, or in lay parlance, multiple personalities! The hair on the back of my neck stands up.

We have been going at it for hours now, working right through lunch, and I desperately need to use the bathroom.

"Annette, this is really tough stuff. A lot of really hard things happened to you," I reflect as we back away from the interview for a few minutes. "I really appreciate you opening up about all of this. But I think now we need to take a short break. You've shared a lot and maybe you need a rest, too. I need to use the bathroom. I imagine you do too after all these hours we've been talking, and I'd like to grab a quick lunch. Is this an okay time to take a break? Will you be okay if we leave you alone for about forty-five minutes?" I ask.

Annette nods and a look of relief crosses her face. It's inconvenient to have to break at this crucial moment, but I know I won't be able to continue on without using the toilet soon and in the interest of keeping steady blood sugar, I know I should eat as well. I decide to trust that she'll be okay when we're gone and Christina and I pack up our things as I say, "I think they will bring your lunch to you," and we leave to walk down the hall explaining to the guard that we will go briefly to lunch.

"You'll bring her lunch to her while we are out?" I ask and the guard nods. "Be really careful approaching her," I warn. "She's been talking about some really sensitive issues and might freak out if anyone tries to touch her." He nods and thankfully he looks like a thoughtful person, so we leave hoping everything will be okay in our absence.

*   *   *

"She's got dissociative identity disorder!" I say with amazement rising within me after the elevator doors close on us. "Multiple personalities!" I explain when I see that Christina's face is blank.

"Yes, it's really bizarre!" Christina looks a bit frightened by it all. "The way her eyes roll back into her head!" she remarks, her eyes wide with astonishment.

"She's talking about three personalities, right?" I ask glad that I can check with Christina to make sure I'm not imagining it.

"Yes!" Christina answers, equally bewildered.

"And she had amnesia for all the abuse until her grandmother died. Then the 'Lara' personality broke through and spilled the beans, but she still doesn't know everything that happened to her! And she loses time and doesn't know what's going on. Lara is probably out then," I muse aloud.

"It's a really strange case!" Christina agrees as she guides us through the jail out to the courtroom building where the cafeteria is. We continue discussing the morning's interview comparing notes on what Annette has shared. "Did you see any of this when you translated for Dr. Pankiewicz?" I ask about the State's expert evaluation of Annette.

Christina should probably not divulge what happened in their interview, but perhaps from the shock we are both feeling in response to this bizarre case, she opens up immediately. "She said she didn't remember the crime and that she didn't do it. She also said that the police told her that she did it and that she confessed, but she claimed she didn't remember any of that," Christina explains. "Dr. Pankiewicz kept trying to get her to talk about the crime, but she claimed she didn't know anything about it and then finally he got frustrated and gave up. It was then that she said that she heard a voice in her head telling her to kill both of us! It was freaky. But she didn't open up to him like this at all! You are really good with her, so gentle and

you talk so softy. I think you are really putting her at ease, making her feel safe."

"I'm trying," I say. "I think she didn't answer him about the crime because she really can't remember it. She may not *be* the one who did it. Maybe Lara did it?" Christina and I stare at each other in astonishment as we hurry through our courthouse sandwiches and tidy up, rise and return back to the prison.

Annette is sitting on a plastic chair shackled outside the interview room, her finished lunch tray sitting on the floor next to her waiting for us when we return. Her dark red prison uniform is the only splash of color in the stark hallway. The guard unlocks the door, Christina and I position our things and he brings her into the room and shackles her legs to the leg of the bench as he seats her there. I pull out my pen and tablet and as he leaves we start again.

"So you were telling me about when you learned that your tubes had been tied and could never be pregnant and Lara was coming out a lot during that time screaming in your head," I recap. Annette nods. "And she was suggesting that you find another pregnant woman and take her baby," I say.

"Yes," Annette answers.

CHAPTER TWENTY-SIX
"REMEMBERING" HORROR

It turns out that Annette does not remember her crime. She knows that Lara proposed to do it and that she refused and after that tried to block Lara's voice from consciousness, most often successfully. It doesn't mean that Lara didn't continue to be active but only that Annette blocked her awareness of what Lara was trying to communicate to her out. Then according to Annette, she woke up at the hospital and found that indeed Lara had been quite active, as Annette began to put the pieces of the story together.

"So the first you were aware of all of this was when you 'woke up' at the hospital, the *first* day after the ambulance took you there, and you had no idea what had occurred?" I ask, trying to grasp the multiple blank spaces and disconnects in Annette's story. I don't realize it at the moment, but my confusion about her reality is an exact mirror of how her life is lived—with too many unaccounted gaps in memory and experience.

"I had an idea, because they said I had a baby and it had died, so I knew she must have done something, but I didn't know what yet," Annette recounts.

"You have complete amnesia when she is out?"

"Yes, I don't remember anything."

"How did you piece it together?"

"When I came home there was a blood stain on the carpet and I asked Ramón what had happened here and he told me. He said I had given birth to a baby boy and he had died and the blood was from the birth," Annette recalls, tears welling up in her eyes.

"Geez!" I exclaim. "So that's when you first realized what had happened?"

Annette nods.

"Did you know she killed the woman?" I ask.

"No. I was really tired and I couldn't think so I put the children to bed and then Ramón helped me get into bed and I just slept. In the morning the medical examiner's office called and said I had to go back to the hospital. The questions they asked told me what had gone on," Annette explains.

"You had a vaginal ultrasound," I remark, mentally recalling the chain of events recorded in the police and medical records.

"Yes."

"You were present for that?"

"No, Lara came out. I wasn't there."

"Do you remember anything from that room?"

"No, just going in and undressing and the doctor coming in, then I was gone and Lara was there."

"When did you 'come to' again?" I ask.

"Here, I think," Annette answers. "In the jail."

Sweet Jesus! I think to myself imagining how it must have gone. "So *Lara* confessed?"

"I think so. I saw the tape. I wasn't there," Annette answers.

"What happened here in jail? How did you piece it together?" I ask.

"She told me some of it and she let me see it in my dreams. I see her choking the woman and I watched the video of the confession—she tells some of it there," Annette answers, her face white and innocent like a child's. *How strange,* I think to myself, *that one part of her could be completely amnestic for the crime and innocent in a way, while the other part is psychopathic enough to commit it!*

"You were angry?"

"I won't speak to her. I don't want to listen to her anymore. I told her if you could do a thing like this I never want to see or hear from you again!"

"She went away?"

"No, but I don't listen to her anymore. I block her out completely. I don't want to know her. She's a killer!"

"What about your children?" I ask, wondering what has happened to them. This is the second time they have been separated from their mother by the authorities.

"I don't know where they are," Annette answers, tears streaming down her cheeks. "They took them again and no one will tell me how they are or where they are."

"Can you write a letter to them?" I ask, worried about their welfare.

"What would I write?" she asks, pain filling her voice.

"That you love them and you are trying to find answers," I suggest. "It doesn't matter how bad it is, they need to hear that from their mother."

Annette nods and asks, "How?"

"Let me ask Pat," I answer, jotting a reminder in my notes, and then flipping back through my notes I explain that I want to make sure I understand everything and we go back over again everything that Annette remembers and what she doesn't know or only knows vaguely, through the filtered and distant memories of "Lara" that she somehow accesses.

"How often was Lara out in the past, when you were living here in Milwaukee?" I ask.

"She came whenever things were difficult—at the doctor's office and also on weekends. She likes to dance."

"She drinks?" I ask.

"Yes, but she likes to dance more than drink, but yes she drinks, too." I ask Annette about the pain medication with codeine that I saw

noted in her records, wondering if one or both of them is an addict as well. It would make sense—a means of escaping from the painful reminders of years of repeated childhood sexual assault. Annette denies any addictive behavior saying the medicine was to treat her painful headaches, but I note to myself to ask those around her more about that. Addicts rarely admit to their abuse of substances.

The wall clock is indicating it's already five p.m. and Christina needs to leave. I can do nothing without her translating, so I wrap up the interview telling Annette we'll return tomorrow to discuss things further.

"We've talked about some really hard things," I say before parting. "Are you going to be okay tonight? Is Lara going to be angry with you for telling?"

"She'll be angry, but I don't talk to her anymore," Annette says. She looks so diminutive now, overtaken in her red canvas prison canvas uniform. "I'll be okay, don't worry."

Lugging my briefcase strap over my shoulder I tell Annette, "Take care and try not to think about it too much tonight. Sleep well." Given she can't shake hands, I warn her that I'm going to plant a kiss on her head, which I do in a maternal fashion as we part. "We will see you first thing tomorrow morning!"

Christina says goodbye as well and we walk out down the white painted cement block corridor toward freedom, leaving Annette shackled to her bench behind us.

CHAPTER TWENTY-SEVEN
FORENSIC CONSULTATIONS

Heidi, my niece, picks me up inside the courthouse lobby. As we emerge out into the blinding white snow and crunch across it to her parked car, I remember all the sensations of Wisconsin's bitter cold winters. I grew up here. After university I escaped the northern climates and never looked back, but right now the cold air feels fresh on my face and the white, just fallen snow is clean and bright washing away the impressions of the dinghy jail and Annette's murderous story.

"The lawyers want to meet briefly to get my read out. Is that okay with you?" I ask Heidi as we climb into her car.

Heidi nods and speeds along on the snow-packed street following Pat's car to the coffee shop where've agreed to briefly meet. There we join Bob D'Arruda, the third lawyer on the case.

This morning I had breakfast with Pat and Mike and both seemed like genuine, cool guys, definitely small town Midwestern but kind and caring and smart. Bob is the heavyweight among them, known for working major felonies and being an expert jury man—he readily takes cases to jury trials versus accepts plea bargains. He's done nearly twenty homicides, getting acquittals on a few and good deals on several others. I'm not sure how I feel about that, given that guilty people are then let back on the streets. But on the other hand, everyone deserves a fair trial and due process.

"I'm quite sure she's got dissociative identity disorder, DID— or multiple personality disorder, MPD, for the layperson," I say,

launching head first into the case as we slide into the booth, Heidi sliding in beside me.

"This is my niece, Heidi. She's an intensive care nurse and she understands about confidentiality," I say as we continue.

Heidi nods and, putting up her hands in mock surrender, says, "I won't leak a thing!"

"She's got three main personalities," I continue. "Two are the most active, and Annette has amnesia when the one that is named Lara comes out. Lara is present when Annette is intimidated or overwhelmed. We see this kind of thing when a person has been chronically sexually abused in childhood or witnessed a great deal of violence."

"Annette was sexually abused by her grandfather and her uncle over a period of years and Lara took it all. Annette didn't even know it happened until her grandmother died when she was sixteen; then Lara broke through and told her the whole story. It's only at that point she understood her history and that she's got another active personality. She's been raped too, again in the Lara personality. Annette doesn't know all the details of any of the abuse, as she was not present and it sounds like she's in a lot of denial about having multiple personalities!"

I look to Bob and Pat as I'm speaking watching their reactions. "I know it sounds crazy—*freaky* really. These cases are rare but I've treated eleven of them and this one, I'm quite sure is for real," I explain. "To the best of my ability to evaluate, she's not faking. And I don't think she could fake this so well, but all the same I'm glad the translator was with me today so it's not just me saying she said all of this. It's bizarre really—kind of makes your skin crawl!"

"MPD! Jesus Christ!" Pat remarks. Bob remains silent, sizing me up.

"I'd like to film her tomorrow and try to get her to 'switch'—that is change into one of the other personalities—and catch it on film. I don't want anyone saying I made all of this up!" I explain. "So, as

far as your case you can definitely argue she didn't know right from wrong at the time she committed the crime. In the Annette personality—her dominant self, she didn't even know she was committing a murder! She had complete amnesia for it until she spent some time in jail. Then Lara clued her in. I don't think she *still* knows the whole story!

"And your state's witness, Dr. Pankiewicz—he didn't catch any of this. It's probably because he only spent an hour and half with her; that's forty-five minutes if you account for the time spent in translation. Christina probably shouldn't have told me but she went over his whole evaluation and she says Annette kept telling him she didn't do it and knew nothing about the crime, that she'd seen the film of her confession but doesn't remember that or anything else. And she said she heard a voice telling her to kill them both!

"I think she was telling him the truth. She doesn't remember the crime and she doesn't remember confessing either. He interviewed Annette just after you brought the DVD into the prison and that's when she attacked the guard too, isn't it?"

"I don't know. That sounds right," Pat answers. "I'd have to check the records."

"I think it is," I continue. "She was probably totally shook up over figuring it all out and from her point of view, she didn't commit the crime; her other personality did, and it's got to be Lara telling her to kill the two of them," I say. "Annette is only now putting all the pieces together. Pretty horrific."

"Do you know why she did it?" Bob asks.

"Yes, in her Annette personality she really believed she was pregnant. I expected we'd find some kind of forced or coerced abortion in her history—something to explain how she could justify taking another woman's fetus from her, but it wasn't that at all. She got a really rude shock when she went to the doctor to confirm her pregnancy that she believed was already far along.

"He told her that her tubes are tied, that she'll never have another pregnancy and this one was psychological—all weight gain and bloat. She freaked out and didn't know what to do, how to tell Ramón. They both really wanted a child together—she especially after they had taken her kids away and the daughter being attacked." I pause to ask, "Can we get the records on that? I'd like to know the whole story. Did she really have a babysitter that night or is she lying about that? They kept the kids for three months according to Annette. That's a long time."

"I've been pinging on CPS [Child Protective Services] for the past weeks trying to get those records. I'll call them again today. They are stonewalling us," Pat answers.

"You think she's fit to stand trial?" Bob asks.

"Yes, as long as she's working with Pat," I say. "It's clear that she's got a good relationship with him. She trusts him, and I think she can stay present as long as things don't get too threatening."

"You've got huge Miranda issues in this case, too," I add. "She had two vaginal exams she didn't want—one that she says she outright refused, but they did it anyway against her will while she was, what looks like to me, in police custody. And no one read her rights to her until she was taken to the station. That's pretty bad isn't it?"

"Yeah, we're looking into that," Pat answers.

"I'd like to see her medical records from the hospital too, see if there's a signed informed consent for the gyn exams. I bet there isn't, at least for the second one that she refused. What's the informed consent protocol here in Milwaukee?" I ask turning to Heidi, suddenly very glad that she's here. Heidi has just graduated in nursing and begun her job at one of the top Milwaukee hospitals. She's very smart, and I smile at her proudly.

"It's *always* written, and if for some reason it has to be verbal, there are always two people in the room—one to be the witness of the verbal consent," Heidi states matter-of-factly.

"That's the word from inside the hospital!" I say. "We've got to get those medical records to see how that went." Pat nods. He's been in charge of gathering all relevant records.

"From what she told me, the police arrived on her doorstep once the medical examiner figured out the case was sketchy. So at that point she is possibly a suspect, and they escorted her to the hospital, maybe for her own well-being but more likely to keep her under their control. And they stood outside her examining room door during the vaginal ultrasound and then escorted her and stayed bedside in the emergency room, too. I don't get why they don't have to read her rights to her if they are keeping her under such close watch?"

"It's debatable," Bob answers, "but we're on top of those issues."

"Yeah, there are major Miranda issues," Pat echoes. "I don't think the Milwaukee police ever encountered a case like this before so they were sort of winging it outside of normal protocols.

"Okay, should we meet again tomorrow for breakfast?" I ask as we wrap things up. "I want to start interviewing her again in the morning and hopefully if she can handle it, go all day. And I want to film her. Can you get a video camera and a tripod for me for tomorrow morning and can we get it into the jail?"

"Mike's got a camera; let me talk to him," Pat answers. "If it's something you need for the evaluation, we should be able to get it in."

"I just want to film her and hopefully catch her switching between personalities. I don't want anyone on the other side to be able to impeach me as a witness and say I'm just making this stuff up. If you see her, you'll realize it's really bizarre. I don't know if she switched today, but she does the classic MPD moves: she does this rapid eye flutter and her eyes roll up in her head and she goes away briefly when we get on tough topics and she is super spacey. It's like this, I say demonstrating the way Annette's eyes roll up on her head as her eyelids flutter rapidly.

It gives me a strange feeling to do it, disorienting as I mimic her, and I imagine how she must feel when this occurs involuntarily in reaction to posttraumatic stressors.

We finish up and Heidi drives me back to Anita's house in the suburbs. "Okay, one more day of this stuff and then I'll be up to your Mom's house in Sheboygan," I tell Heidi, giving her a brief kiss. "Thanks a lot for the ride and all your clinical expertise!" I close the door and Heidi drives off.

Inside Anita and Jeff, her son and two dogs are waiting to see what we will do for dinner. We decide for Japanese food and head off in the darkness to their favorite restaurant while I tell them what I can share from the case.

CHAPTER TWENTY-EIGHT
MORE TRAUMAS

Mike Torphy, the third attorney on this case picks me up in the morning and I spend about twenty minutes telling him about the day before. "You know most people don't realize how devastating it is for a child to be molested repeatedly during childhood," I say.

"A friend of mine was raped in a men's bathroom when we were twelve," Mike suddenly shares.

"Oh geez, I'm sorry," I say, controlling myself to have a steady, calm voice as I react to such horrific news. "A stranger?"

"Yes, he didn't tell anybody until we were fifteen. Then he told us and his mom," he adds.

"I have a relative like that. She was raped on a sleepover at age fifteen and didn't tell her parents until she was almost twenty. Never told anyone except her boyfriend at age seventeen. I guess it's so terrifying to be violently raped, and most abusers make some pretty terrible threats to keep their victims silent. In Annette's case, her abusers choked her and told her they'd kill her if she ever told."

Pausing, I look at Mike. Of the three attorneys on this case, he seems to me to be the most intellectual and sensitive. And right now I feel filled with appreciation for his candor.

"What do you think made your friend open up to you and his mother?" I ask, shifting the focus back to this painful revelation.

"His mom is a nurse and she was talking about some cases from work, and most of us thought she was pretty cool with sexuality. He just kind of spilled the beans," he says.

"You were there? How did she react?" I ask, still recoiling from thinking of a twelve-year-old boy raped in a men's room. *No one realizes how many children are sexual assaulted, molested and even raped! And boys as well as girls!* I think to myself.

"She was pretty cool about it, she took him to the doctor and I think he talked to a social worker for a few sessions." he answers. "I don't remember, but it really didn't come up after that."

We fall silent for a bit reflecting on these sad stories until Mike points across the road. "That building over there is Pat's new offices. He's moving next week so expect some chaos from him," Mike explains.

"He's a funny guy," I comment. "He likes to send a lot of texts and e-mails." *He seems drunk for some of them,* I think reflecting on some of Pat's recent texts, but having decided it's just the friendly Wisconsin side of him coming out, I don't comment more about that.

"Yeah, Pat likes the texts and e-mail, that's for sure," Mike says pulling into Miss Katie's Diner, the place where we had breakfast yesterday as well. "This still okay with you?" he asks.

"Yeah, I loved the omelets and the coffee!" I say as we exit our warm car into the snowy parking lot.

Miss Katie's Diner is decorated in a fifties theme with black and white checked tiles, chrome siding and soda bar style tables and chairs. Pat is seated under a life-size cardboard cut-out of Michelle Obama who visited the diner in 2010 and nearby is another of Hillary Rodham Clinton from her visit in 2008 and beyond that, one of Bill Clinton from his visit in 1996, all suspended from the ceiling in a "just hanging around here" sort of motif.[39]

"We're in good company!" I joke to Pat as I glance around at the power ladies "hanging" around our table.

"Yeah, you want to get a picture with them?" Pat asks and we decide to pose with the cut-outs, laughing as our waitress hands us menus. The place is hopping and we need to keep moving if I'm

going to get a full day in with Annette. I order an omelet and coffee again, the men do the same and then we launch into business.

"After today I'll need all the records like I already wrote to you," I explain. "It will take me at least a week, but given this is a very complex case with the two days of interview material I expect that I'll be sending you a thirty pages or more, single-spaced report at the end of it all."

Mike emits a low long whistle, "Thirty pages single-spaced! That will be the longest expert report we've ever had," he says, turning to Pat smiling.

"I write very exhaustive reports," I explain. "It will discuss *everything* and it will be a completely tight case as far as I can make it. I've done this a lot, and I am good at anticipating anything they might try to impeach me on and I'll have an answer for it."

The guys smile, pleased as they know, as do I, that expert witnesses are always attacked from the other side's lawyers who try to discredit them, and they're glad I'm familiar with this part of the "game".

"Mike's got the camera and tripod," Pat explains. "It's all set up and ready for you, all you have to do is make sure you have Annette in the frame and then push film. The batteries should last for most of the day," he instructs.

"I'm not going to come up into the jail with you today. I've got some appointments, but Pat will go up with you and set the whole thing up. He knows how to run it," Mike adds as I confess to being a bit technologically challenged. We exit and return to his car to drive over to the courthouse together.

CHAPTER TWENTY-NINE

MEETING LARA

Mike parks the car in the basement parking lot underneath the courthouse, and we get a good laugh when he opens the trunk. The camera tripod is in a zip-up army green canvas bag, just under a meter long.

"It looks like a rifle!" I say, convulsing in laughter. "Good luck getting that past the jailhouse guards! They'll probably shoot us all if we approach with that thing!"

"What the hell, Mike?" Pat asks as we laugh some more.

"Come on, they'll have to let it in if it's necessary to your evaluation," Mike says maintaining a serious expression. It feels good to be laughing as I try to gear myself up to face this horror again today.

Christina meets us at the security checkpoint and together we take locker keys and store our things. *No pear today! Just a tripod in a canvas bag that looks like a sawed off shotgun! No worries— none whatsoever*, I think as we approach the guard desk for our second day inside the Milwaukee County Jail.

The clerk at the desk takes our IDs and hands us prison badges as Pat puts the "shotgun" through security. The guard unzips it checking to see what it is and amazingly it passes through along with my phone, Mike's camera and my camera. Phones and cameras are contraband, but I don't say anything. Christina has stored hers. I prefer to have mine on hand, despite also having Mike's at the ready. *You never know if you'll need it,* my inner rebel says, highly satisfied to have cleared it all past the security guard.

We retrace our path of yesterday and set up again in the white cinderblock room. Pat works on setting up the tripod, screwing Mike's camera to the top of it.

"It won't shut itself off will it?" I ask as Pat shows me the right button to push when we are ready to film.

"No, you have to shut it off with the same button that turns it on," he reassures me and takes a seat against the wall on the other side of the room.

"You staying?" I ask.

"Yeah, I want to see this for myself," he answers, surprising me. "I think I know what you are saying about the eye fluttering, but I can't say that I've seen any other personalities."

"Okay," I agree, wondering how it will work with him in the room. Annette seems comfortable with him and he's a bit of a teddy bear type personality with an easy smile and laugh—not very threatening as far as men go. *It will be good to have another witness,* I think to myself as I get used to the idea of two people observing me today instead of just one.

The guard leads Annette into the room. She shuffles along with the leg shackles and sits uneasily while he fastens the chain on the bench to her cuffed feet. She has an easy smile for us today, her face still timid with the big saucer eyes, but her smile is genuine. She's happy to see us all.

"I'm going to stay here today, Annette," Pat explains and she nods, seemingly unperturbed that he will remain.

"How are you today?" I ask worried that she's had a bad night. "Did it go alright for you last night?"

She nods and says, "It was okay."

"Annette, I have this camera here and I'm going to film us today because I want to be able to show some things that you do and say in the courtroom when we go to trial. I know it's weird to be filmed, but are you okay with that? It's really important," I explain.

She nods as Christina translates. I go up to the camera that Pat has already tested out with Christina to be sure it is focused correctly on the spot where they've seated her. It is. Annette is framed well inside the camera aperture. "Okay. We are filming now," I say as I push the button. A red indicator light illuminates and I sit down trusting it will capture our work today.

"So how did Lara handle that you told me all that you did yesterday?" I ask, concerned about the fallout of telling what she'd been warned never to tell. "Was she angry at you?"

"Yes, she's really angry," Annette answers and her eyes begin their rapid eye flutter as her eyes roll back into her head. This time it's longer than before and when she finishes Annette looks different, tougher—but I don't catch the change at first.

"I'd like to go back over what we discussed yesterday," I say, watching Annette closely. She's not afraid anymore and now she looks me aggressively in the eyes.

"Who's here?" I ask, suddenly aware that she's "switched".

"Lara," the new personality answers in a low voice as I feel the hair on the back of my neck stand on end. She's the same person, yet *totally* different, I notice as she throws back her head saucily and arches her neck taking me in as well.

"Okay. We'll then, you can tell us a lot," I say, determined to keep my cool in the face of the totally bizarre having occurred right in front of our eyes. "Could we start with Grandfather?" I ask.

"What do you want to know?" Lara asks me aggressively.

"What he did to you," I answer grimly, bracing myself for the story.

Lara repeats Annette's stories of how Grandfather started molesting Annette at age six, every time Abuela left for town, and how her Uncle also molested her starting at age ten. Lara explains that Annette "left" for these episodes and that Lara emerged each time,

allowing Annette to have complete amnesia for what Grandfather did to her.

Lara on the other hand remembers it. "I was there every time he played this game."

"How often was it?" I ask.

"Every time we went there, which was everyday," she says, anger filling her voice.

"How did it end?" I ask.

"We stopped going there when I was twelve," Lara explains. "Papa thought I was old enough to watch my sisters so we stayed home after that. I never went there without Papa along again."

"And your sisters, did they get molested too?"

"No, never."

"How do you know that?"

"I watched them every minute and I never ever let them be alone with Grandfather or Uncle. I protected them."

"So your function is to protect, and to take the hard things for Annette and keep them from her?" I ask.

"Yes," she answers.

"And she doesn't know what happened? You keep the memories from her?"

"Yes, Annette is weak," Lara answers, her lips curling into a sneer. "She can't take anything bad." The truth though, is that Lara also is not strong enough to contain it all herself all the time. When Abuela died, Lara broke, letting the memories through to Annette.

"What about the rape? When did that happen?"

"I was sixteen."

"Was it Juan, the one she told me she first made love with?"

"No, it was after him. Juan was good to her."

"What happened?"

"It was when Abuela was sick. I was drinking and one of the boys at the bar asked me to go home with him."

"Were you drunk?"

"A little bit, yes."

"Did you want to have sex with him?"

"No, I wanted to keep drinking and the bar was closing. He invited me to come in his car so we drove to his house together and drank some more there. He tore off my clothes and raped me there. Then he called me a whore and said he had gotten what he wanted from me and he threw me out of the house naked along with my clothes.

"How did you get home?" I ask.

"I walked, after I dressed myself. I was crying all the way home," Lara recalls.

"What did you do when you got home? Did you tell anyone?"

"No, I took a very long, hot shower and then I went and got some beers and I sat and drank them. I drank until morning and then I passed out," Lara face's hardening as she recalls.

"What happened with Miguel?" I ask.

"He was Annette's husband," she answers blandly.

"Who had sex with him: you or her?"

"I did. She started it sometimes, but I always finished it."

"What kind of sex was it?" I ask, wondering if she reenacts the traumas of her childhood.

"Rough."

"Did he hit you?" I ask.

"Yes, when I asked him to."

"Did you ask him to call you names and choke you?" I ask.

"Yes, I told him to call me a whore and choke me hard and tell me he was going to kill me."

"Did he do it?"

"Yes."

"And you liked it?"

"Yes, very much."

"You like sex and men?"

"No I hate men. And I hate sex, but I like the pleasure at the end. I like that," Lara answers.

"So did Miguel hit you or Annette other than when you asked him to?"

"No, he wasn't violent. He just drank all the time and went out in the evenings, leaving Annette home alone with the children. They fought a lot."

"And how about Ramón. Who had sex with Ramón?"

"Me, but sometimes she started it and then she was there for the beginning, but I always finished it."

Did you get him to choke you and call you names too?" I ask.

"He didn't like to do that, but I asked him to," Lara explains.

"And what about the bars and drinking? You like to drink?"

"Yes, on the weekends I come out and drink."

"You drink a lot?

"Yes, but I don't get drunk. I like to fight with other women."

"You pick fights with other women? Why?" I ask.

"They are always stupid women who throw themselves like trash at men beneath them. I like to punch them."

"You like to hit them?"

"Yes it feels good to punch them again and again," she says the pleasure of hitting them clear on her face.

"Does Annette know when you are out, or remember what you do?" I ask.

"No, she doesn't know. I come whenever she is in trouble or when I want to drink and dance," Lara says, her arms languidly resting on the table. I can imagine her in a bar stirring up a storm.

"And do you know what's going on when she's out?" I ask.

"Some of it, but I get bored around her friends and stop listening. I don't know them all," Lara explains obviously uninterested with Annette's clean life.

"But you can listen when she's out, but she can't when you are out?" I clarify. "She has amnesia for what you do?"

"Yes."

Glancing at the clock, I pause and explain to Lara that we need to break for our lunch. She nods and we signal to the guard. Pat switches off the camera and we pack up our things, taking them with us, to leave briefly.

"Please be careful approaching her again today," I warn the guard as we exit the corridor to go and get our lunch.

"That's freaking weird," Pat says as soon as we are in the elevator. "I don't think I've ever talked to that part of her, although I've seen the eye flutters with Annette many times when we've talked."

"That's when she's switching or about to switch because the topic is too upsetting," I explain. "It happened all day yesterday, but I don't think we saw Lara yesterday. What do you think?" I ask turning to Christina.

"No, we didn't see anything like that yesterday! This is *so bizarre!* I've never seen anything like this in my life!" Christina answers.

CHAPTER THIRTY
THE PERFECT CRIME

We catch a hurried lunch as the courtroom cafeteria is shutting down their afternoon service, eat quickly and then hurry back upstairs. I see that Lara is still present as we set up again. Pat checks the camera and pushes start as I signal to him that I'm ready to begin again.

Eyeing the clock on the wall I realize we need to keep a fast pace as Christina needs to leave right on time today and we have already spent a great deal of time going back over all the abuse that Lara knows about in detail and Annette could only tell us about in a distant, psychologically removed sort of manner. There is a lot more ground to cover, and time is short.

"Can you tell me what happened with the pregnancy—when Annette found out she couldn't be pregnant?" I ask.

"She miscarried once and then she was pregnant again and she kept going to the doctor and they said she wasn't pregnant—the test came out negative, but she was getting bigger and bigger. Finally the doctor did an ultrasound and then he told her that she couldn't be pregnant and would never get pregnant again, that her tubes were tied."

"Did you know about that?" I ask.

"Not really. I guess they tied them after her third child [Elise], but I don't remember the doctor explaining it. I think they just did it after the pregnancy to stop anymore babies at the time," Lara explains.

"Annette was upset?"

"Yes, she was crying and she couldn't handle it, so I came out and I listened to the doctor. He said unless she had a lot of money it couldn't be changed, that it was final. She wouldn't believe it so we argued at that time."

"How did the argument go?"

"I told her she needs to tell Ramón because she couldn't keep going to doctor appointments and telling everyone she's pregnant when she's not. A pregnancy ends in birth after nine months and it was getting close to the end. She needed a baby or to tell him the truth. She just cried and told me to stop talking."

"And what did you suggest?"

"I told her that if she wants to keep Ramón she needs to find a real baby and that we should find a woman and lure her into the house and then cut the baby out of her. Then this could be Annette's baby," Lara explains matter-of-factly.

"You studied how to cut it out of her body?"

"Yes, I watched a film of a Caesarean section on the Discovery Channel and I learned it."

"You watched it many times?"

"Yes – ten or twelve times."

"You had recorded it?"

"No."

"How did you watch it again and again?" I ask, suddenly realizing the answer—personality fragments formed in childhood often have impressive skills like retaining the photographic memory that preverbal children often display. "You have a photographic memory?"

"Yes, I watched it in my mind again and again until I knew how to do it. I knew I had to work fast because you don't have much time to get the baby out."

"You knew this would kill the woman?"

"Yes."

"What did you plan to do with her body?"

"I was going to wrap her in a blanket and put the body into my car at night after I killed her and then when I could slip away, I'd take her to the lake and tie cement blocks to her body and dump her in so she wouldn't float up. No one would ever find her. It was a perfect crime," Lara answers her face hard, remorseless.

"You knew the place?"

"Yes, I went and checked it. I was going to take her body there as soon as I could slip away after the 'birth'."

"Where did you find this woman?"

"She was walking down the street from the neighborhood clinic, and I stopped and asked if she wanted a ride. She was tired so she said yes and got into my car. In the car I told her I had some things for babies if she wanted to come to my house and get them, I'd drive her home afterward. She needed to stop at the drugstore for a prescription too, so I offered to take her there. I went in with her and translated for her. She didn't speak much English." Lara also doesn't speak much English but knew enough to help out in this situation.

"She came home with you?"

"Yes."

"Then what happened?"

Lara describes how Eva needed to use the toilet and how she waited outside with the baseball bat bludgeoning her as she came out of the bathroom, hitting her over and over again until she collapsed to the floor. "I thought that would knock her unconscious but it didn't, so I jumped on her and choked her," Lara explains.

"She was fighting back?" I ask.

"Yes, I put my knees on her arms while I choked her," Lara says coldly, "Then she finally stopped fighting."

"And then?" I ask.

"I put duct tape over her mouth and her eyes in case she woke up, and I tied her arms and legs with it, too," Lara explains. "And then I got scared. I saw her things laying all around the floor and I jumped up and collected them and ran outside and put them into the garbage can, being sure there were a lot of bags covering her purse and things and then I put the lid back on and ran inside for the knife. Then I lifted her shirt over her face and pulled her pants and panties down around her ankles and I cut the baby out."

"Was it difficult?"

"No, but when I took the baby out he was not breathing, and I was really upset about that. I made a big mistake. I waited too long to take him out."

"So it was you that called 911?" I ask.

"Yes," Lara answers.

"I listened to the 911 tape," I tell her. "You sound very upset on it."

"I was."

"Because of what you did?"

"No, because the baby died. Annette needed a baby and I didn't do it right. I wasn't fast enough. I should have been faster," Lara answers. She sounds like a doctor describing a procedure that went bad rather than someone who has carried out a pre-meditated murder. "My plan went all wrong after that," she adds.

"Did you feel bad for the woman?"

"No, not at all. I didn't care what happened to her. I only cared about Annette and solving her problem," Lara answers coldly.

With that, I see that Lara is a total psychopath and underdeveloped as a person.

But of course she is! I think to myself as horror wrestles in my soul with pity. *She only exists to endure constant daily sexual assault, and she is filled only with terror, horror, anger and the need to survive at any cost. She's never developed as a complete personal-*

154

ity, nor had any need to! I force myself to swallow my disgust and continue on.

* * *

"What happened at the hospital?" I ask going back over what Annette shared the day before.

Lara describes how the Milwaukee medical examiner's office called her back again to the hospital the morning after.

"Did they ask permission to examine you?" I ask.

"No," Lara answers and I feel anger rising inside my belly. Despite her despicable criminal acts, it doesn't sit right. *She's a long-term child sexual assault and rape victim, unable to communicate well in English, in police custody—at least in police intimidation mode as they met her at her house, escorted her to the hospital and stood guard over her during two vaginal examinations forced upon her against her will,* I think to myself.

"Did you tell them no?" I ask.

"I didn't feel I had any choice for the first one, but in the emergency room I said no," Lara recounts. "I refused the second one. They did it anyway."

"The police met you at your doorstep and escorted you to the hospital?"

"Yes."

"And they stayed outside the door while you were being examined the first time?" Lara nods. "And when you went downstairs to the emergency room they escorted you there too? Officer Gomez came in your room?"

"Yes, he came in and spoke to me in Spanish. He asked how I was doing and when the nurse came and told me I had to take my pants off, I told her I didn't want another examination. But she said I had to take my pants off, that the doctor was coming to do another examination. I asked the policeman if he could tell her to go away and he did.

"Then he told me, 'We know everything. Where is the girl?'

"I answered him, 'The girl is safe.'

"[He asked,] 'Where is the body? Is she dead or alive?'

"I told him she's dead.

"'Where?'

"I told him, 'In the basement.'"[40]

"Why did you confess?" I ask confused that she would plan her crime so meticulously and then cave in so easily under pressure.

"I didn't want to have that examination and I thought if I confessed I could go to jail for the crime, and Annette would go free," Lara explains.

I stare at "Lara" speechless. For all the rest of the horror, I can somehow temporarily suspend my emotional responses listening to her, but this spins my mind into total disbelief. *Dissociative disorders are so strange!* I think to myself. *How could she honestly believe such a thing—that confessing in one personality would save the other from going to prison?* I also feel stricken to imagine any woman having her confession extracted from her by threat of another intrusive vaginal exam, especially if she is a former rape and sexual assault victim. *There is something so sick about that,* I reflect as we continue forward.

"But you realize that you share the same body, that what happens to you also happens to her?" I ask, incredulous.

"Yes," Lara answers, looking sadly down at the table. "Now I realize."

"Did you talk to Annette since you've been here?"

"Yes, I tried to tell her what happened and I tried to talk to her, but she won't listen to me. She doesn't want to hear anything from me now."

"Were you the voice that told her to kill Dr. Pankiewicz and Christina?" I ask.

"Yes, I wanted her to try and escape," Lara answers, glancing embarrassed at Christina.

"Was it you that attacked the prison guard?"

"Yes, I wanted to help Annette escape. She needs to get to her children."

"Who is the man's voice she hears now?" I ask, referring to the male voice Annette described hearing since she arrived in prison.

"It's me. I had to change my voice because she won't talk to me anymore. I was trying to explain to her and to help her escape."

"How about the baby crying?"

"I don't know about that. Maybe it's the baby that died? I don't know."

CHAPTER THIRTY-ONE
FILMING A "SWITCH"

"Is the camera still working?" I ask Pat as we pause temporarily. The day has sped by. I glance at the wall clock and see that we have only another forty minutes before Christina needs to leave.

Pat jumps up to check. "Shit! No, it's stopped. The battery died!"

I reach into my bag and pull out my camera, glad I did not surrender it at the guard's desk.

"Can you set this one up on the tripod?" I ask, always intimidated by using new high- tech equipment. Pat takes it and removes Mike camera to place mine there and I stand to check if it's still capturing her image and when I see it is, I press the record button—pleased that I can figure that much out—as I explain to Lara what I intend to do.

"Lara, it's really important for your court case that I catch something that you do on film. I don't want to hurt Annette but this is *really, really* important. Can you go away now and let Annette come out?"

Lara looks into my eyes and slowly evaluates me. I see that she trust me. She nods and suddenly her eyelids start flickering wildly as her eyes roll up in her head. When they open again Annette is back. It's extremely bizarre and again I feel the hairs on the back of my neck standing on end.

Unlike Lara's languid somewhat aggressive and sexualized posture, Annette appears timid, terrified and her wide eyes are back. Her eyes flit from me to Christina and back to Pat as she tries to orient herself.

"Hello, Annette, can you tell us where you've been all day? Where you've spent the day today?" I ask, expecting her to say she was with us.

"In my cell. I was sleeping in my cell all day," she answers looking back and forth between us.

"And how did you get here?" I ask, amazed that the compartmentalization between Lara and Annette and the amnesia for Lara's experiences is so strong—even though she's been telling us that all day.

"The guard brought me here," she answers sincerely.

"When?"

"Just now, a few minutes ago," Annette answers looking around the room, obviously highly disoriented and fearful as she sees the disconfirming looks on our faces. Probably this is a fact of her life: others constantly telling her that what she perceives as her reality is not at all as she experiences it.

"Annette, I'm *really, really* sorry to do this, but I must do something that may be painful for you," I explain, feeling a deep twinge in my heart as I go forward to *knowingly* cause a sexual assault and rape victim deep emotional pain. But I press on speaking firmly to her. "Annette, you've been here all day. You've been here since ten o'clock this morning and you've been talking with us since then, in your Lara personality."

Annette's eyelids flutter wildly and her eyes roll up in her head but Lara doesn't give her any relief. Her eyelids continue to flutter as I pause and Annette briefly returns to stare at us, completely terrified. I press on.

"And Lara's been telling us what happened to *you,* how Grandfather put his fingers inside you and choked you and how Uncle did the same." Annette's eyelids start the wild fluttering again and her eyes roll back again as she struggles to escape, but Lara doesn't give her that possibility.

Annette again recovers herself momentarily staring at me with her eyes wide and terrified. I press on, pushing her into another eye roll and rapid eyelid fluttering by saying, "He made you orgasm. And he said you liked it. The boy who raped you tore your dress and called you a whore, saying that he didn't need you anymore, throwing you naked out his door with your clothes."

Mentally I scroll through the list of abuse, repeating aloud what I know she avoids by switching personalities.

Annette is in overdrive, her eyes rolled back in her head, eyelids fluttering helplessly, trying to escape. I feel so guilty for what I'm doing. But I push onward repeating sick details that Lara has shared, until finally Annette manages to leave and Lara reappears, languid and staring aggressively again.

The transformation is eerie and complete. "Thank you," I say as Pat, Christina and I watch the saucer eyes revert to normal, relaxed eyes, the scared face transform into a languid somewhat aggressive and sexualized look and her body posture changing completely before us, aggressive versus timid.

When it's complete I ask, "Can you go away again?" I ask wanting to be sure to capture the whole thing.

Lara complies, her eyes again rolling upward, the rapid eyelid flutter, this time with no terror involved, until Annette reappears— terrified.

"You can turn off the camera," I say to Pat, and he jumps up obeying my command. I'm clearly upset and he feels it. And I don't feel like recording anymore.

"I'm *really, really* sorry," I say as I look into Annette's terror struck eyes. Suddenly I feel that I have just become another of the abusers in her life. "I had to do that to try and help you. I want the court to understand what happens to you when you go away and come back," I say, but she doesn't comprehend. "Do you know what just happened here?" I ask.

"No," Annette answers, confused.

"I said some things that may have scared you. I'm sorry for that," I say. *I'm a healer, not someone who causes pain*, I think to myself as I wince inside. "I'm *really, really sorry*," I repeat.

Annette seems clueless and wide-eyed. Speechless she watches as we begin to clean up our things.

"I think I have everything I need now," I say, "but if I don't, I'll ask Pat to talk to you or I'll come back and talk with you again," I say. "I hope I can help you Annette, but you do understand that the best I can do is help you to move to a hospital instead of a prison cell, right?"

She nods.

"But I think you can heal if you work at it with a good psychologist. You've already done a lot of the work here in prison understanding what Lara's shared with you—that's a big breakthrough already. I think you can heal, but it will take a long time and you'll have to work at it. And Pat and I will talk about if we can arrange for you to write to your children at least. Good bye, dear," I say as I rise and take my things. I walk over to Annette and press another kiss atop her head, hoping that somehow we can help her.

She's committed a horrible crime in her Lara personality—cold-blooded murder and Lara feels no remorse. But Annette, if it's possible to think of her as another persona, is an innocent and almost childlike personality—that's plain to see.

Poor dissociated woman! I think as I leave the room shaking my head. Silently, I follow Pat down the hallway.

* * *

"We got it on film for sure! Geez that last half-hour was unbelievable!" Pat comments as we descend in the elevator back to reception. "No one can argue with that. She changes into a completely other person!"

"Yeah, I'm really glad I had my camera along," I answer, "but I felt bad doing it, pushing her that way."

"You saw it, too?" I ask Christina, and she nods. "We may need to call you as a witness," I explain and Christina agrees that she can attest to watching this very bizarre phenomena.

We get our things and Christina departs, both of us thanking the other profusely, and then Pat and I go to sit in the courthouse lobby to compare notes while I wait for Heidi to pick me up.

"Okay, now I need you to get me *all* the records—police, child protective services, medical, etc.—and in the meantime I'll go home and write this up," I say as Pat and I confer.

"I have a request for the CPC records, but they can be real buggers," Pat answers in reference to the records I want for finishing her evaluation. "I used to work with them and they are just sandbagging us. Let me see if I can get to their boss."

We part with Pat promising to send me all the outstanding records and to track down and arrange interviews for me with Ramón, Annette's girlfriend and possibly her two oldest children if possible before I leave Wisconsin. "We'll need an interpreter for those," he notes and we discuss if we can engage Christina again possibly on Monday before I leave, as she has been great. We say goodbye, and I disappear again into the snowy Wisconsin street to catch up with my niece.

CHAPTER THIRTY-TWO
EXPERT REPORT

After a weekend spent with my sister in her small town of She-boygan and letting the case sit quietly in my head, I fly home to McLean, Virginia, a suburb of Washington, D.C., and begin making my way through the fifty pages of my handwritten notes from the evaluation. As a clinician, I've learned to take nearly simultaneous notes of what is said in interviews and I have recorded verbatim nearly everything Annette said over the two days spent with her. Now as I sit surrounded by police and medical records and the evaluation notes, I try to make sense of it all.

It takes me about a week and I still don't have everything I want to complete my report. I've already asked Pat to set up interviews with Ramón, Annette's oldest children, and with her closest friends by Skype now that I'm no longer in Wisconsin. "And I need those Child Protective Services records and her charts from the hospital when she was taken there for the examinations before her confession," I also remind Pat.

Pat's been working on collecting documents for some time and is exhausted from it. Before I even went for the evaluation I had sent him a long list of documents that I wanted to look at. On February fifth just days before I met Annette he wrote:

> Anne,
>
> We met with the DA on 1/30/12 to get *missing* police reports, which were not provided to us *for some reason*. I am sending this to you, Mike and Peter Perales [the private investigator]. These reveal that

the children are in a foster home due to the Bureau of Milwaukee Child Welfare (BMCW). There also appears to be an alibi for Ramón. . . . Ramón and Annette's daughters took photos of the deceased infant and they all prayed on the spot. I don't know whose idea it was off the top of my head about actually posting pictures of the deceased baby on Facebook. Annette gave detective Gomez the pswd [password], so it was either her Facebook or Ramón's FB. It appears 100% certain that her family and Ramón (assuming his alibi holds true) totally believed she was pregnant. Her neighbor was not so convinced because of what she told police about Annette not knowing a delivery date and not receiving regular pre-natal care.

So, now it seems we have to obtain the following:

BMCW records

Jail call / visitor records

 Facebook subpoena

Ambulance records (may be contained in ST F records)

St. Francis Hospital records (I have the release for her to sign)

Possibly a court order to speak with the children if Foster parents object

All her medical records going back as far as necessary regarding pregnancy, etc.

Patrick

Prior to coming to Milwaukee I had read most of what Pat sent and I had scrolled through the police photos from the crime scene. They were horrific: pictures of Eva's body with her panties caught around her ankles and her blouse pulled up over her face and her carved open abdomen exposed, her entrails hanging loose. It reminded me of the Charles Manson case when the cultists hung pregnant Sharon Tate up from the ceiling after having stabbed her belly repeatedly and used her blood to write "pig" on the door.

Horrific! Looking at them made me wonder *Am I right to be helping to defend a murderer? But child sexual abuse is horrific too, isn't it?* I ask myself.

And who is the murderer in this case? I seriously ponder as I read and reread the evaluation notes and plow my way through the voluminous records. *How separate are these two personalities?* Annette doesn't seem to know when Lara's present. Her confusion looked genuine when we "called her out" at the end of the second day of the evaluation. She seemed to believe she had been sleeping in her cell all day and was completely terrified when I told her, no—that she'd been with us. And when I repeated the details from the abuse that Lara had shared with us, Annette became so terrified that she immediately went into a sustained eyelid flutter, trying to escape what I was saying.

And she doesn't seem to know the whole extent of the abuse, rape or the even of the crime she committed, I think to myself. Annette is very confused, whereas Lara knows all the details and speaks easily about it, fearless and angry as she spits out her spite over all that's been done to her. Lara doesn't believe that she owes anyone anything and she feels fine to take from others what she thinks Annette needs—even an innocent life.

Lara is *not* separate from Annette, I realize of course, yet I see from the intensive evaluation that she has the ability to rise up and take executive control of Annette's mind and body, causing a complete amnesiac episode.

Only Annette appears completely separate from Lara, knowing only what Lara chooses to share with her and lacking the ability to stop Lara from overtaking her mind and body. *She was able to block Lara from speaking to her, but not from acting on her own,* I reflect. *That must be a terrifying feeling.*

I've often pondered the issue of free will in relationship to the patients I see, especially those who were terribly abused as children. And I sometimes wonder if indeed *all* people have free wills? Possibly those who entered this world amidst conflict, horror, deceit, abuse, hatred—born into war or abusive families where they are not nurtured, are unloved and abused—don't have a chance to humanize.

Indeed, in terms of the mind, we aren't born as full members of humanity. Instead we learn first at our mother's breast and then humanize further in the wider family and community circle through nurture, love and limits about how to function and become fully participating members of humanity.

Perhaps those who grow up abused and severely neglected, even sometimes drug addicted from the womb, develop what Jewish and Christian scriptures refer to as a "hardened heart". And if a child never encounters true love to melt that heart, perhaps it never unhardens, never humanizes.

Or perhaps the "sins of the fathers and grandfathers" are visited upon these children. *How can a child develop a normal conscience, empathy for others and become anything other than a psychopath when he or she has been repeatedly betrayed, severely neglected and used repeatedly as a sexual object?* I ask myself as I read over again and again my notes from the evaluation.

Annette seems to be a timid and easily terrified person but also, by her own report and what I could see of her, to be a kind, hardworking and somewhat self sufficient individual committed to nurturing her partner and her children. Somehow she soaked up some nurture

along the way and seems to have developed a normal conscience and a normal sense of responsibility to her fellow human beings.

Lara on the other hand, is not a completely formed self: she is nothing but a personality fragment really, and she is violent, probably alcoholic or an addict, appears sexually sick in that she reenacts the childhood abuse, and she is completely out for herself—that is for herself and Annette, who she realizes she must keep functioning.

Lara, as a personality fragment, came into being solely to deal with the chronic, inescapable and horrific childhood sexual assaults and she seems to understand that she needs to keep Annette safe and shield her from serious threats—sexual and otherwise—and to solve serious problems for her. But Lara isn't a very good problem solver. She is limited in her moral judgment, detached from real life and emotionally hardened, lacking empathy for others. Her main emotions are anger and spite.

It's Lara that committed the murder! I think to myself. And unlike Annette who even now doesn't know all the details of the sexual abuse, rape and murder, Lara knows it all! And while Annette was not psychologically present for the planning or execution of the murder—and until very recently even had complete amnesia for it, Lara premeditated and carefully planned the murder and fetal abduction and she has *no remorse over it even now. Lara is a psychopathic killer! And Annette—if they are really separate individuals in terms of a truly "split" personality—is completely innocent!*

But how can one argue that in court? I wonder to myself. This is a really tough case and while I see that Annette has a serious dissociative disorder that is not an easy thing to convince a jury of, especially one that is horrified and angered over the despicable crime she has committed. *Perhaps the film of her switching personalities will convince them? But will they really understand that when she is in the Lara personality – which is really only a personality fragment – Annette has complete amnesia and no control over what Lara decides to do? Will they be able to understand that while Lara is guilty*

of a premeditated crime, that Annette should receive the not guilty by insanity defense? Can a jury distinguish these nuances involved in a dissociative identity disorder case?

Annette without her Lara personality might not be a threat to society, but Lara should never be released into the public; she is a sick psychopath who could easily murder again. Lara should spend her life locked up in prison. But Annette is living in the same body and is a person who should go to hospital, not prison. If Annette takes part in intensive therapy, can work through and integrate the now sequestered memories of the sexual abuse and the murder; she can face and process terror, horror, fear, guilt and shame to come out a fully-integrated human being who no longer loses herself whenever a posttraumatic trigger fires up her Lara personality fragment, thereby taking over executive control of her mind and body.

Annette needs round-the-clock, in-patient psychological treatment in a lock ward until she can be rehabilitated and return to society in full control of her mind and body. Our legal system understands and has made provisions for mentally ill people. Now I have to find the way to convince the court that indeed Annette is deeply mentally ill.

*　　*　　*

I clear my calendar and spend the entire week pouring over records, telling Pat I want to speak to potential corroborating witnesses over Skype to find out if they too noticed the personality switches and if they can provide much needed information to corroborate what Annette has told me.

"I'd love to talk to her one still living sister or her other relatives if we can find them," I tell Pat by e-mail. "We need to be as solid as possible that the story she has told us about her childhood is true. Maybe they know details about the abuse? Molesters often don't limit themselves to only one victim. There must be others in the family that know about her grandfather's and uncle's abuse."

Mike who is more knowledgeable about childhood sexual abuse and PTSD in general gets it and agrees, but it's Pat who's working with the private investigator, Peter Perales, trying to track down Ramón, Annette's children and her one close friend, Angelita Rosaria[41], who might be able to shed more light. Of course this is costing a lot of professional time and money for the legal team, and funds are an issue in this case. Annette is indigent with no one helping her but these three attorneys, who aren't charging her but are also not court-assigned lawyers who can tap into State funds to cover some expenses.

And I also have not been paid. The lawyers have promised to pay me at a one third reduction from my fees, but when I submit my bill it goes into someone's inbox with no response. I don't tell them this because once I've gone for the evaluation and I know what needs to be done, I know that to the best of my ability I will do it—paid or not. It's my character and it often means that when I get involved in a case like this one, I don't get paid!

As far as Annette's family and friends in Milwaukee, Pat reports that it isn't easy to get them on board because the children are in foster care and can't be reached. Ramón is an itinerant worker and was briefly considered a suspect, so he is afraid to talk. Pat sends Peter to put Ramón at ease and claims that Ramón may agree to an interview, but we don't know for sure yet. Angelita Rosaria agrees to talk with me over Skype, but has to wait until she has a day off to travel—she has to take two busses to the lawyers' offices to be able to sit in front of a computer. None of these people have personal computers, and we need to get the translator on board at the same time! Nothing is simple in this case and it calls to my attention how difficult it is for indigent people to defend themselves properly in court.

The Child Protective Services are also not easily releasing Annette's records and I cannot verify Annette's story or the exact dates

of how long her children were kept in foster care after he daughter was molested. And no one can find her extended family.

I realize that they will probably not find everyone and I wonder what to do about it. As an expert witness, I like to go into the stand rock solid, having left no stone unturned and ready to answer all questions with corroboration to every claim I make in my expert report and every statement I will make in court.

CHAPTER THIRTY-THREE

MIRANDA RIGHTS

You have the right to remain silent. Anything you say can and will be used against you in a court of law. You have the right to an attorney. If you cannot afford an attorney, one will be provided for you. Do you understand the rights I have just read to you? With these rights in mind, do you wish to speak to me?

Miranda rights: they're on every police show. All Americans know about it. But what about Americans from the territories? Puerto Ricans? Non-English speakers? Do they know that they should be read their rights before being taken into police custody, before confessing to a crime? And what exactly does police custody consist of?

And as I work on understanding the case and pulling my report together, I find that the records from the hospital and police are deeply disturbing in this regard. It's clear that Annette was at some point, while in the hospital, if not before when she was being escorted there by the police, a suspect for a crime related to the death of Eva's fetal child, if not Eva herself. *Doesn't being under police custody require them to read her rights to her?* I wonder as I read over the police reports of their time with Annette in the hospital. Annette is clearly identified as a criminal suspect in the reports even before the second vaginal examination – when she is in the labor and delivery room.[42] Later it even comes out that she was also put under arrest

before being taken to the emergency room, but Detective Gomez who questions her there without reading her rights to her claims to have not known about the arrest.[43]

It's clear in the medical and police reports, as well as in Annette's reports to me, that she did refuse the second exam, yet it was forced upon her *and* she was questioned by more than one of the police officers and confessed to her crime while under this duress. This seems to me a type of horrid female torture! My mind harks back to my work with Iraqi prisoners, where male prisoners told me about torturers anally raping them with bottles and brooms to extract confessions from them. *Is this so different?* I ask myself, although I understand that the vaginal examinations in Annette's case were carried out due to medical concern for her well-being—at least, in the second instance, but I am not convinced about the first.

As I read over the reports and search the news on the case, I find testimony from Detective Gomez, reported from the pretrial hearing by the Milwaukee Sentinel Journal. Gomez, who entered the examining area and talked to Annette when she was trying to ward off the second vaginal exam, is reported as saying:

> ... he was talking to Morales-Rodriguez at a hospital a day after she had reported giving birth at home to a stillborn baby boy, whom medical examiners determined more likely had been cut from his mother's womb. "She said she was 'sorry for the girl,'" Gomez testified at the preliminary hearing for Morales-Rodriguez.
>
> He said she was shaking profusely, under obvious emotional distress. Then she asked him how much time she would do, Gomez said. He said he told her that he didn't know what she was talking about. Then, Gomez testified, she told him that in her basement, Eva Alvarez Mendoza[44] lay dead, and that the

baby Morales-Rodriguez claimed to have delivered
Oct. 7 was not hers.[45]

When I had asked Lara what she recalled of that encounter she told me that Detective Gomez had dismissed everyone from the room and when they were alone, he began aggressively questioning her. Obviously he was treating her as a suspect without first reading her rights to her. And Lara, believing that he could forestall the second vaginal exam (which is clear to me that she viewed as an assault) and believing that she could protect Annette by taking the "rap" for her, confessed to him.

In his records, Detective Gomez reports that after talking with Annette, he sent a car to the house to find the body she had told admitted to hiding there.[46] At that point he must clearly be seeing Annette as a murder suspect—yet he fails to read her rights to her!

I'm not a lawyer and I've never studied Miranda case law, but from lay knowledge it seems to me that he is in gross violation of the law intended to protect suspects who are in police custody to prevent them from confessing without the benefit of a legal consultation and presence of one's attorney during a police interrogation. I become incensed reading it. While I don't deny the sickness of her crime, *isn't something wrong here?* I ask myself, angered that this can happen in my country.

It reminds me of torture stories I heard from terrorists in third world countries—of how their confessions were extorted from them in jails while their heads were repeatedly dunked and held underwater in buckets of dirty water so they could not breathe, or how victims in one cell were forced to listen to the rape or torture of loved ones in cells next door to make them confess. *For a rape victim, isn't have a vaginal exam forced upon her a form of torture?* I ask myself.

In Detective Gomez's incident reports I find that he states that he was informed upon *arrival to the hospital* that Annette had not been pregnant and could not have given birth to the dead infant, so he

obviously knew a crime had been committed and that she was a suspicious person. He then goes on to describe approaching Annette in the ER, introducing himself and conducting a conversation with her in Spanish in which he admits asking her numerous questions about herself and what was going on without reading her rights to her.

Detective Gomez gallingly even writes in his report that Annette declined the vaginal exam that was forced upon her while she was in his "custody", writing "the nurse walked into the room and made an attempt to treat Morales, who refused treatment, demanding the nurse leave the room."[47]

He goes on to state that at that moment, Annette negotiated with him to "cooperate" in discussing the case with him if he would demand that the nurse leave the room. Clearly, even in his own notes, he describes that there is an exchange going on: a confession without the benefit of an attorney being present to hold off the clearly refused, but soon to be forced upon her, vaginal assault.[48]

Detective Gomez also reports that Annette was visibly shaking during this interchange.[49] From my reading, it appears to me that Annette was giving up her rights deprived of understanding and without them being presented to her, in order to protect herself from further vaginal assault. Then according to Detective Gomez, Annette proceeded to confess to her crime in a fragmented manner to which he still did not respond at anytime by reading her rights![50]

Annette then negotiated with him offering, "I'll tell you at the police station if you take me out of here."[51] It appears to me that *obviously* Annette was more terrified of the unwanted vaginal intrusions than she was of confessing to a murder!

While I know she is guilty, I wonder, *What if she was not guilty? Does the state have the right to order a woman to be escorted out of her home to a hospital to be forced to submit to multiple, unwanted, intrusive vaginal examinations? And if the person is guilty, does the state have the right to coerce a confession from her by implying that the vaginal assaults will stop if she confesses and to submit her to*

them without reading her rights to her beforehand and letting her decide for herself?

Detective Gomez, I find, states in his written reports that he told Annette in response to her refusal for another vaginal exam "that I wanted her to get checked by the nurse to ensure that she was physically okay. . . Morales reiterated she was okay and that she had cut herself." He goes on to say that "I did convince Morales to submit to medical examination by medical staff, which she did."[52] His convincing it seems occurred by virtue of his police uniform!

In the St. Francis Hospital Emergency Room records I find a medical notation stating: "Patient arrived via Law Enforcement Agency." Their history repeats this twice noting:

> **Patient reported giving birth to a stillborn baby. Was seen in L&D [Labor and Delivery] and it was determined she had not given birth. Was not bleeding when discharged from L& D but went to the restroom and came out bleeding from the vagina. Patient is in police custody [bold added by me] and needs to be medically cleared. (ABH 17:38).[53]**

In regard to the examination, I find that the St. Francis Hospital records also note her time with Detective Gomez and that she clearly refused further vaginal exams although they were done anyways:

> **MPD [Milwaukee Police Department] in with patient at this time, patient has refused pelvic exam.[54] MD [Doctor] aware. (JRWW 10/07/2011 18:00). Upon entering the room, MD with female MPD officer in with patient along with writer to perform pelvic exam. Will continue to monitor (JRWW 18:20)[55]**

When I asked Heidi about the normal informed consent protocol in Milwaukee hospitals, Heidi explained that informed consent for a medical procedure if collected orally would involve a witness being present.[56] Indeed, conducting any medical procedure *without*

informed consent is generally considered in legal terms, an assault. In this case, in addition to the medical notes clearly documenting her referral, there is a witness—a police officer—who recalls that Annette very clearly declined the procedure!

When I inquired of Lara if permission for the second vaginal exam was sought, Lara told me,"I didn't feel I could say no."

I find in the police records that it's only far later, after taking Annette from the hospital to the police station that there is any evidence of the police carrying out their Miranda duties. Detective Gomez reports in his notes that at 6:57 p.m. that he and Detective Hutchinson "conducted the interview of Morales." Only at that point does he record reading Mrs. Morales Rodriguez her rights and giving her the opportunity to refuse to speak, to call an attorney, etc. He reports, "I advised Morales of her Constitutional Rights, which I read in Spanish, from the MPD [Milwaukee Police Department] card."[57] Officer Deidrich writes in her report that at 6:32 p.m. that she conveyed Annette, already under arrest from the hospital to the Investigative Division of the police station in behalf of Detectives Gomez and Hutchinson. She was already under arrest at 5:25 p.m. and had been in policy custody most of the afternoon and questioned during that time, but her rights were only read to her at 6:57 p.m.[58]

As far as I can see, it appears from all the police reports, the hospital records, as well as from Annette's own report of events that this was the first time Annette was apprised of her rights. When I again watch the DVD of the rights reading, I am struck by what looks to me as though Detective Gomez keeps touching Annette's naked arm while speaking to her and asking if she understands.

When I asked "Lara" about what I viewed during this time, she states that his touching he made her very physically uncomfortable saying, "I didn't have any covering."

Annette as her "Lara" personality recalls those moments, "He explained I didn't have to answer, but I didn't understand." She goes on to say of the beginning of the interview with them, "I was lying

to him. I didn't want to tell him the truth. At the beginning I was lying because I didn't want to confess."

I read on and find that Detective Gomez also reports that in the first moments of the confession that Annette stated that she wanted to separate Ramón from the entire affair because he was innocent and that after doing so, she then she wanted a lawyer.[59] So Annette by her own recall did not want to confess, and by Detective Gomez's report did clearly ask for a lawyer, but she was too discombobulated to insist on the lawyer from the first moments of her "confession".

Knowing how sexual assault victims often dissociate, I can imagine that once the invasive bodily procedures began at the hospital, Annette—even in her cold-hearted and less timid Lara personality—would have been in no psychological shape to understand or act in her own best interest regarding her legal rights *even if they had been read to her.*

I'm exhausted from the case but I force myself to sit at my computer because I am beginning to feel a duty to *all* sexual assault victims to fight for a fair trial—*even given her heinous crime.* After a full week of working long days on it I finally have a preliminary report written detailing Annette's Dissociative Identity Disorder and Posttraumatic Stress Disorder diagnosis and arguing that because her Lara personality is able to take executive control of her mind and body and did so to plan and commit the crime, Annette was unable to judge right from wrong, nor even know what was happening at the time it was committed.

I proofread the report, being careful to document the long list of sources I referred to in writing it, in addition to the two-day evaluation. I carefully note the missing information I still need to finalize, then I send it off to Pat telling him that he should *not* file it with the court until we finalize. And I ask him to share it with Mike and Bob as well, telling them to take a look and proof it from a legal point of view, to remove any comments I may have inadvertently made on

the law which are outside of my expert's purview and to clean it up from the lawyer's perspective.

Pat promises to discuss it with the others and I take off to a NATO sponsored conference in Turkey where I am a speaker on issues of counter-terrorism, letting him know I remain available on another time zone, by phone and e-mail.

Likewise Pat writes me a characteristically funny e-mail after printing out my report:

> Hi Anne,
>
> Your report blew out my toner, lol. I can't wait to drop it on the DA [District Attorney] via certified mail. Maybe the state will need Depends underwear after they read it.

I write to him from Turkey reminding him that we still need to finalize it and that when it's final, I recommend that we send it to the State's expert, Dr. Pankiewicz, as well, with a letter that I draft and send to Pat. In the letter to Dr. Pankiewicz, I share my diagnosis of Dissociative Identity Disorder and point out to him that it seems to me that he only spoke to Annette in her main "Annette" personality at a time when she was still in complete amnesia for what "Lara" had done, and at a time when she was highly distraught just after viewing the DVD of herself confessing as "Lara" and shortly after she attacked the guard. I invite him to spend more time with her and potentially re-evaluate Annette in light of what I found.

I have no interest in embarrassing him in court or getting into a battle of experts. I am confident if he spends a longer time with Annette he will find the same that I did. This actually is exactly what happened in the Lorena Bobbit case. After I sent in my evaluation chiding the Commonwealth of VA for using only male experts to evaluate a woman who had just committed a crime that most males would have a strong reaction to, making it very difficult for her to talk to them openly, and pointing out her PTSD and dissociative

tendencies, the Commonwealth's experts agreed and went back and changed their diagnosis. I prefer to remain collegial among experts and allow the other side to re-evaluate in case I found something they failed to find, which is often the case, because I spend an inordinate amount of time conducting my evaluations whereas most experts are in a hurry and spend a minimum of time.

Pat, however, does not send Dr. Pankiewicz my letter and we exchange a few more e-mails about the need to get all the other corroborating information for me to finalize the report before submitting and that we should not submit different versions with changes in it. In reference to my concerns about collecting all the corroborating information, Pat writes to me while I am in Turkey:

> Anne,
>
> I definitely always try to bust the witness on anything he or she did not put in their original report, so we have to think about that. However, your voice is so soothing (like a waterfall) that Mark Williams won't rattle you. I, ON THE OTHER HAND, will rattle him as much as possible with statements that are designed to make him erupt and look like an asshat.
>
> Pat

Having gotten used to Pat's colorful sense of humor, I laugh and go back to my business in Turkey. Then the shit-storm happens.

Chapter Thirty-Four

Going Public

I am back from Turkey but a bit jet-lagged. In the back of my mind it nags at me to get in touch with Pat and learn if we can now set up the interviews of Ramón, Angelita, Annette's eldest children and possibly her sister or other family members and if we have collected the rest of the records so I can finalize my report. But I wait while I re-acclimate to U.S. time.

Then I get an e-mail dated March 8th, 2011:

> Dear Ms. Speckhard,
>
> I'm a reporter, writing about the Annette Morales-Rodriguez case in Milwaukee. At a hearing today, there was much debate and confusion about your qualifications. Are you a licensed psychologist? What degrees do you have, and where were they earned?
>
> I'm on deadline. Thanks for your cooperation.
>
> Bruce Vielmetti

Attacking the credentials of the other side's expert witness is par for the course, so this does not surprise me. The DA, it seems, is already going after my credentials. I know all the holes where he is likely to take a stab at mine and I've got all my answers prepared. *We have to go over this with Pat*, I think to myself as I answer Bruce Vielmetti. *The legal team needs to be prepared.*

I write back to the reporter:

Hi Bruce,

Psychologist is a licensed term in the U.S. I am licensed in VA [Virginia] as a family therapist and behavioral counselor. I have a Ph.D. in Family Social Science from MN and a Masters of Child and Family Studies from the University of Wisconsin. I am currently an Adjunct Associate Professor of Psychiatry in Georgetown University's Medical School (I do research and teach medical students). I am also a member of the American Psychological Association. I previously taught and developed the psychology courses for Vesalius College in Brussels, Belgium in their psychology department - cognitive, social psychology, psych testing etc. I am enclosing my bio.

One day later, an e-mail arrives from Pat with the link to a Milwaukee Journal Sentinel article by Bruce Vielmetti entitled, "Woman accused of cutting fetus from womb has 2nd personality, report says."[60] It states:

The woman charged with cutting the late-term fetus from a young mother, with hopes of passing the baby off as her own, suffers from a multiple personality disorder, according to the report of a new mental exam. The 57-page report released Thursday concludes that Annette Morales-Rodriguez suffered horrific sexual abuse and abandonment as a child and has adopted extremely dissociative behavior to block it out. The truth only emerged during 13 hours of interviews in which her alter ego, "Lara," emerged, according to the report.

What the hell? I think to myself. *Expert reports as sensitive as the one I sent should be sealed by the court and Pat shouldn't have*

submitted it yet anyway since it wasn't finalized. Reading on, the news article reports:

> Lara admitted to tragically believing that as a separate 'person' she could sacrificially spare Annette from imprisonment by coming forward herself and confessing to the crime," states Anne Speckhard, an adjunct professor at Georgetown University Medical School who was part of the defense team for Lorena Bobbitt, found not guilty by reason of insanity after infamously cutting off her husband's penis.

> Morales-Rodriguez, 34, has entered a similar plea, but a state psychiatrist found in December that she did not suffer from a mental disease or defect. She is charged with two counts of first-degree intentional homicide in the October deaths of Eva Alvarez Mendoza, 23, and her unborn son.[61]

> According to the criminal complaint, Morales-Rodriguez went looking for a pregnant woman near a south side social service agency, found Alvarez Mendoza and offered her a ride. They got some medicine for Alvarez Mendoza, then stopped at Morales-Rodriguez's house to use the bathroom.

> There, the complaint charges, the defendant struck Alvarez Mendoza multiple times with a baseball bat, then choked her unconscious before using an X-Acto knife to cut her child from her womb, trying, she told detectives, to duplicate a Caesarean section she'd seen performed on the Discovery Channel.

> Speckhard, the defense expert, has testified in courts around the country and before Congress about post-traumatic stress disorder and worked

with international committees on terrorism and its sociocultural effects. She also has studied and written about the traumatic stress of abortion, according to her website.

But in court Thursday, Assistant District Attorney Mark Williams questioned her qualifications, noting her doctorate is in family social science, and that federal judges in Wisconsin have declined to recognize her as an expert in two other cases.

That's not true! I think to myself and begin to feel angered, realizing that Pat has surely submitted the un-finalized version of my report and now, without any preparation for attacks on my credentials, the press is questioning them! I had written to Pat telling him about the one—not two—episodes where a judge in Wisconsin, out of political motives wrongly, in my opinion, questioned my credentials. *Pat should have knocked that ball out of the stadium before the DA ever had a chance to try and field it*, I think realizing now we will have to resort to damage control.

Whether it ever becomes evidence, Speckhard's report offers fascinating reading about a condition - dissociative disorder disease, or DID - believed to exist in less than 1% of people.

Switching screens I fire off an e-mail to Pat. "Did you file my unfinished report?" I ask and hit send as I switch back to the article:

According to the report, in the first several hours of an interview at the jail, Morales-Rodriguez spoke of a fairly happy, normal childhood. But eventually, Speckhard noticed that when the conversation turned to the facts of the case or other trauma, Morales-Rodriguez's eyes would roll up and her eyelids would flutter rapidly, as "Lara" would emerge.

According to Speckhard, Lara is only a personality fragment, developed to absorb the most traumatic experiences and memories of Morales-Rodriguez's abuse and abandonment by her mother and the death of her grandmother. Like those events, the October slayings don't register in Annette's memory, while Lara can recall them in numb detail. The report includes lengthy accounts of each personality speaking of the other and mentions a videotaped emergence of Lara during the second daylong interview.

"The change was quite dramatic in bodily posture, musculature, emotional tone, etc.," the report states.

Okay at least they got that right, I think to myself clearly peeved. How can this be out in the public? Pat should have asked the judge to seal the record! I fire off a text message to Pat again asking, "Did you file my unfinished report?!!"

Then I read on:

Speckhard concludes that Morales-Rodriguez continues to suffer from a severe mental defect that affects her capacity to "understand and morally evaluate her decisions and actions" and is in dire need of lengthy therapy.

According to the report:

Morales-Rodriguez suffered long-term sexual abuse until about age 12. Her mother left the family, and her grandmother, who had taken over parenting, died when Morales-Rodriguez was 16, a traumatic event that triggered her first realization of Lara.

> After moving to Milwaukee, she met a boyfriend who she said wanted to have a child with her. She believed she was pregnant in 2010 and had physical signs that she was, but learned at a clinic that she was not, and that she'd undergone tubal ligation in Puerto Rico years earlier. She was unaware she was sterile and really wanted to have a baby with her new boyfriend and so was devastated. Early in 2011, she began her next "psychological pregnancy."

> When that was coming up on nine months, Lara took over, somehow concocting the plan to get a baby for Morales-Rodriguez so she wouldn't suffer so much and taking over "executive control of her mind and body."

As I read on, I see that it's not just that my report that has somehow been filed without my knowledge and permission, or that it's gone public and is being quoted extensively in the press, or that my credentials are being questioned publicly by the DA with no answer from our side, but that our legal team also seems to be having some serious problems:

> Morales-Rodriguez's case took an odd turn recently when the prosecutor asked the court to hold a hearing at which she would be required to waive any potential conflicts of interest by two of her attorneys. One, Patrick Rupich, is facing charges of drunken driving, and another, Robert D'Arruda, is the victim in a domestic violence case being prosecuted by Williams' office.

Drunk driving? Domestic violence? Oh my God! I think. *Who are these clowns? What kind of a defense team have I gotten myself involved with?*

Milwaukee County Circuit Judge David Borowski admonished the defense lawyers Thursday for not yet
explaining the situation in detail to their client. As
a result, she could not waive the possible conflict
issue at the hearing. Attorney Michael Torphy had
tried to argue that there's no basis for the state's
motion.

My mobile rings. It's Pat. "Did you file my report?" I ask tersely.

"Yeah, they were sandbagging us and they insisted we had to meet the deadlines so I put it in," Pat answers sheepishly.

"You didn't have my permission to do that! It wasn't finalized, and now the DA is jumping all over my credentials! I sent you an entire e-mail telling you the things he would likely try to attack. *Did you even read that e-mail?*" Anger fills my voice.

"Ugh, I don't know if I got that one," Pat stumbles.

"And the report—it's a matter of public record now? *Journalists have it?*" I ask, although the answer to that is obvious.

"Uh, yes it looks that way," Pat responds.

"You didn't ask to have it sealed?" I demand.

"Uh, no the judge would normally be the one that does that. I guess he didn't seal it." Pat answers.[62]

"So any journalist can read the report in its entirety and quote from it as they like?" I ask.

"Yeah, I guess so," Pat answers.

"We've got some work to do then," I say. "You have to try to direct the public sentiment a certain way if you want to win this case—that is, if it's going to being tried in the press. I wouldn't normally as an expert ever talk to the press but I think maybe we need to do something now to try to make sure this doesn't get sensationalized and that we explain the DID diagnosis well, from a professional point of view."

"Yeah, you're probably right," Pat agrees. "Let me talk to Mike and Bob and we'll decide how to respond." We hang up and I bang my hand down on my desk. *You can never trust lawyers!* I remind myself. I am so glad I put the report in its correct format and notated what was missing from it along with a header calling it an incomplete draft. *Jokers!* I say slamming my hand down again on my desk. *Now how do we handle this?*

With a few hours Pat forwards me an e-mail from Fox 6 requesting an interview and Pat asks me if I will talk to them.

> Anne,
>
> Do you feel comfortable talking to these people? We can talk about it. I want to create enough media action that will help us sway Judge Borowski and the DA about shutting their pie holes.

I laugh reading it and can't stay angry. I call Pat to discuss, telling him I think it's the only thing we can do at this point to try to control the "media storm". I also resend him my previous e-mail outlining where I think the DA will try to attack my credentials—I have already anticipated all their attacks and where they may try to impeach me.

But Pat has not. He writes back:

> Nice.
>
> I'm giving myself the rest of this day off to recuperate from this week, but feel free to call or email.
>
> We have to be careful about what you say because your own comments could be played in court and used against Annette.
>
> You've probably done this a lot, but perhaps the media could give you a list of questions in advance like what they do for politicians.

We want as little sandbagging from them as possible.

The judge was possibly talking about a gag order, which probably will go down after we stoke the fire.

Maybe we can get the media to do some work on your credentials.

We need a counter strike on any attack on these 7th circuit cases.[63]

Pat and I talk on the phone again, and after that I talk to Fox News via Skype and answer questions from another print journalist.[64] Deciding that the only way to quell crazy speculation about the bizarre nature of this case and her diagnosis, I also post my expert report to my website with a brief introduction to the concept of dissociative identity disorder and the idea that chronically sexually abused children who find no escape often have no choice but to defend themselves psychically by splitting off the reality of their abuse and developing alternate personalities that hold the horror. I explain also that when they grow up they may not be capable of coping with normal life and commit crimes until they are treated for the horror they underwent as children.

Pat and I hope for the best, but two days afterwards Judge Borowski calls Pat, Mike and Bob into his courtroom and according to Pat's recall of it literally shouts them down saying something to the effect of, "How could you be arguing for a change of venue saying it will be a media circus in Milwaukee over this case, but your expert is talking to Fox News and even making legal statements that your client is guilty and saying she should be sent to hospital, not prison!"

It's true I had unknowingly overstepped into legal territory on the Fox News report, speculating that given Annette's confession and the body in her basement, she had clearly committed the crime and

that mentally ill patients like her need to be locked up in hospital not prison.

As Pat explains the judge's anger, I get a clearer picture of what we are facing and of the steps they have already taken in this case that have put me on the wrong side of the judge. They previously, prior to my involvement, had requested a change of venue citing the media coverage as making it impossible in Milwaukee to find jurors who hadn't already made up their mind about the case. The change of venue motion was in part to get away from Judge Borowski and the Milwaukee DA's office. Known to be a tough judge and with the DA's office already angry at Bob that he had gotten so many murderers off on technicalities, both were (according to Mike and Pat) determined to make this case stick.

So when Pat encouraged me to talk to the press he was in a sense thumbing his nose at the judge. They had already complained to the judge about too much publicity and now they were creating their own. And when Pat filed my expert report he should have requested that the judge seal it so that it could not fall into the hands of journalists and require a response on our side.

In addition to this I had already been aware that when the lawyers brought me into the case they had sought State funds to pay my expert fees because Annette is indigent and they too were not being paid. This caused complications because while the court would normally pay for an expert for a poor client, the judge insisted to use a local expert while Pat and his team refused. I knew this had already caused numerous arguments with the judge who cited the current infamous Wisconsin Governor Walker's numerous budget-cutting measures, including rescinding all collective bargaining rights of state employees. Given that political climate, the judge wasn't about to allow submission of an expensive bill higher than anything they would normally pay local experts. I had told Pat and Mike to back off on that, that we would find the funds another way, but Pat had kept insisting, likely also raising the judge's ire against me.

Likewise, as I read Vielmetti's coverage again I understand that the attorneys have their *own* issues to contend with. I ask Pat about the drunk driving charge and domestic abuse issues they are facing in their own personal lives. On March 12th he writes back answering:

> I feel outrage about being attacked because I have an OWI (Operating While Intoxicated) [from before the trial now] pending, which compares to your outrage at the state questioning your credentials. I have an OWI case, but it has been alleged that I would tank Annette's case to get an advantage in my own personal case. I will withdraw from this case before I see Annette prejudiced by any of my actions. The State has also said that Bob may tank this case to curry favor with the DA's office so that they prosecute his ex GF [girlfriend] to the fullest extent of the law. THEY DON'T WANT ANNETTE to have a defense. If we wouldn't have stepped in she'd have some useless public defender who would plead her to life automatically.
>
> I stopped keeping track of all the hours I worked on this case months ago because it has been so much.
>
> The Judge has been against you from the beginning saying, "Why do we need someone from out of state and why can't you get someone locally?" This has been repeated many many times by Judge Borowski. He's said it privately in chambers at least 3x and he's said it from the bench.
>
> Nothing has changed. It's not like the DA was rolling out the red carpet for you either.

CHAPTER THIRTY-FIVE

CONTEMPT OF COURT

Later in the day Pat writes again:

Hi Anne

Mike is doing the bulk (if not all) of the research regarding the admissibility of your testimony under Daubert[65] as he has a lot more resources for databases. We have been ordered in to Judge Borowski's Court tomorrow because the DA is making a big deal over you posting your report online. They are "concerned about the jury pool being tainted." We know you're qualified and have to get your testimony admitted. The DA (and even the judge) does not want your opinion being admissible because it causes them problems.

Don't worry, we have no doubts about you. The state wants Annette to go down hard and they are doing everything they can do to prevent Annette from having a defense.

We will deal with the Judge Crabby etc.[66] The judge is going to order us to ask you to take the report off your website. Please remove it as soon as you can, but you may not get to it until much much later. We just need it off ASAP because a gag order will probably be issued. But, we had to make a response to what they said.

The BMCW / CPS wants an additional release for Annette, so I will be seeing her tomorrow.

Pat

And later Mike calls saying, "The judge has summoned us to the court tomorrow morning to discuss your qualifications and your report being up on your website. Can you help me put together a good answer?"

"Sure," I answer, telling him I've already spoken to Pat and that I've already taken the report down from my website. We then spend the next four to five hours talking on the phone and putting together an airtight list of my credentials in response to seven or eight charges the DA has made against them.

Normally it wouldn't bother me to undergo this attack because I am used to the expert witness routine. This is par for the course. It's a joke among experts that the other side practically asks you, "So Dr. Bonehead, you went to a stupid school, did ridiculous research and couldn't possibly know anything to say about the facts of this case, so why *are you* here?" Indeed the last case in which I had appeared as an expert witness had gone like that. For nearly four hours, the opposing side's lawyer had asked me in nit picking detail about each and every one of my credentials. She asked how I knew I had an appointment at Georgetown and how I knew for sure it was real. By the time she got through questioning all my honors, schooling and publications she had begun to make me doubt if I had any credentials at all or if my name was even Anne Speckhard!

But this time it does get to me because the DA's attack has gone public with no response from our side—yet. In this case, I know one thing in particular will come up and it already has. A Wisconsin judge had years ago attacked my credentials on a political basis when I testified there on an abortion-related case. Angered that I testified that *some* women suffer emotionally after abortions, which unfortunately they do, she went on the attack and wrote in her sum-

mary judgment that I had no published peer reviewed articles on the subject and that my education was substandard.

It was actually a humorous thing for her to say since I was educated at the University of Wisconsin—in the State she was representing! And she was factually incorrect as I had at the time published my research supporting my testimony in a number of journals—all peer reviewed—and one of them even in an American Psychological Association sponsored journal. So she was wrong, but her remarks followed me into every case I testified in from there on in and I had of course gotten used to countering her attack. Luckily in the next case I appeared in, in which the opposing side tried to use her remarks to disqualify me, the judge, of the same standing as her, realized the political tenor of Judge Crabb's remarks and that she was erroneous in her statements about me, overruled it, and I was recognized as an expert.

So I am confident that we can refute all attacks this time as well. And one thing I particularly relish in this case is that only a year earlier I had appeared as an invited expert to address the 7th Circuit Bar Association, the very one that the DA is probably a member of, and thanked profusely by the Bar as well afterward. *If that doesn't mean I'm an expert for their court, I don't know what does!* I laugh to myself.

When Mike calls on the phone to discuss some details for the document he is preparing about me for court I bring it up. "That doesn't make any sense, if they invite me to come speak to them as an expert for their 7th Circuit Bar Association and then turn around and say I'm not expert enough to testify in their courtroom, does it?"

Mike laughs in agreement and I add, "And really what more do they want? Where can they find someone who is on the staff of a prestigious Medical School in the Psychiatry Department, a member of the American Psychological Association, a researcher and who is a licensed clinician who has treated DID? It's a rare disorder you know, and I've treated eleven cases of it and presented profession-

ally on the subject in medical and psychological settings. Can they find a better-qualified expert than that?"

"No, that actually sounds very good," Mike answers gleefully.

"You can apologize to the judge on my behalf about putting the report up on my website if it helps smooth things over," I say. "Pat told me it's the judge's fault he didn't seal the record, but please tell him that when the DA is publicly attacking my credentials and allowing my preliminary report to be filed unsealed, of course I want to defend both my professional opinion and my qualifications. When it went public Pat told me it became public record. I would not have posted it otherwise."

The next day, Mike arrives at the courtroom with a nine-page document that he intends to file to the court stating why I have expertise for this court and this case.[67] Pat and Bob file in with him, and Mike takes his seat next to Annette. When Judge Borowski sees the three lawyers in his courtroom, he begins to bellow loudly again about the publicity and my report appearing on my website asking: "Counsel, do you think that's a good idea? Do you think that's appropriate? Because in 20 years of practicing, and it's almost nine years as a judge, I have never seen anything like this. This is turning into a three-ring circus and I've had it!"[68]

Mike begins to answer but the judge continues to shout over him until Mike takes his pen and strikes it down hard on his tablet and shouts back, "I am *trying* to answer you judge!"

The judge does not recognize that he has created this situation by shouting while also demanding answers. Already livid, he immediately reacts with more anger shouting to the court bailiff to arrest Mike and remove him from the court.[69]

"We might all withdraw from the case," Mike tells me later when we speak over the phone, filling me in on all that happened. "Our problems with this judge might not result in a fair trial, and I'm afraid maybe all of us now have a problem defending her," Mike explains. "Pat would never do this, but it can be argued that Pat

might throw the case so that the DA goes easy on him for his DWI, and it's not Bob who is being charged for domestic abuse. It's *his ex-girlfriend.* But they can argue the same about him – that he could give a poor defense in Annette's case to get what he wants from the judge and DA in his case. And now I was arrested in court today!" Mike explains. "They took my belt, my wallet, my shoelaces and they had me in cuffs! I knew I was getting out, but I wondered *how is this good for our client? What is she thinking when she sees her attorney getting arrested and hauled out of the courtroom?*"

"She saw you get arrested?" I ask, imagining how terrified and out of control Annette must now be feeling. *This is a regular circus!* I reflect to myself as I listen to Mike describe the day's events.

"Yep, she saw it all, and we are just beginning to think maybe it's better if we all withdraw and at least then whoever takes her case could perhaps insist on a new judge."

"But Mike, you at least *understand* the long-term and devastating effects of child abuse, and you will know how to frame this case," I argue. "There aren't many attorneys that really get it when it comes to how child abuse damages the mind. She doesn't have a chance without a good expert and an attorney who can help the judge and jury understand what it means to be sexually assaulted for years at a time—that the mind is no longer normal."

Mike agrees, but we end the conversation with him telling me that the three of them are going to meet that evening to decide if any of them will continue on the case. Just before their evening meeting I decide to send out a "pep talk" e-mail encouraging them to stand strong. I write:

> I think you guys are all as emotionally exhausted as me on this case and tired of getting character assassinated?? I don't think you should give up though... She is a very sad person that needs a good defense. I think if we proceed in a very calculated way, form the arguments in her behalf carefully

and argue them calmly it will be very hard for the judge to rule against. She's insane and did not have a clue what she was doing when she did it and only after a considerable length of time gained memory of it. We all know it. It just takes carefully and deliberately convincing the judge and jury now. If you do your jobs as the attorneys I am confident we can do that well and no one can impeach us. Don't get thrown by a DA throwing around accusations and Mike ending up in hand cuffs...and all the rest. I promise you will have a good laugh about this over beers when it's all over. I'm committed now and want to see her sent to a psychiatric facility where hopefully she will be treated with some dignity and where she can hopefully heal vs. rot in a airless, sunless dark cell. And we do all know——contrary to what the judge said today—she's guilty but insane so now we just need him to think that is his bright conclusion—not ours (smile).

In his usual style, Pat sends me the court report which states among other things that on March 13th there was "discussion regarding Dr. Speckhard interview with the media and posting on her website. During the discussion attorney Torphy [was] placed in temporary custody." Pat writes:

Yes, indeed. I predicted that someone was going to get cuffed and stuffed today. It was almost me last time, as I was "admonished". [Today] Judge B became "agitated" when either Mike or Bob reminded him that he never ordered either report sealed. We did not give it out even though it was a public record. The Journal-Sentinel and other news media went and made copies of it. As for your website? That was an accident and we apologized for that. OOPS!

The judge did see your interview on TV and expressed his displeasure that:

1. You said she was guilty;

2. You gave an interview regarding the merits;

3. That you suggested how long Annette should be in a hospital and;

4. That you gave a legal opinion about the admissibility of Annette's statements in the hospital.

Well, we just said we wouldn't do any more interviews and neither would you. This is like a self-imposed gag order. But we got our use out of it. The judge used to refer to you as "Speckhard or Ms. Speckhard." I think he actually used the name "Dr. Speckhard" several times today. So at least that is improving.

I already had a meeting scheduled with Annette with interpreter Horacio Ferreira for 9 am this morning (until we were ordered in today). I went to the jail after court and spent an hour with her. We discussed everyone's legal issues (including mine), and I told her she could fire us if she wanted to. I told her we were trying to do our best for her and that is why Mike got cuffed today and I got beat-down the last court date.

Mike had to stand up to the judge and that was that. Have you ever seen "Casino" with Robert De Niro and Joe Pesci? Well there was a scene at the end where Pesci and his brother were stripped, beaten with baseball bats nearly to death and then buried

alive in the desert. That happened to me last time
in chambers and then it was going that way today.

As usual I laughed and scratched my head thinking *Pat is a kind of crazy guy.* But at the same time I am relieved that he and Mike and Bob are still on the case. I can just imagine Annette sitting doe-eyed listening to Pat explain the near-violent and chaotic court proceedings. I wonder, *What are her fear levels at right now after having seen her attorney hauled out of court in handcuffs?*

CHAPTER THIRTY-SIX
LOSING THE LEGAL TEAM

The judge continues to insist that Pat and Bob cannot represent Annette Morales Rodriguez at the same time that they have cases pending in front of him unless she waives her rights, and he also will not allow the case to be switched to a new venue, which would mean a new judge and a new DA. Pat goes to explain to Annette the situation and to ask if she is okay with it. He explains that of course, despite the potential conflict of interest, their team of three attorneys have full intention of defending her to the limits of the law, because to do otherwise would be bad for them and because they actually do care.

The judge wants a written statement signed by Annette, but Pat insists that he doesn't know who is signing it or if Annette can even understand what he is telling her about such legal intricacies. The team decides against having her sign away her rights, and they opt to withdraw if the judge continues to insist.

Their response also brings up the whole issue of if Annette is even competent to stand trial. In the U.S. legal system, a person who by reason of mental illness or mental defect cannot understand and rationally participate in court proceedings is deemed incompetent and cannot be tried.[70] My opinion in the beginning when I evaluated her is that Annette is competent to stand trial. At that point I saw that she has a trusting relationship with Pat, appears to stay present with him and can understand what he is explaining to her enough to understand the nature of the proceedings and to assist properly in her defense. *But now that she has watched one of her attorneys being arrested and hauled out of the courtroom and put in handcuffs,*

maybe she no longer is in a safe enough place in her mind to be processing what is going on around her? I wonder to myself. She is after all severely mentally ill with a dissociative disorder.

As things progress, Judge Borowski basically orders Pat and Bob off of the case since they don't allow Annette to sign off, leaving Mike to decide if he can try it on his own.

I speak with Mike on the phone, encouraging him to stay with it. Mike expresses his disappointment explaining to me that they are all withdrawing from the case, "Pat has a drug and alcohol problem," Mike says bitterness filling his voice. "He's my good friend and I really care about him, but he has to stop using drugs and drinking. He made some bad decisions on this case, like submitting your report before it was done and telling you to talk to the press. And now we are all paying for his problems. I really wanted to try this case, but it's just not feasible anymore. Annette deserves a good defense, and both Pat and Bob are compromised and Pat has so angered this judge that it's impossible for any of us to go forward now. This judge is angry at me too. We can't give her a good defense."

"What will happen to her?" I ask. "Are you going to try to interest anyone else to take her case?"

"She will probably be assigned to the public defender," Mike replies.

"And my involvement? Will I stay involved as the expert?" I ask. I've never been involved in a case where the attorneys withdrew.

"That is up to the next attorney," Mike explains. "We will of course pass all the materials we have, including your expert report, to the next attorney and recommend that they use you. But it will be up to them to decide. I can't imagine why they wouldn't want to use you though."

I ask Mike if Bob will be paying my fees for my work up to this point, as promised. Mike says he will, but as the weeks go on I receive no payment and no word on the new attorney.

Later when I am writing this book and ask Pat in October of 2012 to explain why they withdrew from the case, he explains his frustration and recalls having been very moved by Annette's disorder:

> I wanted to see it all the way through no matter what. I took an interpreter (Horacio) to the jail and explained it all to her and even showed her my alcohol-monitoring bracelet and that I had not drank in almost a year. . . .
>
> She said she would waive the conflict. But I had seen Lara and Annacita in the jail with you.
>
> Which persona was going to sign the waiver or waive it in open court, Annette or the other 2? She would have waived her right to ineffective assistance of counsel for appeal purposes. We were all convinced she was DID and had three personalities. I saw it.

Pat, I already know, despite whatever trouble he has with drinking, is a kind-hearted person and had decided to follow his conscience. While I am quite sure that Annette could remain present with him, he didn't want to violate any confidence she had placed in them. And he especially didn't want her to sign an agreement that would cause her to lose her right to appeal if things went badly. And the judge had made it clear he was squarely against this legal team so things going badly wasn't just conjecture in this case.

Chapter Thirty-Seven

The Public Defenders

Eventually a public defender is named for the case, a female attorney named Reyna Morales along with her assistant Deborah Patterson.[71] Mike and Pat send all their files to her, including my expert report and Mike tells me that they've discussed the case and let her know I am willing to continue serving on the case. When I don't hear anything I contact her myself.

Sending an e-mail on April 20, 2012 I write:

> Hello Reyna, I left a message on your office phone. I'd like to talk over the Annette Morales Rodriguez case, as after evaluating her I became quite concerned about her. I'm glad she has another attorney now!
>
> All the best!
>
> Anne

The public defender, Reyna Morales writes back on April 20, 2012:

> Hello,
>
> Thank you for your contact and contact information. Attorney Patterson and I took over the case this week and will be reading all of the materials pertaining to the case in the very near future.
>
> Reyna

Unable to contain my anxiety over Annette, I write to Reyna again the next day highlighting the hospital exams under police custody in which her rights were not read to her. I point out that the police and hospital reports even document Annette refusing the second forced examination, which many would thus term an assault, and that her confession appears to me as coerced under such conditions. I tell her, "I am not a lawyer, but having treated scores of sexual abuse survivors I find this very disturbing and to me a great violation of her Miranda rights."

And I write to Reyna again at the end of April again expressing my concerns over Annette. But I hear nothing back until the middle of May when I write two more times asking if we could please discuss her case.

Pat in the meantime keeps in e-mail and phone contact (by texts) and continues to share his distress that the public defender seems disinterested in the case and may even fail to argue insanity as a defense. He tells me that Reyna just had a baby and is working from home. Nothing wrong with that, but it also appears to me that she isn't very interested in discussing the case.

I am meanwhile wondering if Annette is even competent to stand trial at this point. It seems to me that since coming to the U.S., Annette has had a series of crises: first, losing her children after her eldest daughter is sexually assaulted; second, finding out she is not pregnant; third, learning she has been sterilized and will likely never be able to reverse it; and fourth, "waking up" to find that the Lara part of her personality has committed murder.

In therapy with dissociative identity disordered individuals, one of the main tasks is to help the core personality integrate the splinter personalities which means coming to grips with the traumatic memories and experiences they store. *Annette is not in therapy but she is basically doing her own integration process in jail in a state of acute psychological crisis, and I would not be surprised if she tried to commit suicide or had a serious psychotic break,* I think as I reflect

on her case. The amnesia and psychological barrier that walled Lara off from Annette's consciousness has been seriously breached by all of these crises. And now in jail, according to Annette, the memories from Lara keep "flooding" in during daytime and sleep. The impenetrable barrier that previously kept Annette separated from Lara and from her traumatic memories is now breaking down, and she has no real help in dealing with this.

In her evaluation, Annette told Dr. Pankiewicz, "From noon on it gets bad. That's when I lose it and start to see things. Sometimes I see a woman with a knife in her hands and I get desperate and call the guards." Clearly Lara is no longer able to keep the horrors of the past or of the terrible crime she committed separate from Annette's consciousness, and Annette is suffering.

In posttraumatic stress theory, psychologists refer to a break in the ability to keep dissociated, traumatic memories at bay as "flooding", and it is something we work hard to avoid in therapy. I always tell my patients that when it comes to working through a trauma that they have kept dissociated from consciousness, and now are in a hurry to get up and dealt with, that *slower is actually faster*. This is because I know that patients fall apart when a flood of memories hits them. The sensory recall, overwhelming emotions, confusion between past and present, terror, horror and sense of inescapability can make them feel and even act like they are at the age and place when the original traumas occurred. And this can make them look and act totally nuts.

This is what I think Annette is experiencing in prison right now and I am finding that I am completely powerless to help her, which disturbs me greatly.

At the end of May I write again to Annette's new attorneys telling them that I am very concerned about Annette, that she may be in need of psychiatric hospitalization. I also state my concern and that I don't appreciate that given the switch in the legal team, that no one has answered the DA's attack on my credentials despite that Mike

and I put together a nine-page document listing in detail my many accomplishments, scientific presentations, forensic experience and so forth.[72]

Debra Patterson writes back referencing the "great deal of controversy surrounding her [Annette's] previous lawyers" and saying that the DA has put forth an attack on my ability to testify, and that the judge (without having seen any rebuttal to date) has indicated that he likely would not admit my testimony and that they are trying to decide how they are going to put their defense together.

I write back encouraging her to take a look at the document Mike and I put together; and her assistant, Karen Mosley, suddenly requests it, so obviously Annette's new attorneys have not yet read the rebuttal to the attacks on my credentials and are perhaps believing all that the DA said about me. I find that also worrisome.

In addition to reassuring her about my credentials, I tell her that although I started out neutral on this case, that at this point I have grown to care about it's outcome, that I find the vaginal examinations and coerced confession so disturbing that I will even waive my fees and testify for free.

In the meantime Pat writes to me telling me that the new legal team may not even argue insanity as a defense. When I ask if there is anything we can do, if Annette can request another lawyer, he answers:

> We were disgusted by the fact that now those attorneys are not even sure they will be pursuing an NGI [not guilty by reason of insanity]. It's ridiculous that they may just lay down for Judge Borowski.
>
> We can't make them do anything. I cannot contact (nor can another attorney contact) a person who is represented by an attorney. Hypothetically speaking, a private person could write her a letter in Spanish reminding her she has the right to an NGI plea

and that she can fire her two lawyers. Then the
SPD would have to appoint someone from the private bar, like Attorney Richard Hart.

A Daubert hearing has to be scheduled and then
it has to be immediately appealed if you are not allowed to testify. But it looks like they are going to
fold like chairs and have a sham trial or guilty plea.

We go back and forth in e-mails and I decide that Annette deserves a fair defense and that if Pat can do nothing, then perhaps I
should try. Public defenders are usually not well paid and sometimes
do the bare minimum for poor clients, and I am very concerned that
perhaps that is happening now, although I have no way of judging.

I decide first to try to contact the American Civil Liberties Union
to see if given what I see as police misconduct and Miranda issues,
they might be interested to take her case. I find that it is not possible
to simply call up the ACLU. One has to write a letter describing the
case and requesting assistance. I don't feel up to that so I decide
to call Attorney Hart and ask if he indeed would take the case. I
describe it to him, and he says he would and would do it pro-bono
as well. I ask him about what Pat has proposed about writing to Annette to inform her of her choices. He agrees that is a fine way to go
ahead and that if Annette wants his services I should let him know.
Grateful, I now have to figure out how to approach Annette and decide if I can ethically do so. It seems that I can.

I decide the best way to approach her is to contact Christina
Green and ask if she would be willing to help by translating a letter
from me explaining to Annette that she has the right to a not guilty
by reason of insanity (NGI) defense and that if her public defenders
aren't willing to entertain that option, I have found an attorney willing to argue that for her pro-bono and she can switch if she wants
to. Anxious about going around the public defender this way, I wait
anxiously for Christina's reply, which never comes. And I conclude
she is uncomfortable with the request.[73]

In early June, I return to Wisconsin for a family wedding and I consider trying to visit Annette in jail as I'm traveling through Milwaukee, but I would need an interpreter along as well and Christina still has never replied to me. When I ask Mike about the possibility of visiting Annette, should I find an interpreter to work with, he informs me that since I am not treating her and not a family member I would not be allowed in. So I give up and simply let her public defenders know that I am in town and available to meet in person if they wish. They don't even bother to reply, and I assume they have decided they don't want my help.

On my return home, I get a nasty surprise in the mail. My husband who often opens our official-looking mail brings me a letter from the Virginia State Board of Counseling—my licensing board—dated May 22, 2012. Some how it's been overlooked till now in June, but it's opened now. Dan has a serious look on his face and when handing it to me sits on the couch next to my desk.

"You have an ethics complaint against you," he says, obviously disturbed by this fact. "Those investigators can be really horrible. They have to justify their existence. Do you think you can lose your license over this?"

Taking the letter from his hand I read it over. It's a list of accusations that they want me to answer, all in relationship to my involvement in Annette's case. *It must be the DA behind this—he probably wrote an ethics complaint to my licensing board trying to silence me!* I think as I read it, disgust mounting in my gut as I do.[74] The letter states that I worked without a license in Wisconsin, that I breached my client's confidentiality by speaking to the press and putting my report up on my website, that I listed my work as an expert in Lorena Bobbit's case, breaching confidentiality with her as well—despite the fact that was a matter of public record—and so on.

"This is ridiculous!" I say, looking up at my husband. "I can answer everything! I did speak to the press, but I did not violate her confidentiality because I have a signed waiver from her giving me

permission to write up her case, *and* I spoke to the press and put the report up with her attorney's full permission and by his request and only after my report had become a matter of public record because they failed to seal it! And I don't need a license to do an evaluation in another state or to give testimony as an expert. Experts testify in other states all the time! I have nothing to worry about. This is an obvious attempt to silence me!"

And no one is going to silence me! I think to myself as I fire off a reply to the investigator. In a few days, she calls and we discuss the case by telephone and I feel confident after speaking to her that I have nothing to worry about. Although, I still find that it is extremely disconcerting to have an ethics investigator call to ask me in detail about my dealings on a legal case. Even though I know opposing attorneys commonly use ethics complaints as a tactic, I feel so angry when I think about it that it makes me want even more to find a way to help Annette.

I write again to Annette's public defenders asking if they have made any decisions in her case and if they are going to be using me as their expert. Expressing my lingering sense of responsibility, I write:

> As a professional, I approach each case neutrally, but after forming my expert opinion, I do have an opinion which I am quite sure of; and in this case I see an indigent woman who was, in my opinion, badly treated by the police and medical personnel at the hospital, who has DID, and I am very concerned about her welfare now and in the future. I am not sure she is competent to stand trial unless someone who is aware of her condition is working with her, nonthreatening and carefully explaining things to her. I saw that she trusted her former attorneys and could communicate with them. I am not sure if that remains the case. And during all of the "hoopla"

of her case, she has already witnessed one of her attorneys getting arrested and taken from the court while trying to defend her!

In any case I would appreciate when it becomes a public matter if you could inform me who the judge will be in this case and what your plea in her behalf will be.

They write back that they cannot discuss their decision making with me about the case, as to do so would violate confidentiality unless they decide to retain me as their expert, which they have not yet made a decision to do.

For me, the sense of responsibility I feel toward Annette remains a heavy burden that I cannot easily shed. Since they cannot share their strategy with me, I am not confident that her new legal team is making good decisions on Annette's behalf or that she can communicate effectively with them and trust them as she did her previous team. And I am one hundred percent confident she has dissociative identity disorder, and I can even show her switching personalities on film in front of two witnesses.

If this legal team engaged another expert to make the same diagnosis and who could argue well that Annette's dissociative disorder made it impossible for her, in her core personality, to know right from wrong, or even to know what she was doing when the murder was committed, I could walk away from it without feeling badly. But I am now intimidated, despite myself, by the prospect of approaching Annette myself to see if she would like to have another attorney who would give her the insanity defense that I think she needs, and I become hesitant to act. In mid June I write to the investigator Kimberly Wood and to my licensing board asking for any advice the board might give as "to the best ethical way for me to proceed to help ensure that she receives a good defense and a fair trial. I want to discharge my moral obligation to Ms. Morales Rodriguez in the best way possible."

At the end of June I receive the following disappointing reply

> Hello. Board staff is unable to provide advice on legal and/or ethical matters.
>
> Catherine Chappell Executive Director Virginia Boards of Counseling, Social Work, and Psychology

Uncertain how to proceed and certainly not wanting anymore trouble from the DA or whoever made the complaint or from my licensing board, I decide to call the American Psychological Association of which I am a member, to find out if they can help. I get no better response from them.

Then at the end of June I read a news report that states:

> New lawyers for Annette Morales-Rodriguez, charged with cutting a late-term fetus from his young mother with the plan of passing the baby off as her own, said Thursday they don't plan to rely on a diagnosis of multiple-personality disorder that had been prepared for a prior defense team.
>
> The lawyers did not even confirm they will pursue any kind of insanity defense.[75]

And in July another new twist appears in the case. On July 26th, 2012 Bruce Vielmetti of the Milwaukee Journal Sentinel writes of a potential scandal involving the detective who took Annette's coerced confession:

> Milwaukee police homicide Detective Rodolfo Gomez was arrested and briefly jailed last month before the district attorney's office announced that no charges would be issued and he was released. At the time, details about the alleged incident were not made public.

In court Thursday, an assistant city attorney said Gomez remains the subject of an ongoing internal investigation, and that records related to his arrest should not be turned over to defense attorneys for Annette Morales-Rodriguez.

. . . Gomez took the initial statement from Morales-Rodriguez at a hospital, when she told authorities her own baby had been born dead at home and investigators had not yet figured out the whole story. Defense attorneys have sought to suppress those statements, since Gomez had not read Morales-Rodriguez her rights against self-incrimination at the time.

"A decision to not charge him (Gomez) at this time may be consideration given to him by the state in an attempt to protect his credibility at trial," the defense wrote in a motion to compel.

Prosecutor Mark Williams has argued that Morales-Rodriguez was not in custody at the hospital and, even if she was, she volunteered incriminating statements to Gomez on her own. Furthermore, he said, the decision not to charge Gomez last month could hardly be connected to the murder case, because his reports of Morales-Rodriguez's statement had already been committed to writing months before.[76]

As I read this I think to myself, *Geez, it seems they try to silence me with an ethics complaint, they don't file charges against their shady policeman, the dedicated attorneys get kicked off the case . . . what is going on?*

In early August when I see that the public defenders make a motion to suppress her initial "confession", I write to them encouraging the move. I also write "off the record" to Bruce Vielmetti to encour-

age him to write more about the Miranda rights aspect of the case since I am not certain if I am free to comment publically on the case until it goes to trial. Vielmetti appears an extremely thoughtful reporter. He puts out a good article a few days later:

> The woman charged in last fall's disturbing fetal abduction homicides made incriminating statements to a detective who asked her for "the truth" before he told her she had the right to remain silent - even though she'd already been put under arrest.
>
> Annette Morales-Rodriguez has lawyers now, and they're arguing the statements from an emergency room bed should not be allowed as evidence at her trial next month. They also challenge more admissions she made in a recorded interview at police headquarters after saying she wanted a lawyer.
>
> Milwaukee County Circuit Judge David Borowski, who heard testimony on the matter Thursday and Friday, said he'll need more time and research before making a decision.
>
> At the suppression hearing, officers and detectives detailed how the story unfolded. While they described an uncertain situation, defense attorney Debra Patterson suggested they must have considered Morales-Rodriguez a homicide suspect almost immediately.[77]

But we've already seen that this guy is shady haven't we? I think to myself. *He was under police investigation for other serious issues including disorderly conduct and sexual assault, but did not get charged...can we believe him when he says he didn't know she was under arrest? And does it matter anyway? She was under arrest – they admit it now – and she should have had her rights read to her. If he didn't know, he still screwed up didn't he?*

A few days later another report by Mike Johnson of the Milwaukee Journal Sentinel comes out:

> Defense attorneys for the woman charged with cutting an unborn child from a young mother, killing them both, will get to see some of the records related to a sexual assault investigation of the lead Milwaukee police detective in the case, a judge decided Friday.
>
> Attorneys for Annette Morales-Rodriguez had asked to review the records, saying that the state's decision not to charge the detective might have been a move to protect his credibility during Morales-Rodriguez's trial.
>
> . . . The city had attempted to block the release of the records in the investigation of homicide Detective Rodolfo Gomez. He was arrested and briefly jailed in June before the district attorney's office announced that no charges would be issued and he was released.
>
> Milwaukee County Circuit Judge David Borowski had ordered the records turned over to him so he could review them.
>
> On Friday, he said he would turn over a portion of the written materials to the defense but would allow the city to first propose a redaction of the material. He said he would not turn over DVDs from the investigation.
>
> . . . Gomez took the initial statement from Morales-Rodriguez at a hospital, when she told authorities her own baby had been born dead at home and investigators had not yet figured out the whole story.

Defense attorneys have sought to suppress those statements, since Gomez had not read Morales-Rodriguez her rights against self-incrimination at the time.

Prosecutor Mark Williams has argued that Morales-Rodriguez was not in custody at the hospital and, even if she was, she volunteered incriminating statements to Gomez on her own. Furthermore, he said, the decision not to charge Gomez in June could hardly be connected to the murder case, because his reports of Morales-Rodriguez's statement had already been committed to writing months before.[78]

Annette's trial is scheduled for September 17th. On the 12th of September, Judge Borowski rules that despite the defense's argument that interrogation was improper and Annette's statements while in police custody at the hospital should be suppressed, they should be allowed under a public welfare or emergency rescue exception. Officer Gomez's actions are characterized by the court's ruling, as asking questions in order for a victim to potentially be saved rather than interrogation of a potential suspect. And Annette's constitutional right not to incriminate herself is put aside.

CHAPTER THIRTY-EIGHT
TRIAL

As Annette's trial looms closer on the horizon, Pat starts sending me a series of agitated e-mails and texts telling me that Annette's court-appointed lawyers, Reyna Morales and Debra Patterson, are dropping the insanity defense. I ask if there is any way that I can come to the trial and offer *my* opinion or file a brief as a friend of the court (i.e. amicus brief)—or anything like that.

"No," Pat answers, "the judge is the gatekeeper" and it wouldn't work, meaning that unless someone argued that my opinions satisfied the Daubert rules of evidence—which Annette's new attorneys don't seem interested to do, even though they have a nine page document arguing just that, my opinion, no matter how it arrived to the case, would not be allowed. I ask if I can send Judge Borowski a letter before the trial, but Pat doesn't think that's a good idea either. As we pass e-mails and texts back and forth, it's clear that for both of us the distress is mounting.

Indeed I feel that I cannot shrug off my responsibility in this case. It's just so bothersome that she has no family shielding her, and I don't get the sense that her court-appointed lawyers get it how mentally ill she is. On September 13th, Pat, knowing that I am seriously contemplating flying in for the trial and thinking of even at this last moment somehow trying to contact Annette, writes to me.

> Anne,
>
> A friend told me a story. A person was in jail, and someone came to see them. The inmate was told by the visitor that the inmate could fire the inmate's attorney. The inmate (any client) has the right to fire

his or her attorney. The judge is supposed to honor that request. However, the judge may not if the defendant has fired at least one attorney. Defendants sometimes fire their attorneys for a strategic advantage. Other attorneys have advised their clients to do this because they get a delay or a new judge rotates in. But, I think the trial starts Monday.

I think the judge is stuck if the defendant's previous attorneys withdrew and the defendant wanted to keep them. No one got fired; and the judge doesn't want to get overturned on appeal for violating a defendant's right to choice of counsel.

Here is the visitation policy at the jail. My case is till pending, but I will have to wrap it up soon. I would gladly get back on the case. Torphy and D'Arruda will call me an NGI case just for suggesting it. The 8th amendment prohibits cruel and unusual punishment; and to put Annette in prison for the rest of her life, if she was not legally responsible for her acts, would violate that amendment.

http://county.milwaukee.gov/Visiting15657.htm

I cannot contact another lawyer's client, but there is nothing to prohibit a non-attorney from doing so. The question is whether someone would be allowed to visit a high profile defendant unless they are family. But you have seen her before.

One thing I know about myself is that I am a person who was raised to "speak truth to power" and I have often stood up for justice when others remained silent. The pitfall of being such a person, however, is that others who are more timid often recognize this trait and egg me on to stand up when they are too afraid to do so. And I pay the price while they get off as a bystander, paying nothing. Hav-

ing recognized this in myself, I have learned the hard way to stop myself from acting in behalf of the downtrodden when others encourage me without insisting that they stand up as well. In this case Pat is doing this to me, although he has a good reason for not acting. He has his hands tied by the laws contravening his interfering in the case and offering her another legal defense, whereas I do not.

Intrigued by the possibility he offers, I write to Pat and ask if I can write ahead to the sheriff and get permission to seek Annette. I can arrive on Sunday to do so. Pat writes back:

> I would not ask the sheriff because it gives them an opportunity to ask and say no. All you can do is gamble and show up and just say you've seen her b4. Or see if someone down here can show up and test the waters.

"Who can we send?" I ask.

Pat writes back suggesting sending Christina Green, but I tell him that I already asked her months ago to translate and carry a letter to Annette informing her that she has a right to an insanity defense if she wants it and that Christina never wrote back. "I think she is intimidated to be involved."

Then I share with him that I called Vicki Thorn, the professional who first told me about this case, asking for advice and asking her if she knows a local attorney who can advise me on how to intervene in an ethical manner. I tell her that I am distraught because I believe something very unjust is about to happen.

"My friend advised me to speak with W. Michael McCann, the former DA, and ask his help," I tell Pat. "Please tell me how to reach Mr. McCann. Vicki told me through the law school." Vicki is referring to Marquette Law School, Pat's alma mater where the former DA is now serving on the faculty.

When Pat does not offer any help in that regard, I find the former DA's office phone number and leave him an urgent message ask-

ing if he can advise me and explaining that I am worried about the police misconduct, forced vaginal exams, coerced confession and failure to read her rights to her. I am candid that there seem to have been attempts to discredit and silence me after I did her evaluation and wrote an opinion in support of a "not guilty by insanity plea". It's already Friday afternoon and Annette's trial is scheduled to begin on Monday. Perhaps because it's the weekend, he does not call back. But, in fact, he never returns the phone call.

I tell Pat that I will come to the trial or beforehand if that is the right course of action.

> Okay, I could understand the ruling that the cops could question her without reading her rights because they were trying to save a life, but I cannot understand attorneys that won't defend her.

> I offered to fly out and testify for free. They just blow me off.

> It's a tough week for me next week, but I will come if I can help.

The final blow comes when I belatedly ask Pat who the new judge is going to be and Pat tells me it's still Judge Borowski. I cannot believe it!

"I thought he was supposed to move off of the case!" I write back.

"Yeah the scuttlebutt on the streets was he was being rotated Aug 1st," Pat writes, "and he did not. No NGI defense [either]. I think you should evaluate her attorneys."

Laughing at that suggestion I write back, "I guess we are both crazy for caring so much," adding, "But I prefer to be a person that cares rather than a creep."

I write to my friend Anita, who very graciously offers me her guestroom again should I decide to come. Then I check flights and my schedule. I am about to book one when my husband, Daniel,

tells me not to go. "It's too expensive and it won't do any good," he counsels. "We need you here," he adds. Indeed he has to travel and I often help my daughter with our granddaughter—my schedule is already very full. I'd have to cancel many professional meetings and back out from a long-standing invitation to a dinner party with friends—the husband a gourmet chef who always goes to a lot of trouble to prepare for guests. I decide to wait and see.

On Saturday night I check my messages to see if the former DA has replied to my pleas and e-mails for help, but there is no answer from him. I check the price of airline tickets the next day and look again at my calendar.

I can still go, I think to myself, but I feel uncomfortable going when my husband really doesn't want me to. I think he is worried about the DA going for blood if I show up and mess up his case at the last minute.

Daniel may be right, I realize. *There's no telling what could happen if he goes after me. He's a lawyer after all and I don't know the law. But I do know she is definitely a Dissociative Identity Disorder case with two very separate personalities – one a psychopath and the other is being punished for that.* I worry as I lay my head on the pillow. Sleep as usual, comes quickly for me, but tonight it doesn't last. After a few hours of deep sleep I suddenly wake up horrified. *I can't do it!* I suddenly think to myself. *I can't be a coward and do nothing when something very wrong is about to happen. I have to book my tickets and go in the morning—no matter what it costs me!* I get out of bed, grab my bathrobe in the darkness and head for the door.

"What's the matter?" my husband says, also waking and sensing my determined mood.

"I cannot stand by and do nothing. It isn't right," I tell him.

Always the voice of reason, he asks me what I feel I need to do and why. That prompts an hour-long discussion in which I vent my frustration and sense of powerlessness while my husband, sitting up

wearily in bed while I pace around the room waving my hands in the air as I speak, reminds me that I have done everything humanly possible to help her and that now it is actually out of my hands. And he also stresses that just because I am convinced that she is mentally ill does not mean that I am for sure right nor that I can make the justice system function.

"Don't mentally ill people go to prison all the time?" he asks.

Indeed, I know it's the case but I shoot back, "So those who have money and resources get a good defense and those who don't go to prison? Only rich people can use the insanity defense?"

"Yes," he says. "Poor people often don't get good representation. And he goes on to help me realize that Pat is transferring a lot of his guilt and anxiety over what is happening in this case to me and making me feel that I personally need to fix it. "If he didn't have his DWI, he would still be her attorney," Dan points out.

Finally exhausted from talking it through, Dan convinces me that it would be like Don Quixote going to dual with windmills to fly to Milwaukee the next day.

"Find an attorney who can advise you," Daniel counsels and we agree the case will try for more than just one day so there is time. He tells me that James Santelle, the U.S. Department of Justice Attorney (for the Eastern District of Wisconsin) who had invited me to speak at the 7th Circuit Bar Association was just in town and that we can give him a call the next day. Perhaps he will help. And he reminds me that we have another friend who is a high-powered attorney who may agree to advise us, or we can use our family attorney, although we both agree this is probably beyond his expertise.

I go back to bed peaceful for the first time in weeks over the case and my responsibility in it and fall into a deep sleep. We keep our dinner party plans, I keep all my appointments and on Monday Daniel calls the two attorneys. One of them answers on Tuesday and Dan explains the case.

"You mustn't intervene; you shouldn't write to the judge or otherwise try to contact him," Dan informs me. "It could cause a mistrial and you would be held responsible. It's better to let the case go on as it is and if it's true they didn't get another expert in and have her evaluated again, and if your finding is correct, she can appeal that she wasn't given an appropriate defense, the lawyer told me." I take a sigh of relief. I am sure of my findings.

Pat continues to write to me and I tell him that if he and the other attorneys want me to speak to the press during her trial, I will do so, but I want the request from them put in writing because they need to take responsibility for that. I feel by doing this I put some of the responsibility back on his shoulders instead of continually letting him tranfer such a heavy weight to me.

Pat writes back saying it's impossible as the others are in Las Vegas (!) and that they would need to get an ethics determination if they can even do it before proceeding. *So he wants me to take risks to intervene in her behalf, but is not willing to take risks himself,* I think to myself, putting up a wall from his attempts to transfer his anxiety to me and to motivate me to act. And I finally feel comfortable just waiting it out.

I know I will write this book afterward since I have a written agreement with Annette that permits me to write about her case, and hopefully she will get an appeal after the trial that I am most certain she will lose. *That is all I can do*, I think to myself as I watch from the sides powerless.

Monday, September 17th arrives, and Annette goes to court charged with two counts of first-degree intentional homicide for murdering Eva Alvarez Mendoza and her unborn son. A conviction on either count carries a mandatory life sentence, although the judge could allow for the possibility of parole. Thankfully, Wisconsin does not have the death penalty. Reyna Morales and Debra Patterson, Annette's court appointed lawyers, as Pat anticipated, do not enter an insanity defense, and they change her plea "to not guilty".[79]

The argument put forward by the defense is that while Annette did commit the crime, she did not ever intend to kill Eva Alvarez Mendoza. In her opening statements to the court, Debra Patterson argues: "We submit to you that Annette engaged in criminally reckless conduct, but she did not intend to kill Eva."[80] Likewise as the trial ensues, Patterson does not deny the prosecution's arguments that Annette had faked two previous pregnancies and miscarriages and was desperate to produce a child from this one or that she plotted to take a baby from another woman. Instead she argues that Annette entertained various possibilities: telling her boyfriend the truth, faking another miscarriage, taking a baby from a pregnant woman and even committing suicide—but that those were just *thoughts* Patterson argues and Annette really didn't know what to do.[81]

Patterson paints a picture of confusion, self-doubt and anxiety as she states that when Annette offered Alvarez Mendoza a ride while considering cutting her baby from her, she became so terrified that she considered simply driving her home. However when she stopped off at her own home to change her shoes, leaving Alvarez Mendoza alone in the car, Alvarez Mendoza activated the murder by knocking on the door asking to use the bathroom. Patterson states "it was at that point she acted on an extreme desire to acquire a baby."[82]

Reyna Morales tells the court that if Annette had intended Alvarez Mendoza to die, she would have had a plan for disposing of her body instead of hiding her corpse in her basement.[83]

To me this argument makes no sense given that Reyna has already told the court that Annette did contemplate taking a fetus from a Hispanic woman and did intentionally pick Alvarez Mendoza up with the terrifying intent to cut her baby from her. That she hesitated in fear does not seem like a convincing argument to me that she did not premeditate and then carry out her evil plan.

Morales also argues that Annette wanted the baby to live so she could claim him as her own, which I agree is accurate.[84]

The defense does not have Annette testify, nor do they call any other witnesses in her behalf. And they don't deny that she attacked Alvarez Mendoza and cut her baby from her. They simply argue that the deaths were unintentional acts of recklessness. And they argue for a conviction to a lesser charge of first-degree reckless homicide, a crime that carries a maximum penalty of forty years in prison versus a mandatory life sentence.[85]

"We never said she didn't do it. She told the cops she did," Reyna Morales tells the jury in her closing statements. But, she argues that the evidence shows "from the very beginning all the way to the last minutes, reckless, reckless, reckless."[86]

In response, DA Mark Williams has an easy day in court. He is allowed to admit Annette's video confession and he also comes armed with stacks of medical and forensic evidence, graphic pictures, including an autopsy photo of Alvarez Mendoza's disemboweled lower torso.[87] He builds his case by creating a picture of a gruesome and premeditated murder.

He shows the videotape of Annette confessing, as she explains to the police that she was desperate to give Ramón a baby and that she had already faked two pregnancies because she couldn't "stay pregnant" and admits on the film to claiming to have miscarried each one. Annette describes on the film to the police how during the third "pregnancy" she plotted to take a baby from a Hispanic near-term pregnant woman and to pass the newborn off as her own. On the video, Annette describes how she executed the crime.[88]

The DA presents pictures to the jury of Eva Alvarez Mendoza's disemboweled body and evidence that police found her body in Annette's basement. And he emphasizes Annette's intent to kill, stating that Alvarez Mendoza must have gasped for air and pleaded for mercy as she was choked while Annette likely looked her in the eye. He also points out that Annette admitted to taping the Alvarez Mendoza 's mouth and nose and placing a plastic bag over her head.[89]

"Now what did she think was going to happen when she did that?" he asks the jury, clearly refuting any arguments by the defense.[90]

Williams plays Annette's call to 911 in which she tells the dispatcher she has just delivered a baby but did not know she was pregnant. One juror gets teary listening to Annette sobbing when she tells the dispatcher that the baby isn't breathing and has probably died.[91]

The prosecution calls a medical examiner to testify as to the cause of death of the two victims. He states that Alvarez Mendoza died due to a combination of blood loss, blunt trauma and asphyxiation and that her fetal child died as a result of her death. He also refutes Annette's claim to police investigators that she thought Alvarez Mendoza was dead when she cut her open and that she just wanted to save the baby, testifying that the blood found in the victim's abdomen suggests her heart was still beating when Annette cut her baby out. The medical examiner confirms evidence that in the autopsy they found that the baby wasn't the product of a natural birth and had cut uterine and ovarian parts still clinging to him.[92]

The DA shows medical evidence that a subsequent examination verified Morales Rodriguez hadn't given birth at all.[93]

The DA also calls Wendi Coon, one of the first EMT responders who arrived at the scene. She testifies that she and the other paramedics swaddled the infant after he was declared dead and that she handed him to Annette for emotional closure. "It struck me as odd how she held him," Coon states. "She held him away from her, and she kind of looked at him as an object."[94]

Christian Mercado, Eva's husband and father of their three surviving children—two daughters, ages five and seven, and their three-year-old son, attends the trial in an effort to cope with the excruciating testimony and horror of what has happened. News reports about him state that the children are seeing a psychiatrist trying to deal with the reality that their mother is not ever coming back.[95]

When I see pictures of Annette in court, I cannot tell which personality she is in. She doesn't have the scared saucer eyes I saw her with in prison so it is most likely Lara. According to one reporter, "Morales-Rodriguez sat in silence throughout the proceedings, her eyes fixed on the table where she sat and her expression unchanged."[96]

When all the arguments are made, a jury of six men and six women deliberate for about an hour on September 20, before finding Annette Morales Rodriguez guilty of two counts of first-degree intentional homicide in the deaths of Eva Alvarez Mendoza and her preborn child. Annette Morales Rodriguez, who is now age 34, faces a mandatory life sentence. The sentencing hearing is set for December 14, 2012.[97]

When I read the news reports of her trial outcome it seems predictable to me. I don't see what defense she was really given. I write and ask Pat if he will try to be involved in the appeal. He writes back:

> The appeal would take place after sentencing on December 14, 2012. The state office of the public defender was her trial counsel; therefore, they would have to refer to a private bar attorney who is an independent contractor of the state public defender's office.
>
> Trial counsel cannot do their own appeal because they could try to cover up their mistakes, so it has to be done by another attorney.

I shake my head with sadness thinking, *We live in a sorry world where sexual abuse victims grow up never getting any help and finally snap, committing crimes that just keep the cycle of violence going. And I had hoped she might get treatment in a locked psychiatric ward. Perhaps on appeal?*

CHAPTER THIRTY-NINE
CLOSING THOUGHTS

I'd never heard of fetal abduction before getting involved in this case—the kidnapping of an unborn child by forcing the mother to submit to a forced Caesarean section—a crime that often results in her death and is most often carried out by another woman. The National Center for Missing and Exploited Children (NCMEC, in the U.S.) reports nine fetal abductions compared to two hundred fifty-one cases of infant kidnappings between 1987 to 2007.[98] Twenty fetal abduction cases have been reported worldwide.

A 2002 study of six such cases in the United States suggests that there is usually premeditated planning before the act is carried out and that the female abductor has two motives: to fulfill a "child-bearing and delivery fantasy" and thereby to cement the relationship with her partner.[99] Pregnancy is often faked beforehand, and desperation to have a child is the motivation that crosses the board of all cases, often due to pressure to keep a partner. NCMEC spokesperson Cathy Nahirny stated in 2007, "Many times the abductor fakes a pregnancy and when it is time to deliver the baby, must abduct someone else's child."[100] Vernon J. Geberth, who analyzed nine cases, wrote that many of the attackers were motivated to kidnap the newborns in order to maintain relationships with their partners and that seven of the women had pretended to be pregnant.[101]

Labeling fetal abduction as "Caesarian section murder" and as a new category of homicide, a Canadian researcher notes that in most case of fetal abduction, "the abductor befriends the pregnant victim, all the while planning to kill her" and that she is so desperate to give

birth to a child that "she actually acts out the fantasy of delivering the baby herself, rather than kidnapping one already born."[102]

It's unclear if the other fetal abductors were mentally ill or just desperate to fake birthing their own baby.[103] Psychologist Cheryl Paradis notes of Kathy Michelle Coy, who confessed to fetal abduction in Kentucky, that it seems that she had "tunnel vision" and that although Coy's crime was carefully planned, it was not well-thought through, causing her to be quickly and easily apprehended afterwards.[104] Psychiatrist Brett DiGiovanna and her colleagues presented their findings from their analysis of eighteen cases referring to them as "womb raiders". They identified only one as psychotic, five with personality disorders, one with major depression, another with substance abuse issues and five that had undergone previous psychiatric treatment. They also noted that six of the perpetrators had previous miscarriages or hysterectomies and that of the thirteen for whom data was available, nine were married or had a partner. These authors also noted that unlike psychological pregnancy (pseudocyesis, or the delusional belief that one is indeed pregnant), "the majority of the perpetrators made planned and willful attempts to feign pregnancy" and that these were premeditated crimes. Only one of the cases they analyzed received a "guilty but mentally ill" verdict, and none received a "not guilty by reason of insanity" verdict.[105]

When I reviewed news reports on the fourteen cases occurring in the U.S. and compiled data on them, I came up with the following:

All the perpetrators were women, ranging in age from nineteen to thirty-nine. While some already had children, the ability to conceive or carry a pregnancy to term was an issue at the time of the crime. Two of the perpetrators acted with male partners, one who believed he was "abducting" the fetal child he had impregnated his previous partner with. In eight cases the women were murdered before the baby was cut from them: three strangled, three shot in the head, two stabbed to death, and in one case the woman was knocked uncon-

scious before her baby was cut from her. Four were left to bleed out or otherwise died. Of the thirteen cases carried to completion four of the newborns died. In one case, the victim escaped, although severely injured, she and her baby both lived.

The motivations of the abductors appeared to fulfill their dream to complete a pregnancy by a faked delivery of the abducted fetal child, and it seemed that they often believed this would seal their male partner relationship. The perpetrators engaged in some degree of premeditation—faking a pregnancy beforehand and stalking their intended victims. In at least five cases they befriended or offered some inducement to the pregnant women to accept a ride, an invitation home, to come to a location for gifts, etc. Only four of the attacks involved complete stranger attacks with no confidence trick involved. Only two of the victims had been actual friends of the perpetrator beforehand.

While the crimes involved a degree of premeditated intent, planning and trickery, many aspects of the crime also demonstrated a lack of awareness, attention to detail and clear thinking. For instance five of the Caesarians were crudely performed—by scissors in three cases, a box cutter in one and by car keys in another! Abductors often failed to conceal the body well or appeared with the infant in the emergency room without a convincing story and willingly submitted to a physical exam, which of course immediately laid bare the truth.

It was hard to find much data on the abductor's psychological state at the time of the crime and only one other was argued to have been dissociative.[106] One researcher argued that most abductors are not mentally ill.[107] However, the lack of attention to detail and cover-up suggests that they were so strongly overcome with their obsession that rather than facing the reality of their non-pregnant condition they took some one else's fetal child to carry out their own delivery fantasy without thinking through all aspects of the crime in order to carry it out successfully. It also appears that these perpetra-

tors were also highly narcissistic and even psychopathic in that they could murder another woman in order to fulfill their own needs to fake a delivery.

The case of Annette Morales Rodriguez and her attempt at fetal abduction was the fourteenth such case reported inside the U.S. since 1987. In Annette's case I feel I got my answers as to why she committed her crime—why she resorted to murdering a pregnant woman rather than abducting a newborn and why she would do either. But becoming involved with this case opened up a whole new set of questions I still wrestle with. Can our authorities order bodily searches—even ultrasound and internal vaginal searches—without consent? Share the results with law enforcement without consent? Can Miranda rights be waived and invasive bodily searches—even vaginal searches—be performed simply because there is concern for public safety? How much leeway should police be given when there is public endangerment?

When I was studying terrorists, I often came across the ticking bomb theory that justified the use of torture on behalf of public safety, arguing that torture is justified if authorities have a terrorist in custody who possesses critical knowledge that could prevent an imminent attack with the potential to cause great loss of life. But where do we draw the lines? Aren't these just excuses for violating human rights?

I am convinced that Annette Morales Rodriguez has Dissociative Identity Disorder. In such a case, can we expect that the main "host" personality who has amnesias for the other personalities (or fragments) and no control over them to be held responsible the same way a healthy, sane person is? Doesn't the insanity defense allow for if the person was "out of their mind" they can be deemed as having been unable to realize what they were doing and knowing right from wrong at the time the crime was committed? To me, this is at the heart of Annette's case.

And we must ask ourselves how many indigent people are being tried when not mentally competent? How many are not given the insanity defense when they are mentally ill? And how many are already languishing in prisons who are seriously mentally ill? Surely having no money and no good family and community advocates diminishes one's ability to get a good legal defense.

I once heard a criminality expert say that *all* prisoners of serious crimes are child abuse survivors. I begin to wonder to myself, *Are **most** criminals mentally ill? Victims of abuse? Are we going about this all wrong? Are we acting wisely when we incarcerate but do not treat mentally ill abuse victims who continue to cause more violence, pain and suffering in our society? Could we do better? How?*

For me, most mental illness relates back to development versus current popular theories of "chemical imbalances". The human brain is genetically programmed to unfold and develop based on an expected set of nurturing experiences. And it will predictably go off course if the expected experiences turn into the unexpected— becoming horrible experiences of childhood neglect, sexual and physical abuse, rape, death, and desertion and the myriad of other traumatic and bereaving experiences that children undergo.

In my therapy practice, I always know if I dig deep enough I can usually find the origins of most psychological dysfunction. Then it is a matter of rebuilding the cognitive structures, emotional modulation, attachment functions, and expressive abilities necessary to heal and to grow into a healthy fully functioning human being. My belief is that a healing attachment relationship, much like the good parenting and loving, nurturing community that was expected at birth, can offer a means to rebuild and reformulate much that's gone wrong. But of course not everyone is going to be able to seek, tolerate, afford to pay for and endure a healing therapeutic relationship. And those that don't get treated will struggle, function poorly, self-destruct, and in some cases even harm others.

Interestingly, after the case was finished I had the chance to speak to Christina Green. She informed me that she hadn't been able to speak to me during the trial due to the gag order, and that is why she did not answer my e-mail and phone call. She also shared that the public defenders did bring in another expert, the chief psychiatrist of the Mendota Psychiatric Hospital where the first group of attorneys and I were hoping Annette would end up incarcerated and treated. According to Christina who gave the psychiatrist a brief background of the two other evaluations she had translated for (Dr. Pankiewicz's and mine), this psychiatrist sat down with Annette and she immediately told him, "I'm Lara".

"I'm not interested in Lara," he immediately replied. "I'm here to talk to Annette." Christina recalled that Annette then dropped the whole charade as Christina saw it and went on to admit coldheartedly to the crime saying her only regrets were that she was caught and that she was no longer with Ramón. To me this sounds like Lara continued in her Lara personality but did not bother to try to convince the doctor of the two personalities. For me this would seem authentic to everything I had learned, as Lara came out when Annette was intimidated and certainly after so much time locked in jail, watching one of her attorneys be arrested, losing her legal team and starting anew she must have been frightened. And Lara was totally cold hearted and felt no sympathy whatsoever for her victim.

I asked Christina if she recalled how Annette's eyes would roll back in her head and her eyelids fluttered when we talked to her and she did. She said that Annette did none of that while she talked to the third doctor—to me another sign that she remained firmly in her Lara personality. Christina also told me that she even mentioned that to the doctor—that we had seen that in our evaluation, and he answered that it is common with patients who lie compulsively. I don't know if that is true but I would certainly say that DID patients do lie a lot because they have complete amnesias and blank spots for entire parts of their lives and they simply have to fabricate things to appear to have an integrated life!

In any case, I was heartened that the public defenders had at least brought in another expert to evaluate Annette but disappointed that evaluator did not see the same things I saw and became convinced of. It is noteworthy, however, that both evaluators for the state were men, and this might have made it more intimidating for Annette to tell them the truth given she had been abused—if she told me the truth—by men.

So after the case is over, I have many questions that I still don't have answers to and remain deeply troubled by the case. I am convinced that Annette Morales Rodriguez suffers from Dissociative Identity Disorder and should have received the insanity defense. Insane persons should be locked in psychiatric wards and treated, not incarcerated like criminals who know right from wrong. And I believe that if offered intensive psychotherapy by a qualified, sensitive and skilled practioner, Annette could be healed and returned to society to parent her own children and to do her best to make amends for her crime and to contribute to society rather than spend her life inhabiting a prison cell.

My hope is that some attorney will read this account and offer Annette Morales Rodriguez a chance at an appeal and that there will be an expert who can help to argue her case so that she will get sent to a locked psychiatric facility where she receives treatment and heals. That will be one less person causing harm in this world. As sorely disappointed as I am by the outcome in this case, I remain hopeful.

ACKNOWLEDGEMENTS

I'd like to extend my heartfelt thanks once again to my editor Jayne Pillemer for her help in formulating this text and bringing it to life. It's a difficult subject, and she never flinched. Thanks also to Jessica Speckhard for the cover design and to Nikki Hensley (www.hensleygraphics.com) for the interior book design. Thanks to Christina Green and Marcos Arvelo who translated for me (Christina while doing the evaluation and Marcos for the Facebook translation). Thanks to Heidi Harry who provided medical information regarding informed consent procedures in the Milwaukee area hospitals. Thank you to psychologist in training Lauren Poppalardo for reading early drafts of the manuscript and offering moral support in writing it. And thanks to Beatrice Jacuch who did early research to find similar cases. Thanks to Michael Torphy for reading a draft of the book and Richard Zevitz for offering legal commentary. Thank you to Molly Larkin Library Information Services Assistant of Marquette University for assistance in researching articles and cases on fetal abduction. Thanks also to Evi and Andonis Camborakis, who offered me a home for a week in their fantastic hotel, Rodos Palace in Rodos, Greece where I finalized the book. Rodos Palace (http://www.rodos-palace.com) is a fantastic tourist destination and a great place to write a book! Thanks also to Anita and Jeff Zagrodnik who put me up in their Milwaukee home while I worked on this case.

APPENDICES

Appendix A

Disclaimer to my report when I posted it to my website after it had been filed in court records without my knowledge and permission and left unsealed and was "discovered" by journalists who were writing about and quoting from it in the news.

Annette Morales Rodriguez

In February of 2012 Dr. Speckhard spent two days in the Milwaukee County jail with Annette Morales Rodriguez a woman who allegedly lured Eva Alvarez Mendoza to her home, murdered her and cut her fetus out of her body. Tragically both Eva Alvarez Mendoza and her baby boy died as a result.

A horrific crime of this magnitude is hard to understand. In the two-day evaluation and review of records related to her case, Dr. Speckhard learned that Annette Morales Rodriguez has numerous gaps in her memory and frequent amnesias that all relate back to years of early childhood sexual abuse that she survived only by dissociating into an alternate personality that became known inside Annette's head as "Lara".

"Lara" originally emerged to endure the abuse, and it became a pattern in which "Lara" involuntarily overtakes Annette's personality whenever she is terrified or overwhelmed and reminded of the traumatic past. In these moments "Lara" emerges and attempts to make protec-

tive decisions from the standpoint of an emotionless and severely damaged personality fragment.

There can be no excuse for murder. According to Dr. Speckhard's exhaustive evaluation, Annette Morales Rodriguez suffers from Posttraumatic Stress Disorder and Dissociative Identity Disorder (formerly called Multiple Personality Disorder) and her case is severe and chronic. When "Lara" overtakes her main personality, Annette has little to no direct memory of, and no control over what occurs. In the evaluation Dr. Speckhard witnessed this personality "switching" and amnesia. Dr. Speckhard's professional opinion is that Mrs. Annette Morales Rodriguez is not in control of herself, is unable to account for her actions, nor control them, and is in dire need of psychiatric treatment.

On March 8th, 2012 a hearing was held in which Dr. Speckhard's preliminary report was filed in the court and made available to the public. Perhaps it can answer some questions of how a seemingly normal community woman could become so deranged as to carry out such a horrific crime.

Dr. Speckhard has treated DID and PTSD patients and has also testified in numerous court settings and before the US Congress. She has also consulted with and spoken for numerous governmental agencies including the UK Home Office, the US Pentagon, and many others. In May 2012, Dr. Speckhard was an invited guest speaker of the 7th Circuit Bar Association that met in Milwaukee, Wisconsin.

Appendix B

Defendant's brief in response to the DA's attack on my credentials and expertise to testify in behalf of Annette

STATE OF WISCONSIN   :
CIRCUIT COURT   :MILWAUKEE COUNTY
BRANCH 12

STATE OF WISCONSIN,

Plaintiff,

v. Case No. 11-CF-4871

ANNETTE MORALES-RODRIGUEZ,

Defendant.

DEFENDANT'S BRIEF IN SUPPORT OF THE PROFFER OF TESTIMONY OF DEFENSE WITNESS ANNE SPECKHARD

I.   **Law.**

In January, 201, Wisconsin amended Wis. Stat. § 907.02 to adopt the Daubert reliability standard as it relates to testimonial evidence submitted at trial. The

Daubert Standard arose from three cases: Daubert v. Merrell Dow Pharm. Inc., 509 U.S.

579 (1993), General Electric Co. v. Joiner, 522 U.S. 136 (1997), and Kumho Tire v. Carmichael, 526 U.S. 137 (1999), and was generally modeled on the Federal Rules of Evidence 701 and 702.

The modified code looks primarily at indicia of reliability. The statute also speaks to the witnesses' qualifications, the relevancy of the testimony and whether the testimony will be helpful to the trier of fact in determining a fact in issue or in understanding the evidence. Under the amended section 907.02, the qualification element should be addressed by an examination of the witness's principles and methods and their application to the facts. Lee v. Anderson, 616 F.3d 803, 809 (8th Cir. 2010) (in a civil rights action, holding that expert's opinion, based on a surveillance video, that the deceased had a gun before he was fatally shot by police would not have assisted the jurors; rather, it would have told them what result reach).

Expert opinion testimony must be based on reliable principles and methods. In determining reliability, the Court may consider a wide range of factors. There are

two distinct considerations: (1) What factors should the judge consider in determining whether the witness's principles and methods are reliable? (2) When weighed against those factors, are the witness's principles and methods indeed reliable? Both issues are preliminary questions of admissibility that are for the judge alone under Wis. Stat. §901.04(1). Which factors apply and how they are weighed are within the court's discretion.

One aspect of this is the acceptance of the work of the expert whose testimony is being offered. One manner to assist the Court in evaluating the acceptance of the work of a proffered witness is to evaluate their current and past employment and educational qualifications.

Expert opinion must be based on specialized knowledge including scientific and non-scientific expertise. Section 907.02 applies to all forms of specialized knowledge. Experience alone, or experience in conjunction with other knowledge, skill, training or education, may provide a sufficiently reliable basis. In certain fields, experience is the predominant, if not sole, basis for a great deal of reliable expert testimony. Fed. R. Evid. 702 advisory committee note (2000 amendment).

The primary challenge to the defense proffered testimony is to the qualifications of its witness, Anne Speckhard.

II. Argument.

This court should allow the testimony of Anne Speckhard as valuable and assisting to the trier of fact. The issues presented by this case are complex and will likely confound many as they attempt to evaluate the ability of the defendant to appreciate the wrongfulness of her conduct and her ability to conform her conduct to the requirements of the law.

A. Licensing

The State makes argument that Anne Speckhard is not a licensed psychologist. While this is accurate it is neither dispositive nor does it assist the Court with evaluating Dr. Speckhard's qualifications. Qualification of an expert is a matter of experience, not licensure. *Karl*

v. Employers Insurance of Wausau, 78 Wis. 2d 284, 254 N.W.2d 255 (1977). Dr. Speckhard is a licensed behavior counselor and member of long and good standing in the American Psychological Association. Further, she is an adjunct faculty member in Georgetown medical school in their Department of Psychiatry. She has developed coursework and taught many psychology classes as an adjunct professor at Vesalius College at the Free University of Brussels and served on the graduate faculty of a psychology department for the American University of Greece. These psychology credentials are of enough merit that Georgetown University Medical School has supported her research and public policy work and asked her to teach in their psychiatry department. This is also true for the two other psychology faculty positions. She would hardly qualify for these positions if she did not have the adequate knowledge, skill, training and experience.

Dr. Speckhard is widely published in peer-reviewed journals. These include the Journals of the American Psychological Association. Her written peer reviewed works include specific articles on the subject of post-traumatic stress disorder and dissociation.

She has given presentations on dissociation and trauma in several medical and psychological settings.

B.   The witness has never testified in an insanity defense case

While this is an accurate statement, Dr. Speckhard did produce reports in the Bobbit and Sperle cases identified below. Additionally, it does not assist the court in its evaluation as the clearly-sought conclusion is that if you have not testified you are not qualified to tes-

tify. The logical extension of such logic will render the Court without experts in short order as those who have now testified retire or pass on.

C.   The Witness has never testified in a criminal case

Anne Speckhard has been asked to do evaluations and give expert forensic witness reports for insanity defense cases and has in fact crafted these defenses in two cases.

It is accurate she did not testify in either case. In the Bobbit, case they had already passed the time for stating who their experts were by the time Dr. Speckhard was asked to join the case. One defense expert had labeled Ms. Bobbit as mentally retarded, the other had diagnosed a psychotic dissociative episode but neither had diagnosed her PTSD and neither had all four, male, prosecution experts.

Dr. Speckhard evaluated Lorena Bobbit for a full five days, wrote up her report and it was submitted to the State's experts and they changed their views based on that report. Dr. Speckhard did not testify because the time before the trial was too short. Her report and work on the case however were essential to it.

Dr. Speckhard also did the evaluation of Jennifer Sperle at her and her attorney's request and wrote up an expert forensic witness report that was submitted to the U.S. government. Up to the point of reading of that report the government had denied any possibility of a plea bargain and she was going to be tried for mandatory sentencing of 25 or more years in prison. When they read Dr. Speckhard's report they allowed the defendant to take a plea bargain of seven years,

which she decided to do versus go to trial. As a result, Dr. Speckhard did not testify but the expert witness work and report in the case were essential to its outcome.

D.   Connection to the Lorena Bobbit case

This argument has been addressed above.

E.   The Witness does not understand the NGI defense

Dr. Speckhard's expert witness report in this case was submitted before it was finalized and in a preliminary state without her knowledge. She had requested the defense counsel read the report to remove any statements that are of a legal nature giving a legal opinion. Without the final report the court would be premature to conclude that Dr. Speckhard cannot adequately address the issues present by an NGI defense.

F.   The witness has been rejected as an expert by the 7th Circuit.

This is not an accurate statement. Further, it does not address the fact that Dr. Speckhard, like many experts, is requested to address issues which having varying degrees of controversy surrounding them. Such political gamesmanship likely does little to assist courts and the trier of fact but it does occur. In many instances Dr. Speckhard has been requested to give testimony concerning the issues surrounding abortion. This is the one of the most controversial issues of our time. That her testimony was rejected by one judge in a case involving this divisive issue should not be weighed significantly in relation to the matters put before the court on this case, which not similar in any way. Of

additional concern to the Court should be the fact that this case was being decided five years ago.

Further, the 7th Circuit Criminal Bar Association very recently asked Dr. Speckhard to speak at its judicial conference in a presentation which was very well received and for which she received a congratulatory letter.

G.   The witness report includes opinion for which she is not an expert

As indicated previously, it was Dr. Speckhard's belief that she was not submitting a preliminary report. It was the concern of defense counsel that the State be apprised of the significant issues raised by the report in as timely a fashion as possible. As the report is not final, claims against are premature and should not be weighed in the Court's evaluation of Dr. Speckhard or of her possible testimony. Finally, the Court is certainly within its discretion to craft orders, which might limit the areas in which Dr. Speckhard might assist the trier of fact, without completely disallowing any of her testimony.

H.   Analysis of Dr. Speckhard's CV

The cases listed by Dr. Speckhard in her CV are those in which her testimony and clinical reports were submitted to the Court. In many case she gave depositions, in some she only provided written reports after clinical or forensic review, Dr. Speckhard has indicated she previously participated as follows:

Planned Parenthood Minnesota v. Mike Rounds, D.C. So. Dak., 05-4077 (2005).

-expert report for Black Hills Crisis Pregnancy Center, Intervenor

- post-abortion psychological consequences

- deposed by plaintiff

- all eight issues ruled negatively by district court judge were appealed

- seven of the eight have been overturned and eighth is pending

Planned Parenthood of the Rocky Mountains, Inc.v. Ownes, D.C. Col. 1:99-cv-00060 (2000).

- submitted affidavit

- post-abortion psychological consequences

- motion filed to exclude testimony – denied

A Choice for Women v. Butterworth, et al., S.D. Fla, 1:98-cv-00774 (1999).

- expert report for N. Florida Women's Health & Counseling Services, Inc.

- report filed with the court but Dr. Speckhard was not called as a witness

Karlin v. Foust, 975 F. Supp. 1177 (W.D. Wis. 1997)

- interviewed several Wisconsin abortion patients

- filed expert report, report concerned PTSD and abortion

- testified as to incidence of PTSD associated with abortion

- testimony was excluded

-judge inaccurately indicated witness had no publications in peer reviewed publications

U.S.A v. Jennifer Patterson Sperle, E.D. VA, 4:96-cr-00018 (1996).

- interviewed client filed expert report, report concerned PTSD and DID

- case was criminal prosecution which resulted in plea bargain

Darlene Greifenberger v Fairfax Ob/Gyn Associates, P.C. et al., Cir. Ct. Fairfax Co., Virginia (1995).

- interviewed client filed expert report

- report concerned PTSD

- case was personal injury case following failed mid-term abortion

Crystal Alexis Osler v. Rose Clinic & Others, Durban, South Africa 18708/04 (2007).

- interviewed client filed expert report

- report concerned PTSD

- case was civil matter young woman subjected to abortion procedure very late term followed by live birth

III. Conclusion

This case has significant issues that the Court is challenged to address without the assistance of experts. A review of Lexis/Nexus seems to indicate there are only 7 prior cases involving similar alleged conduct in the recent history of the United States. The conduct alleged is without question extreme and should give pause to everyone forced to confront it as to the sanity of the perpetrator. The purpose expert testimony is to Assist the trier of fact with complex issues which may confound simple solutions.

Dr. Speckhard is a member of several national organizations and her work involves clinical and education practice in psychology in a career spanning decades.

To be sure her work on sensational cases may require steps to be taken by the court concern the range of her testimony and the specific issues addressed. Likewise, the Court and the trier of fact may benefit from the experience she has dealing with extreme and violent psychology. The Court should avail itself of its experience as it attempts to provide for the fairest exposition of the issues presented in this unusual case.

Dated this ___th day of _____,
20_____.

_____

Attorney Michael F. Torphy
State Bar No. 1019572

Law Offices of Michael F. Torphy, S.C.

12605 W North Ave 251

Brookfield, WI 53005

(414) 975-5686

michaeltorphy@michaeltorphy.com

GLOSSARY

Alter personality – A distinct identity or personality state with its own relatively enduring pattern of perceiving, relating to and thinking about the environment and self.

Amnesia – A partial deficit or total loss of memory.

Competent/competence to stand trial – Established via a competency evaluation performed by a forensic expert to determine the defendant's current mental state at the time of the trial and establish his ability to consult rationally with an attorney to aid in his own defense and to have a rational and factual understanding of the charges against him.

Daubert – The standard of admissibility for expert scientific evidence under the Federal Rules of Evidence, requiring that expert testimony be based upon pertinent items such as: scientific knowledge; that the theories and techniques used by the expert have been tested, subjected to peer review, published and enjoy widespread acceptance. Under Daubert, the trial judge is the gatekeeper for determining that the expert's testimony rests on a reliable foundation and is relevant to the task at hand.[1]

Depo Provera – A method of birth control relying upon medroxy-progesterone injections (in the arm or buttocks), usually administered by a healthcare provider every three months.

Dissociation – A psychological symptom following deep traumatization, the essential feature of which is a disruption in the usually-integrated functions of consciousness, memory, identity or perception. Can include the unconscious erection of a barrier walling off negative emotions and memories of a negative event.

Dissociative Identity Disorder/DID – A diagnosis found in the American Psychiatric Association's Diagnostic and Statistical Man-

---

1 For more information see: The Daubert worldview http://www.daubertontheweb.com/Chapter_2.htm

ual of Mental Disorders (DSM-IV-TR, 2000) and also known prior to 1994 as Multiple Personality Disorder-MPD. DID includes the presence of two or more distinct identities or personality states, each with its own relatively enduring pattern of perceiving, relating to and thinking about the environment and self. According to the DSM-IV-TR, at least two of these identities or personality states takes control of the person's behavior on a recurring basis; the condition includes the inability to recall important personal information that is too extensive to be explained by ordinary forgetfulness, and the disturbance is not due to the direct physiological effects of a substance (e.g., blackouts or chaotic behavior during alcohol intoxication) or a general medical condition (e.g., complex partial seizures).[2]

DWI/OWI – Drinking or operating a motor vehicle while intoxicated.

Fetal Abduction – The kidnapping of an unborn child by forcing the mother to submit to a Caesarean section—a crime that often results in her death and is most often carried out by another woman.

Flashback – An unbidden intrusion of a traumatic memory or fragment of it which can include vivid full-sensory reliving of the memory in total or in parts made up of images, sounds, smells, tactile sensations or emotions. Flashbacks may cause a person to lose touch with reality and reenact the event for a period of seconds, hours or longer.

Hallucinate/hallucination – A seemingly real sensory perception—visual, auditory, tactile, olfactory—of something not actually present.

Homicide – The killing of a human being by another human being, including murder and non-criminal killings considered justifiable (such as in self-defense or an unintentional killing that is considered excusable).

---

2 American Psychiatric Association. (2000). Diagnostic and statistical manual of mental disorders (Revised 4th ed.). Washington, DC: Author.

Host personality – The distinct identity or personality state in a dissociative identity disordered person that maintains the majority of daily functioning. Often this personality state does not have memories about past abuse that other personality states hold.

Hyperarousal (traumatic) – Bodily arousal after a trauma causing difficulty concentrating, irritability or outbursts of anger, hypervigilance, sweaty palms, racing heart or difficulty falling or staying asleep.

Insanity defense/NGI – The standard by which each state and the District of Columbia determine whether a defendant was legally insane and therefore not responsible at the time his crime was committed. There are two general categories for an NGI (not guilty by reason of insanity) defense. Approximately half of the states follow M'Naughten, a rule based on an 1843 case in the UK stating that a defendant may be found not guilty by reason of insanity if "at the time of committing the act, he was laboring under such a defect of reason from disease of the mind as not to know the nature and quality of the act he was doing, or if he did know it, that he did not know what he was doing was wrong." Some states modify M'Naugthen to include a provision for defendants suffering "an irresistible impulse" which prevents him from being able to stop himself from committing an act that he knows is wrong. The American Law Institute (1962) set a standard followed by twenty-two jurisdictions in which a defendant is not held criminally responsible "if at the time of his conduct as a result of mental disease or defect he lacks substantial capacity either to appreciate the criminality (wrongfulness) of his conduct or to conform his conduct to the requirements of law." The A.L.I. rule is generally considered to be less restrictive than the M'Naughten rule.[3]

Miranda rights – Relate to Fifth Amendment rights regarding self-incrimination. Law enforcement officials are required before interrogation of a suspect put under custody to give the following warn-

3 For more information see: Frontline. Insanity defense FAQs http://www.pbs.org/wgbh/pages/frontline/shows/crime/trial/faqs.html

ing, *"You have the right to remain silent. Anything you say can and will be used against you in a court of law. You have the right to an attorney. If you cannot afford an attorney, one will be provided for you. Do you understand the rights I have just read to you? With these rights in mind, do you wish to speak to me?"*

Multiple personality disorder/MPD – See Dissociative Identity Disorder.

Narcissist/narcissistic – An egotistical preoccupation with the self in which others are viewed without empathy and as objects to be used.

Peri-traumatic dissociation – Dissociation at or around the time of a trauma. (See definition for dissociation above.)

Photographic memory – A rare type of eidetic memory in which visual and auditory memory in particular are vividly recalled in great detail and over long periods of time.

Posttraumatic stress disorder (PTSD) – A severe anxiety disorder lasting for longer than one month after the experience of a traumatic event, including traumatic intrusions (flashbacks, nightmares, etc.), avoidance and bodily hyperarousal that cause significant difficulties in functioning normally.

Pseudocyesis – False pregnancy in which actual symptoms of pregnancy are experienced, such as cessation of menstruation, swollen belly, enlarged breasts, weight gain, etc.

Psychotic – A loss of contact with reality often including delusions, hallucinations, etc.

Public defender – A lawyer appointed by the court to represent a person who cannot afford to hire an attorney.

Quinceañera – The celebration of a girl's fifteenth birthday in some parts of Latin America.

Sonogram – An examination using ultrasound echo equipment that makes a picture of internal organs via sound waves.

Sterile/Sterilization – Surgery to prevent pregnancy that is meant to be permanent.

Tubal ligation/tubes tied – Surgery to block a woman's Fallopian tubes, often performed immediately after a woman gives birth.

ENDNOTES

[1] American Psychiatric Association. (2000). Diagnostic and statistical manual of mental disorders (Revised 4th ed.). Washington, DC: Author.

[2] See Maldonado, J. R., Butler, L. D., & Spiegel, D. (2002). *Treatments for dissociative disorders. In A Guide To Treatments That Work* (2nd Edition ed.). New York: Oxford University Press.

[3] See Perry, B. D., Pollard, R. A., Baker, W. L., Sturges, C., Vigilante, D., & Blakley, T. L. . (1995). *Continuous heartrate monitoring in maltreated children.* Paper presented at the Annual Meeting of the American Academy of Child and Adolescent Psychiatry, Chicago.

[4] For more scientific information on dissociation and Dissociative Identity Disorder the reader is referred to Sidran Institute and the International Society for the Study of Trauma and Dissociation as well as scholarly works by Peter Barach, James Chu, Christine Courtois, Richard Kluft, Richard Loewenstein, Frank Putnam, Colin Ross, Marlene Steinberg, David Siegel, Joan Turkus and Bessel van der Kolk.

[5] A pseudonym.

[6] A pseudonym for the town Annette was raised in.

[7] A pseudonym.

[8] All of Annette's family members names are pseudonyms.

[9] A pseudonym.

[10] A psychological or false pregnancy in humans is termed pseudocyesis, and it occurs in one to six of every twenty-two thousand pregnancies. Before good diagnostics, it occurred in one out of every two hundred fifty pregnancies in the U.S. Two thirds of women who suffer this condition are married and it's believed to occur more frequently in women who have been victims of incest. In pseudocyesis, the woman becomes convinced that she is pregnant; menstruation may stop or become irregular, breasts may enlarge and become tender and the abdomen may distend as in a normal pregnancy. In some cases even doctors are fooled diagnosing a real pregnancy. Pseudopregnancy also

occurs in other mammals with dogs for instance preparing a nest, getting enlarged mammary glands and beginning to lactate.

[11] A pseudonym.

[12] This chapter is written based on my transcription of the actual 911 call made by Annette Morales Rodriguez. All thoughts and emotions are attributed according to my interpretation of the events occurring during that call and from what Ms. Morales Rodriguez told me in her evaluation interview.

[13] A pseudonym.

[14] Translated from his Spanish, "Mi morito nacio ayer y se me murio al hora d nacido iba hacer tan bonito mi mujer esta destrosada no deja d library."

[15] This is a pseudonym. I have based this section on the police reports and what Annette told me about the police calling her back to the hospital. The police were quite detailed about their calls from the medical examiner's office and their interactions with Annette at the hospital, but some conversations in this chapter and the thoughts of the medical examiner are reconstructed in part along with my attributions of their thoughts and statements. Part of this conversation is reconstructed from Police Officer Elm's report.

[16] See Milwaukee Police Department Incident Report 112790067 (by Patrick Elm) filed on October 7, 2012 in which he recounts his discussion with Michael Braunreiter who told him that Annette could be suffering from a life threatening medical condition requiring her to go to the hospital for immediate medical clearance.

[17] See Milwaukee Police Department Incident Report 112790067 (by Patrick Elm) filed on October 7, 2012 in which he recounts his discussion with Michael Braunreiter who told him that Annette could be suffering from a life threatening medical condition requiring her to go to the hospital for immediate medical clearance. He recalls arriving at 11:49 a.m. and that they followed Annette and Ramón to the hospital where "we stood by with Morales-Rodrigeuz and informed St. Francis staff members of what was reported to us and that we were concerned that Morales Rodriguez's medical condition could be life threatening."

[18] A pseudonym.

[19] The police names and much of what they said in this and subsequent chapters are based

upon their incident reports but all their reflections and some of their dialogue is attributed to them and reconstructed in parts from what their reports state.

[20] See Milwaukee Police Department Incident Report 112790067 (by Latanya Diedrich) filed on October 7, 2012 regarding her recall of the incident. She clearly states that at 3:25 pm she was called to respond to St. Francis Hospital Labor and Delivery Room #1 and stand by Annette Morales Rodriguez "who was a suspect in an incident".

[21] This is his real name, and the conversations are based on his police reports as well as Annette's recall. All of his inner thoughts and feelings are attributed to him.

[22] A pseudonym.

[23] This and the following police dialogue are reconstructed based on the officer's notes and Annette's recounting to me.

[24] This is her real name, and much of the action recorded here comes also from her police reports.

[25] See Milwaukee Police Department Incident Report 112790067 (by Latanya Diedrich) filed on October 7, 2012 regarding her recall of the incident, in which she states that upon her admission to the ER that Annette "stated she did not need to be seen" and that she gave an explanation for the bleeding and was then nonetheless treated by Dr. Rachel English after which she was conveyed to the police station for interrogation.

[26] This conversation is reconstructed nearly verbatim from the police report filed by Officer Rodolfo Gomez on October 7, 2011, Milwaukee Police Department Incident Report (by Rodolfo Gomez) 112790067

[27] See Milwaukee Police Department Incident Report 112790067 (by Latanya Diedrich) filed on on October 7, 2012 regarding her recall of the incident.

[28] This conversation is greatly condensed and reconstructed from the police video of Annette's confession. Both police officers names are actual.

[29] According to Michael Torphy, Bob's record on homicide includes twenty total cases: one reduced to non-homocide; five reduced from first degree intentional to lesser homicide (reckless for example). Of these twenty he took ten to jury trials and achieved two acquittals by jury trial.

[30] Both are names of the actual persons. Christina shared some of her impressions of this

meeting later when she also served as interpreter for my later evaluation of Ms. Morales Rodriguez. Much of this chapter is reconstructed, based on the doctor's formal report to the court, as well as Christina Green's and Annette's recall of his evaluation. By chance, I happened to cross paths with him as well in the elevator on the first day of my examination but we did not introduce ourselves.

[31] While these are direct quotes from his expert report which went public during the time period in which it was unsealed, I have changed the victim's name here to match the pseudonym used throughout the book.

[32] Durante, T. (October 11, 2011). Woman 'beat pregnant mother to death and cut our child from womb in C-section she had seen on Discovery Channel. *Mail Online*. Retrieved from http://www.dailymail.co.uk/news/article-2047376/Annette-Morales-Rodriguez-beat-pregnant-mother-death-cut-child-womb-C-section.html

[33] Laasby, G. (October 9, 2011). Suspect pretended to be pregnant for months, neighbors say. *Milwaukee Journal Sentinel*. Retrieved from http://www.jsonline.com/news/crime/suspect-pretended-to-be-pregnant-for-months-neighbors-say-131427953.html

[34] Gitte emails encouraging me to search their website for Morales-Rodriguez at http://www.jsonline.com/news/crime/

[35] For more on this research see: Speckhard, A. & Mufel, N. (2003). Universal Responses to Abortion? Attachment, Trauma and Grief Responses in Women Following Abortion. *Journal of Prenatal & Perinatal Psychology & Health* 18 (1), 3-37.; Mufel, N., Speckhard, A. & Sivuha, S. "Predictors of Posttraumatic Stress Disorder After Abortion in a Former Soviet Union Country" *Journal of Prenatal & Perinatal Psychology & Health* Vol 17 (1) 2002. pp. 41-61.; Speckhard, A. "Traumatic Death in Pregnancy: The Significance of Meaning & Attachment in Death & Trauma: The Traumatology of Surviving" Charles Figley, Brian Bride, & Nicholas Mazza, Eds. Taylor & Francis, 1996.; Speckhard, A.. "Adolescents & Abortion: When Coping Mechanism Turns Traumatic Stressor" *The Brown University Child & Adolescent Newsletter*, 1996.; Speckhard, A.. "Abortion: Coping Mechanism Turned Traumatic Stressor" *Psychotherapy News* 1996.; Speckhard, A & Rue, V. (1993). Complicated Mourning: Dynamics of Impacted Post Abortion Grief. *Journal of Pre- and Peri-Natal Psychology*, 8, 6-12.; Rue, V. &

Speckhard, A. "Informed Consent & Abortion: Issues in Medicine and Counseling," *Medicine & Mind* (invited article) 1992. 7 pp. 75-94; Rue, V. & Speckhard, A. "Post Abortion Trauma: Incidence and Diagnostic Considerations," *Medicine & Mind* (invited article) 1992 6 (1-2), pp. 57-73.; Speckhard, A. & Rue, V. (1992). Post Abortion Syndrome: An Emerging Public Health Concern. *Journal of Social Issues* 48(3): 95-119.; Speckhard, A. Psycho-Social Stress Following Abortion , 1987, Sheed & Ward Publishers, Kansas City, MO.

[36] Vielmetti, B. (January 3, 2012). Expert in fetal abduction case helped Lorena Bobbit defense. *Milwaukee Journal Sentinel*. Retrieved from http://www.jsonline.com/news-watch/136391148.html While Bruce Vielmetti lists me as a psychologist in his article, I should clarify that while I am a member in full standing of the American Psychological Association, I do not mean in any place in this book or elsewhere to imply that I hold a license as a clinical psychologist. My licensing credentials in the Commonwealth of VA are Licensed Professional Counselor and Licensed Marriage and Family Therapist. I clarify this for Bruce as noted later in a subsequent chapter.

[37] Scholz, A. (November 15, 2011). Fetal abduction suspect attacked guard in Milwaukee County jail. *Today's TMJ 4*. Retrieved from http://www.todaystmj4.com/news/local/133932413.html

[38] All of Annette's partners are referred to by pseudonyms.

[39] For more on Miss Katie's diner see their website: http://www.miss-katies.com/ Accessed August 6, 2012.

[40] This is the conversation with Officer Gomez as reported to me by Lara.

[41] A pseudonym.

[42] See Milwaukee Police Department Incident Report 112790067 (by Latanya Diedrich) filed on on October 7, 2012 regarding her recall of the incident. She clearly states that at 3:25 pm she was called to respond to St. Francis Hospital Labor and Delivery Room #1 and stand by Annette Morales Rodriguez "who was a suspect in an incident"

[43] See Milwaukee Police Department Incident Report 112790067 (by Latanya Diedrich) filed on on October 7, 2012 regarding her recall of the incident. She states "At 4:40 pm, Detective Rodolfo GOMEZ and detective James HUTCHINSON responded and took

over the investigation," and she explains that she stood by outside the labor and delivery room "until they were ready to interview her" and that she investigated the room and questioned Annette about cutting herself—without recording reading her rights to her. She goes on to note: "I advised Detective HUTCHINSON of the incident at which time he told me to place MORALES-RODRIGUEZ under arrest and convey her to the Emergency Department for medical clearance," and she continues "At 5:25pm, MORALES-RODRIGUEZ was arrested and conveyed to St Francis Hospital ER for clearance." See also: Vielmetti, B. (August 10, 2012). Questionable questioning could jeopardize fetal homocide case. *Milwaukee Journal Sentinel*. Retrieved from http://www.jsonline. com/news/crime/questionable-questioning-could-jeopardize-fetal-homicide-case-r96e-uii-165791466.html

[44] Pseudonym inserted to replace the victim's actual name.

[45] See: Vielmetti, B. (October 19, 2011). Detective testifies in fetal abduction case. *Milwaukee Journal Sentinel*. Retrieved from http://www.jsonline.com/news/crime/detective-testifies-in-fetal-abduction-case-132204523.html and Milwaukee Police Department Incident Report (by Rodolfo Gomez) filed October 7, 2011. Number 112790067

[46] See: Milwaukee Police Department Incident Report (by Rodolfo Gomez) filed October 7, 2011. Number 112790067

[47] See the five police reports filed by Officer Rodolfo Gomez on this case:

10-6-2011 Milwaukee Police Department Incident Report (by Rodolfo Gomez) 112790067

10-6-2011 Milwaukee Police Department Incident Report (by Rodolfo Gomez) regarding his interview with Brenda Melendez 112790067

10-6-2011 Milwaukee Police Department Incident Report (by Rodolfo Gomez) regarding his interview with Jose Ramirez 112790067

10-7-2011 Milwaukee Police Department Incident Report (by Rodolfo Gomez) filed October 7, 2011. Number 112790067

10-19-2011 Incident report (by Detective Rodolfo Gomez) of the Milwaukee Police Department 112790067

[48] See the five police reports filed by Officer Rodolfo Gomez on this case:

10-6-2011 Milwaukee Police Department Incident Report (by Rodolfo Gomez) 112790067

10-6-2011 Milwaukee Police Department Incident Report (by Rodolfo Gomez) regarding his interview with Brenda Melendez 112790067

10-6-2011 Milwaukee Police Department Incident Report (by Rodolfo Gomez) regarding his interview with Jose Ramirez 112790067

10-7-2011 Milwaukee Police Department Incident Report (by Rodolfo Gomez) filed October 7, 2011. Number 112790067

10-19-2011 Incident report (by Detective Rodolfo Gomez) of the Milwaukee Police Department 112790067

[49] See: Milwaukee Police Department Incident Report (by Rodolfo Gomez) filed October 7, 2011. Number 112790067

[50] See: Milwaukee Police Department Incident Report (by Rodolfo Gomez) filed October 7, 2011. Number 112790067

[51] See: Milwaukee Police Department Incident Report (by Rodolfo Gomez) filed October 7, 2011. Number 112790067 in which Officer Gomez attributes this exact statement to her.

[52] See: Milwaukee Police Department Incident Report (by Rodolfo Gomez) filed October 7, 2011. Number 112790067

[53] From St. Francis Hospital Emergency Room notes on the case.

[54] The bold in this quote is added by me.

[55] From St. Francis Hospital Emergency Room notes on the case.

[56] Heidi Harry, a nurse working in a Milwaukee area hospital advised on January 10, 2012 that informed consent in the hospital setting is always sought in writing, or if verbally with a witness present to record that fact. Likewise when I check the previous days records, I find another note showing Annette refusing medical treatment after she has been taken by ambulance to the hospital – after her at-home "birth" – and notes of her discharging herself from the hospital against medical advice. Clearly she did not want to be examined at *any time, either day* and this was noted in the hospital records!

[57] See: Milwaukee Police Department Incident Report (by Rodolfo Gomez) filed October

7, 2011. Number 112790067

[58] See Milwaukee Police Department Incident Report 112790067 (by Latanya Diedrich) filed on October 7, 2012.

[59] See: Milwaukee Police Department Incident Report (by Rodolfo Gomez) filed October 7, 2011. Number 112790067

[60] Vielmetti, B. (March 8, 2012). Woman accused of cutting fetus from womb has 2nd personality, report says. *Milwaukee Journal Sentinel*. Retrieved from http://www.jsonline.com/news/crime/woman-accused-of-cutting-fetus-from-womb-has-2nd-personality-report-says-nn4gaoh-142012313.html

[61] I have changed the victim's name to the pseudonym used here throughout his article.

[62] I later learn from Mike that although Pat blamed the judge for not sealing the report, it was his responsibility to request that it be sealed.

[63] Pat is referring to a case in which I was, in my opinion, wrongly impeached as an expert, that was later overturned by a judge of equal standing.

[64] See: Brewster, C. (March 9, 2012). New twist in murder case involving Morales-Rodriguez. *Fox6Now*. Retrieved from http://fox6now.com/2012/03/09/new-twist-in-murder-case-involving-annette-morales-rodriguez/

[65] Daubert is the rule of evidence upon which expert opinion is evaluated for admissibility into court. It basically allows the judge to be the "gatekeeper" to ensure that the expert's testimony is relevant to the task at hand and rests on a reliable scientific foundation—that it has been accepted by a relevant scientific community, published, passed peer review, etc.

[66] Pat is referring to Judge Barbara Crabb who wrote the negative opinion of me that was later disregarded and evaluated as a politically motivated commentary by another judge of equal standing.

[67] See: Torphy, M. (2012). *Defendant's brief in support of the proffer of testimony of defense witness Anne Speckhard.*

[68] Vielmetti, B. (April 18, 2012). Attorney team quits fetal abduction case. *Milwaukee Journal Sentinel*. Retrieved from http://www.jsonline.com/news/crime/attorney-team-quits-fetal-abduction-case-bv52gc3-148032475.html

[69] This is according to Mike and Pat's recounting of the incident to me, and a report filed by Bruce Vielmetti.

[70] See: USC. 18 USC 4241 - Determination of mental competency to stand trial to undergo postrelease proceedings? Retrieved from http://www.law.cornell.edu/uscode/text/18/4241

[71] These are their real names.

[72] See Appendix B.

[73] Indeed after the trial I contact Christina Green again and she tells me that the reason she did not answer was due to the gag order she was under during the trial.

[74] I should make clear that I was never informed who lodged the complaint and I have no information nor proof it originated from their office. This was simply my conjecture given that the complaint referred to my activities in Wisconsin and related to this case.

[75] Vielmetti, B. (June 28, 2012). Multiple-personality diagnosis dropped in fetal homocide case. *Milwaukee Journal Sentinel*. Retrieved from http://www.jsonline.com/news/crime/multiplepersonality-diagnosis-dropped-in-fetal-homicide-case-7v5uipi-160771655.html

[76] Vielmetti, B. (July 26, 2012). Prosecutors told to explain charging decision in cop case. *Milwaukee Journal Sentinel*. Retrieved from http://www.jsonline.com/news/crime/prosecutors-told-to-explain-charging-decision-in-cop-case-0068rqs-163923636.html

[77] Vielmetti, B. (August 10, 2012). Questionable questioning could jeopardize fetal homocide case. *Milwaukee Journal Sentinel*. Retrieved from http://www.jsonline.com/news/crime/questionable-questioning-could-jeopardize-fetal-homicide-case-r96euii-165791466.html

[78] Johnson, M. (August 31, 2012). Judge to release records to defense in fetal abduction case. *Milwaukee Journal Sentinel*. Retrieved from http://www.jsonline.com/news/crime/judge-to-release-records-to-defense-in-fetal-abduction-case-v26mpu9-168176236.html

[79] Ramde, D. (September 19, 2012). Wis. woman didn't mean to kill mother, fetus, lawyer says. *Associated Press*. Retrieved from http://bostonglobe.com/news/nation/2012/09/18/defense-argues-intent-wis-fetal-abduction-case/rsRo9KnhxBgu5uPg-GPownO/story.html

[80] Ramde, D. (September 19, 2012). Wis. woman didn't mean to kill mother, fetus, lawyer says. *Associated Press*. Retrieved from http://bostonglobe.com/news/nation/2012/09/18/defense-argues-intent-wis-fetal-abduction-case/rsRo9KnhxBgu5uPg-GPownO/story.html

[81] Associated Press. (September 19, 2012). Woman who 'cut unborn baby out of mother's womb' pictured in court as jurors hear 911 call of her claiming she had given birth in the shower after she killed mother and son in botched c-section kidnap. *Mail Online*. Retrieved from http://www.dailymail.co.uk/news/article-2205376/Annette-Morales-Rodriguez-trial-Woman-cut-unborn-baby-mothers-womb-pictured-court-jurors-hear-911-claiming-given-birth-shower-killed-mother-son-botched-c-section-kidnap.html

[82] Associated Press. (September 19, 2012). Woman who 'cut unborn baby out of mother's womb' pictured in court as jurors hear 911 call of her claiming she had given birth in the shower after she killed mother and son in botched c-section kidnap. *Mail Online*. Retrieved from http://www.dailymail.co.uk/news/article-2205376/Annette-Morales-Rodriguez-trial-Woman-cut-unborn-baby-mothers-womb-pictured-court-jurors-hear-911-claiming-given-birth-shower-killed-mother-son-botched-c-section-kidnap.html

[83] Ramde, D. (September 20, 2012). Annette Morales-rodriguez convicted in fetus abduction murder case. *Associated Press*. Retrieved from http://www.huffingtonpost.com/2012/09/20/annette-morales-rodriguez-guilty-conviction_n_1901939.html

[84] Ramde, D. (September 20, 2012). Annette Morales-rodriguez convicted in fetus abduction murder case. *Associated Press*. Retrieved from http://www.huffingtonpost.com/2012/09/20/annette-morales-rodriguez-guilty-conviction_n_1901939.html

[85] Ramde, D. (September 20, 2012). Annette Morales-rodriguez convicted in fetus abduction murder case. *Associated Press*. Retrieved from http://www.huffingtonpost.com/2012/09/20/annette-morales-rodriguez-guilty-conviction_n_1901939.html

[86] Ramde, D. (September 20, 2012). Annette Morales-rodriguez convicted in fetus abduction murder case. *Associated Press*. Retrieved from http://www.huffingtonpost.com/2012/09/20/annette-morales-rodriguez-guilty-conviction_n_1901939.html

[87] Ramde, D. (September 19, 2012). Wis. woman didn't mean to kill mother, fetus, lawyer says. *Associated Press*. Retrieved from http://bostonglobe.com/news/na-

tion/2012/09/18/defense-argues-intent-wis-fetal-abduction-case/rsRo9KnhxBgu5uPg-GPownO/story.html

[88] Ramde, D. (September 20, 2012). Annette Morales-rodriguez convicted in fetus abduction murder case. *Associated Press.* Retrieved from http://www.huffingtonpost.com/2012/09/20/annette-morales-rodriguez-guilty-conviction_n_1901939.html

[89] Ramde, D. (September 20, 2012). Annette Morales-rodriguez convicted in fetus abduction murder case. *Associated Press.* Retrieved from http://www.huffingtonpost.com/2012/09/20/annette-morales-rodriguez-guilty-conviction_n_1901939.html

[90] Ramde, D. (September 20, 2012). Annette Morales-rodriguez convicted in fetus abduction murder case. *Associated Press.* Retrieved from http://www.huffingtonpost.com/2012/09/20/annette-morales-rodriguez-guilty-conviction_n_1901939.html

[91] Associated Press. (September 19, 2012). Woman who 'cut unborn baby out of mother's womb' pictured in court as jurors hear 911 call of her claiming she had given birth in the shower after she killed mother and son in botched c-section kidnap. *Mail Online.* Retrieved from http://www.dailymail.co.uk/news/article-2205376/Annette-Morales-Rodriguez-trial-Woman-cut-unborn-baby-mothers-womb-pictured-court-jurors-hear-911-claiming-given-birth-shower-killed-mother-son-botched-c-section-kidnap.html

[92] Ramde, D. (September 20, 2012). Annette Morales-rodriguez convicted in fetus abduction murder case. *Associated Press.* Retrieved from http://www.huffingtonpost.com/2012/09/20/annette-morales-rodriguez-guilty-conviction_n_1901939.html

[93] Associated Press. (September 19, 2012). Woman who 'cut unborn baby out of mother's womb' pictured in court as jurors hear 911 call of her claiming she had given birth in the shower after she killed mother and son in botched c-section kidnap. *Mail Online.* Retrieved from http://www.dailymail.co.uk/news/article-2205376/Annette-Morales-Rodriguez-trial-Woman-cut-unborn-baby-mothers-womb-pictured-court-jurors-hear-911-claiming-given-birth-shower-killed-mother-son-botched-c-section-kidnap.html

[94] Associated Press. (September 19, 2012). Woman who 'cut unborn baby out of mother's womb' pictured in court as jurors hear 911 call of her claiming she had given birth in the shower after she killed mother and son in botched c-section kidnap. *Mail Online.* Retrieved from http://www.dailymail.co.uk/news/article-2205376/Annette-Morales-

Rodriguez-trial-Woman-cut-unborn-baby-mothers-womb-pictured-court-jurors-hear-911-claiming-given-birth-shower-killed-mother-son-botched-c-section-kidnap.html

[95] Associated Press. (September 16, 2012). US fetal abduction, murder trial to begin. Retrieved from http://www.azcentral.com/news/articles/2012/09/16/20120916US-fetal-abduction-murder-trial.html

[96] Associated Press. (September 19, 2012). Woman who 'cut unborn baby out of mother's womb' pictured in court as jurors hear 911 call of her claiming she had given birth in the shower after she killed mother and son in botched c-section kidnap. *Mail Online*. Retrieved from http://www.dailymail.co.uk/news/article-2205376/Annette-Morales-Rodriguez-trial-Woman-cut-unborn-baby-mothers-womb-pictured-court-jurors-hear-911-claiming-given-birth-shower-killed-mother-son-botched-c-section-kidnap.html

[97] CBS News. (September 20, 2012). Annette Morales-Rodriguez. *Crimesider*. Retrieved from http://www.cbsnews.com/8301-504083_162-57517214-504083/annette-morales-rodriguez-wisconsin-woman-convicted-in-fetal-abduction-deaths/

[98] Summers, C. (October 27, 2007). The women who kill for babies. *BBC News*. Retrieved from http://news.bbc.co.uk/2/hi/americas/6990419.stm

[99] Burgess, A. W. B., T.; Nahirny, C.; and Rabun, J. B. . Newborn kidnapping by Cesarean section. *The Journal of Forensic Science*, 47, 827-830.

[100] Summers, C. (October 27, 2007). The women who kill for babies. *BBC News*. Retrieved from http://news.bbc.co.uk/2/hi/americas/6990419.stm

[101] Geberth, V. (March, 2006). Homocides involving the theft of a fetus. *Law and Order,* 54(3), 40-42, 44-46.

[102] Dalley, M. (Summer, 2005). Abductions from the womb: Caesarian section murder a new category of homicide. *Crime Trends*. Retrieved from http://www.rcmp-grc.gc.ca/pubs/omc-ned/caesar-cesarien-eng.pdf

[103] See Yutzy S., W. J., Resnick P. (January, 1993). Child stealing by Cesarean section: A psychiatric case report and review of the child stealing literature. *Journal of Forensic Sciences,* 38(110), 1520.

[104] Paradis, C. (April 28, 2011). The measure of madness. *Psychology Today*. Retrieved from http://www.psychologytoday.com/blog/the-measure-madness/201104/womb-

raider-kills-again

[105] Yutzy S., W. J., Resnick P. (January, 1993). Child stealing by Cesarean section: A psychiatric case report and review of the child stealing literature. *Journal of Forensic Sciences*, 38(110), 1520.

[106] Yutzy S., W. J., Resnick P. (January, 1993). Child stealing by Cesarean section: A psychiatric case report and review of the child stealing literature. *Journal of Forensic Sciences*, 38(110), 1520.

[107] Frieden, J. (January 1, 2010). Fetal abductors are often not mentally ill. *Clinical Psychiatry News*. Retrieved from http://www.clinicalpsychiatrynews.com/views/commentaries/single-article/fetal-abductors-are-often-not-mentally-ill/d01338608dd1df099b-620c3ae72bbbc4.html

BIBLIOGRAPHY

American Psychiatric Association. (2000). Diagnostic and statistical manual of mentaldisorders (Revised 4th ed.). Washington, DC: Author.

Associated Press. (September 16, 2012). U.S. fetal abduction, murder trial to begin. Retrieved from http://www.azcentral.com/news/articles/2012/09/16/20120916US-fetal-abduction-murder-trial.html

Associated Press. (September 19, 2012). Woman who cut unborn baby out of mother's womb' pictured in court as jurors hear 911 call of her claiming she had given birth in the shower after she killed mother and son in botched c-section kidnap. *Mail Online.* Retrieved from http://www.dailymail.co.uk/news/article-2205376/Annette-Morales-Rodriguez-trial-Woman-cut-unborn-baby-mothers-womb-pictured-court-jurors-hear-911-claiming-given-birth-shower-killed-mother-son-botched-c-section-kidnap.html

Brewster, C. (March 9, 2012). New twist in murder case involving Morales-Rodriguez. *Fox6Now.* Retrieved from http://fox6now.com/2012/03/09/new-twist-in-murder-case-involving-annette-morales-rodriguez/

Burgess, A. W. B., T.; Nahirny, C.; and Rabun, J. B. . Newborn kidnapping byCesarean section. *The Journal of Forensic Science*, 47, 827-830.

CBS News. (September 20, 2012). Annette Morales-Rodriguez. *Crimesider.* Retrieved from http://www.cbsnews.com/8301-504083_162-57517214-504083/annette-morales-rodriguez-wisconsin-woman-convicted-in-fetal-abduction-deaths/

Dalley, M. (Summer, 2005). Abductions from the womb: Caesarian section murder a new category of homicide. *Crime Trends.* Retrieved from http://www.rcmp-grc.gc.ca/pubs/omc-ned/caesar-cesarien-eng.pdf

Durante, T. (October 11, 2011). Woman beat pregnant mother to death and cut our child from womb in C-section she had seen on Discovery Channel. *Mail Online.* Retrieved from http://www.dailymail.co.uk/news/article-2047376/Annette-Morales-Rodriguez-beat-pregnant-mother-death-cut-child-womb-C-section.html

Frieden, J. (January 1, 2010). Fetal abductors are often not mentally ill. *ClinicalPsychiatry* News. Retrieved from http://www.clinicalpsychiatrynews.com/views/commentaries/single-article/fetal-abductors-are-often-not-mentally-ill/d01338608dd1df099b620c3ae72bbbc4.html

Geberth, V. (March, 2006). Homocides involving the theft of a fetus. *Law andOrder*, 54(3), 40-42, 44-46.

Johnson, M. (August 31, 2012). Judge to release records to defense in fetal abduction case. *Milwaukee Journal Sentinel.* Retrieved from http://www.jsonline.com/news/crime/judge-to-release-records-to-defense-in-fetal-abduction-case-v26mpu9-168176236.html

Laasby, G. (October 9, 2011). Suspect pretended to be pregnant for months,

neighbors say. *Milwaukee Journal Sentinel*. Retrieved from http://
www.jsonline.com/news/crime/suspect-pretended-to-be-pregnant-
for-months-neighbors-say-131427953.html

Maldonado, J. R., Butler, L. D., & Spiegel, D. (2002). *Treatments for dissociative disorders. In A Guide To Treatments That Work* (2nd Edition
ed.). New York: Oxford University Press.

Mufel, N., Speckhard, A. & Sivuha, S. (2002). Predictors of Posttraumatic
StressDisorder After Abortion in a Former Soviet Union Country.
Journal of Prenatal & Perinatal Psychology & Health. 17 (1) pp.
41-61.

Paradis, C. (April 28, 2011). The measure of madness. *Psychology Today*.
Retrieved from http://www.psychologytoday.com/blog/the-measure-
madness/201104/womb-raider-kills-again

Perry, B. D., Pollard, R. A., Baker, W. L., Sturges, C., Vigilante, D., & Blakley, T. L. (1995). *Continuous heartrate monitoring in maltreated
children*. Paper presented at the Annual Meeting of the American
Academy of Child and Adolescent Psychiatry, Chicago.

Ramde, D. (September 19, 2012). Wis. woman didn't mean to kill mother, fetus,
lawyer says. Associated Press. Retrieved from http://bostonglobe.
com/news/nation/2012/09/18/defense-argues-intent-wis-fetal-abduc-
tion-case/rsRo9KnhxBgu5uPgGPownO/story.html

Ramde, D. (September 20, 2012). Annette Morales-rodriguez convicted in fetus
abduction murder case. *Associated Press*. Retrieved from http://
www.huffingtonpost.com/2012/09/20/annette-morales-rodriguez-
guilty-conviction_n_1901939.html

Rue, V. & Speckhard, A. (1992). Informed Consent & Abortion: Issues in
Medicine and Counseling, *Medicine & Mind* (invited article) 7 pp.
75-94.

Rue, V. & Speckhard, A. (1992). Post Abortion Trauma: Incidence and Diagnostic Considerations, *Medicine & Mind* (invited article) 6 (1-2), pp.
57-73.

Scholz, A. (November 15, 2011). Fetal abduction suspect attacked guard in
Milwaukee County jail. *Today's TMJ 4*. Retrieved from http://www.
todaystmj4.com/news/local/133932413.html

Speckhard, A. (1987) Psycho-Social Stress Following Abortion, Sheed & Ward
Publishers, Kansas City, MO.

Speckhard, A. & Rue, V. (1992). Post Abortion Syndrome: An Emerging Public
Health
Concern. *Journal of Social Issues* 48(3): 95-119.

Speckhard, A. & Rue, V. (1993). Complicated Mourning: Dynamics of Impacted
Post
Abortion Grief. *Journal of Pre- and Peri-Natal Psychology*, 8, 6-12.

Speckhard, A. (1996). Adolescents & Abortion: When Coping Mechanism Turns
Traumatic *The Brown University Child & Adolescent Newsletter*.

Speckhard, A. (1996)."Traumatic Death in Pregnancy: The Significance of

Meaning & Attachment" in <u>Death & Trauma: The Traumatology of Surviving</u>" Charles Figley, Brian Bride, & Nicholas Mazza, Eds. Taylor & Francis,

Speckhard, A. & Mufel, N. (2003). Universal Responses to Abortion? Attachment, Trauma and Grief Responses in Women Following Abortion. *Journal of Prenatal & Perinatal Psychology & Health* 18 (1), 3-37.

Summers, C. (October 27, 2007). The women who kill for babies. *BBC News.* Retrieved from http://news.bbc.co.uk/2/hi/americas/6990419.stm

Torphy, M. (2012). *Defendant's brief in support of the proffer of testimony of defensewitness Anne Speckhard.*

USC. 18 USC 4241 - Determination of mental competency to stand trial to undergo postrelease proceedings? Retrieved from http://www.law.cornell.edu/uscode/text/18/4241

Vielmetti, B. (October 19, 2011). Detective testifies in fetal abduction case. *Milwaukee Journal Sentinel.* Retrieved from http://www.jsonline.com/news/crime/detective-testifies-in-fetal-abduction-case-132204523.html

Vielmetti, B. (January 3, 2012). Expert in fetal abduction case helped Lorena Bobbit defense. *Milwaukee Journal Sentinel.* Retrieved from http://www.jsonline.com/newswatch/136391148.html

Vielmetti, B. (March 8, 2012). Woman accused of cutting fetus from womb has 2nd personality, report says. *Milwaukee Journal Sentinel.* Retrieved from http://www.jsonline.com/news/crime/woman-accused-of-cutting-fetus-from-womb-has-2nd-personality-report-says-nn4gaoh-142012313.html

Vielmetti, B. (April 18, 2012). Attorney team quits fetal abduction case. *Milwaukee Journal Sentinel.* Retrieved from http://www.jsonline.com/news/crime/attorney-team-quits-fetal-abduction-case-bv52gc3-148032475.html

Vielmetti, B. (June 28, 2012). Multiple-personality diagnosis dropped in fetal homicide case. *Milwaukee Journal Sentinel.* Retrieved from http://www.jsonline.com/news/crime/multiplepersonality-diagnosis-dropped-in-fetal-homicide-case-7v5uipi-160771655.html

Vielmetti, B. (July 26, 2012). Prosecutors told to explain charging decision in cop case. *Milwaukee Journal Sentinel.* Retrieved from http://www.jsonline.com/news/crime/prosecutors-told-to-explain-charging-decision-in-cop-case-0068rqs-163923636.html

Vielmetti, B. (August 10, 2012). Questionable questioning could jeopardize fetal homicide case. *Milwaukee Journal Sentinel.* Retrieved from http://www.jsonline.com/news/crime/questionable-questioning-could-jeopardize-fetal-homicide-case-r96euii-165791466.html

Yutzy S., Wolfson. J.K., & Resnick P. (January, 1993). Child stealing by Cesarean section: A psychiatric case report and review of the child stealing literature. *Journal of Forensic Sciences*, 38(110), 1520.

INDEX